BY **Patrick V. Murphy**
AND **Thomas Plate**

Commissioner

*A View from the Top
of American Law Enforcement*

Simon and Schuster · New York

Photo editor: Vincent Virga
Designed by Irving Perkins
Manufactured in the United States of America
1   2   3   4   5   6   7   8   9   10

Library of Congress Cataloging in Publication Data

Murphy, Patrick V   date.
   Commissioner.

   Includes index.
   1.   Murphy, Patrick V., 1920-   2.   Police chiefs—
New York (City)—Biography.   I.   Plate, Thomas Gordon,
joint author.   II.   Title.
HV7911.M89A32   363.2′092′4   [B]   77-21876

ISBN 0-671-22751-3

5/78

Authors' Note

The occasional dialogue and the frequent anecdotal material have been reconstructed primarily on the basis of the principal author's recollection, notes, and documentary material regarding the actual events.

For their assistance in many ways, the authors would like to thank with gratitude, especially, New York Police Commissioner Michael Codd, Deputy Commissioner Frank McLoughlin, the Public Information Office of the N.Y.P.D., Peggy Triplett, and William H. T. Smith.

To my wife Betty

Contents

Picture section follows page 128.

Looking Back, 1973

At times like this, with City Hall now only minutes away and my last day as Commissioner drawing rapidly to a close, the oddest things occur in my mind. For of all the thoughts that might have been knocking around in my head at the moment, the one thing that I could not get rid of was the thought that I was losing this car.

In itself the car was not much. A black Mercury—not a Cadillac (not even a Chrysler Imperial, which had been furnished when I was Detroit Commissioner)—it was provided for official business by the City of New York. Except for the extra horses under the hood and the unusual radiotelephone installation, it was, on the face of it, nothing more than a nice black car.

But in my nearly three years as Commissioner, I had grown awfully fond of what this car offered. There had been times when it had been my only psychological resting place in the city. At Headquarters, downtown, where the atmosphere was usually one of crisis and the mode of thought, such as it was, entirely operational, it was difficult to see beyond the smoke and fire of the day's pitched battles. Staff aides, city officials, high brass, and what have you were constantly hovering about, hoping for a word or two with the "P.C.," as the Police Commissioner was usually referred to at that level. There was—to add to my point—even a peephole in the door of the P.C.'s office, through which staff aides could peer to see whom "the Boss" was with—or whether the Boss might be alone, and therefore ready to receive the next scheduled appointment or some surprise visitor. Whatever its utilitarian value, the peephole made me feel like an exhibit at the zoo.

The daily commute home from Headquarters took me to Staten Island, one of the five boroughs of New York, and to Betty and four of our eight children still at home. There were no peepholes in our home, thankfully, but there were few closed doors either. We were a close family, a loving one, and we tended to do everything together. Privacy was for single people and orphans. Besides togetherness, home was also where the special phones were—connecting me to Command and Control, where crisis information was collected and dispatched; and to the Mayor's office, where people were often worrying about what that unpredictable Police Department was up to. Sometimes the phones at home never stopped ringing.

True, there were phones for me in the Mercury, installed in a box on the back of the front seat, but here in the car it was possible to beat the system. For one thing, it was easy to let the driver answer the phone. Dan and Dave were skilled stallers as well as drivers, and they knew how to take care of the pests found in any large bureaucracy who make a career out of devising excuses to talk to the top man. Unless it was actually a matter of high priority, the driver would try to handle the call, so that I could be left alone, for once, in the company of my thoughts.

This was what the Mercury did for me: It gave me a place to think —a world apart from the internecine infighting at Headquarters, from the savage political warfare over at City Hall, from the increasingly inconclusive struggle against the criminals roaming around in the city. On some days it got so that it was almost a relief to be stuck in snarled Manhattan traffic; for a delay, you see, might give me some more *time* to think—and one of the most difficult aspects of being Police Commissioner was that however much you might wish to think of things the way they should or even could be, you were often simply overwhelmed by the way things were.

I suppose, therefore, that one reason why I could not stop thinking about losing the dear Mercury was, simply, the memories. For the memories which this car held for me spanned one of the most electrifying and disquieting epochs not merely in the history of the New York Police Department but also in the modern history of crime and policing in the United States. When I informed the Mayor of my intention to step down, I realized that the three years as Commissioner had been like an entire life, with the experiences of having been head of police in Syracuse, Washington, and Detroit occurring quite possibly in a previous life. In a way, though, I had asked for what I got. I knew when I left in 1970 for New York from Detroit, where I had been Police Commissioner, that this was my chance to do something about policing in America through its largest police department, and that I could either represent myself as I believed I really was, which was an activist administrator and innovator, or I could pretend to be what I wasn't, which was an old-school don't-rock-the-boat cop in gold braid. Of course, the choice was an entirely theoretical one, existing only on a blank page in my mind. In reality, I wanted to leave the job with banners flying, and there was only one way for me to come out ahead—reform, innovate, give it my best shot.

To some extent, the chaos of these three years was a case of a certain personality meeting a certain set of circumstances. As a former New York official looking back over those years put it (most generously, from my point of view): "Patrick Murphy took over a Police Department in 1970 demoralized from a combination of publicly exposed corruption and five years of maladministration . . . An epidemic of narcotics corruption was raging throughout the city, creating a large class of predatory criminals who were destroying the fabric of the city's civic life. Investigations were well on their way to demonstrating that corruption was pervasive throughout the anti-narcotics effort of the Police Department. . . . Murphy's job was to turn the department around and restore public confidence before it was irretrievably lost. . . . The city's five district attorneys had already said they couldn't do the job, and the police unions had declared they wouldn't permit drastic changes in established procedures. So the new commissioner had to do battle on two fronts, to respond to the avalanche of bad publicity coming out of the Knapp Commission hearings, the 'French Connection' heroin theft, and federal investigations, and at the same time shake up the department from within without cracking the pillars of the structure."*

And so it was in this back seat that I thought the bigger thoughts. For in the course of a typical day at the office, the Police Commissioner is forced to conduct a stubbornly invariable percentage of his business with the usual assortment of bores, self-inflated personalities,

* Frederick O'R. Hayes, *New York Affairs*, Vol. II, No. 1, 1974, pp. 88 ff.

hopeless incompetents, pitiful phonies, and obnoxious self-seekers. But by starting every day just a little bit behind, I could work it so I could squeeze out the undesirables and thereby spend more time on the legitimate business of the citizens; only when my schedule ran well ahead would I run the risk of not being able to cut short an unavoidable appointment with the words "Sorry, gotta run." Indeed, only by running slightly behind was I able to stay ahead.

The bigger thoughts were not simply New York issues. New York is as much a state of mind as it is a special place. Things and trends tend to happen in New York *first*, but not in the long run in New York *exclusively*. This is why the N.Y.P.D. is probably the most closely watched police department in the country, why its ups and downs are more likely to wind up on the network evening news than the trials and tribulations of other departments. It is not just size but history; watching New York and its police department is like getting an advance preview of the country's future. The heroin torture in New York of the early 1970s is now being suffered in the major cities of Europe. The pornography boom that once seemed a perversion solely of racy Times Square is now a commonplace in towns across the land. The police strikes and job actions that once seemed explicable solely in terms of the city's unique lunacy now plague other local governments. (Some police departments have been unionized by the Teamsters, of all unions.) The N.Y.P.D., like a weather vane, tips us off as to which way the country's crime and police winds are blowing.

So the bigger thoughts for New York reverberate elsewhere. How can a city's streets be made safe and crime reduced if we don't (and we don't) have enough money in the treasury to station a uniformed cop on every street? But do we need more cops in uniform even if the size of our police force remains about the same? What about detectives? They cost a lot, but what is the payoff? Should they be put out on the streets, too, where the dangerous crime is? What kind of impact can a police force really have on crime? How much is just window dressing? How much is real? Are, for example, more cops the answer? Or fewer police officers but *better* ones? If half the Police Department were suddenly female, would that make the department better—or worse? Were taxpayers spending too high a proportion of the criminal justice dollar on the police, not enough on the courts and the prosecutors' offices? If the Mayor came to me to take a big slice out of the police budget, how should I react? Cry wolf and go to the people and scare them into making the Mayor put the money back? Or accept the common sense of the cut, tell the people the truth, and let out from the closet of American policing the dirty little secret that the relationship between crime in America and police protection in America was curiously, paradoxically, but also truly—tangential.

It was odd. On almost every single occasion in the past three years that I got out of the Mercury I had at least one briefcase or attaché case in hand filled with work—and sometimes two. But now, this sunny April morning, I got out empty-handed. Which was also how I was feeling.

Slamming the door behind me, I also realized that I would not be getting into the back seat of this old companion again.

I headed for the Blue Room, City Hall's ceremonial place. It was the ceremonial room, one could tell, because it was just about the only place inside the Hall where good manners were ever displayed. In a city of sharks, the Blue Room was the shallow water at lowest tide, safe even for wading infants.

At the far end of City Hall was the City Council chamber. Every city has something like a city council, though it may be called something else. This was where city legislation was discussed, where Mayor John V. Lindsay and his political operatives maneuvered, or had chunks of their political program taken from them. Outside the building, in the immediate periphery, were the city bureaucracies, huge monuments to inertia and governmental red tape. Down the road a good six blocks was Police Headquarters.

I walked into the Blue Room, and immediately the camera lights went on and the flutter of shutters filled the air, almost drowning out the din of the press corps. I worried that I was going to miss the attention. Betty was seated on the dais with other notables, but I wasn't worried about my wife. I knew she wasn't going to miss the attention, the wee-hours calls about another cop being shot, the corruption revelations, the enervating and demoralizing crime. Oh, maybe she would miss the contact with Mary Lindsay, the Mayor's wife, for whom genuine affection had developed, and surely all those inside stories about what really went on behind the scenes at the N.Y.P.D. . . . Suddenly John Lindsay came into the room, and the photographers launched a second round of picture taking.

In my mind, Lindsay would always remain more than just another handsome face, another politician who became New York's Mayor and thereby signed his own political death certificate. In the police world, mediocre mayors were an occupational hazard, but the problem with Lindsay was not surface mediocrity but dense ambiguity. He had managed to attract to his governing team a glittering array of talent from the business, foundation, and academic worlds, but somehow the city still seemed to drift, like a space station that had lost its orbit.

"This is a sad day for me," the Mayor said to the room packed with press and friends. "This is a sad day for the city. Pat Murphy has been tough as a commanding officer, and fair. The Police Department is now at its strongest point in history."

The Mayor's statement was arguably hyperbolic, but it was not demonstrably false. And this was pleasing. I scanned the eyes of the cynical New York press corps, the best there was, for a snicker or an upward roll of the eyes, but there was none. Lindsay's concern about my departure was even perhaps genuine. After all, his first appointment to the job hadn't worked out all that well. When I had informed him of my intention to take the offer from the Police Foundation in Washington—a research institution funded predominantly with Ford Foundation grants—he had tried to talk me out of it, going so far as to set up a breakfast with McGeorge Bundy, who as president of the Ford Foundation naturally had some influence over Police Foundation affairs. Lindsay sought out Bundy to persuade me to remain, but the shrewd Bundy would not allow himself to get caught between us. And so I was going. Because I knew that it was time to go.

Still, I remembered what I had said three years before when in the same Blue Room I had been sworn in. "Police officers do not think of becoming Mayor, or even President," I said, "but of being Police Commissioner of New York." And so, perhaps oddly enough in retrospect, for all that had happened, if I had to do it over again, I would.

We—Betty and I —walked out of the Blue Room alone. No aides followed in our trail. No reporters peppered me with questions. No flashbulbs went off in my face. When I got to the family car, parked in the drive near the Mercury, I realized that no detective was jumping out to open the door. I opened the door myself. I was no longer the P.C.

Behind the wheel, I glanced at the mirror. In full view was the black Mercury. The new Commissioner—a protégé—was now getting into the back seat. Detectives were clucking over him like nervous hens.

I started up the family car and headed home.

On the Narrows bridge I thought back to that first day when I became Commissioner. I knew then that any commissioner who took the N.Y.P.D. through the coming storm, with all the corruption revelations, might be consumed emotionally by the effort. I came to that realization on the very first day I was in the back seat of the old Mercury being driven home to Staten Island as the new Police Commissioner.

Now, driving home myself as the *old* Police Commissioner, I think I understood the lesson well. I knew now that the job of chief of police anywhere in America, a country with notable crime, was a visible one, and a risky one. The commissioner might well be held accountable for events that were not within his control, such as a rise in crime, and yet at the same time be encouraged by the politicians not to lift a finger about problems that were within his reach and grasp, such as corruption in the department.

The police commissioner might be asked to be a mere figurehead, leaving the actual running of the police to city hall aides, or to take a fall for the mayor whenever called upon. He might spend most of his energies fighting not crime but rival power factions at police head-quarters—or not so much corruption as the worst kinds of incompetence. He might get involved, in fact, in any number of things except that for which a police department was believed designed to affect: the safety of the community.

The difference between the reality of American policing and its appearance is very great indeed. I suppose this is primarily what my story is about.

Chapter One

The Red and the Black

I was born in a family of cops—and nuns. My father was a sergeant in the New York Police Department. So was my eldest brother. Another brother rose to the rank of captain. My two older sisters became nuns—one was a Maryknoll missionary in Korea. My mother always wanted me to be a priest, but I went into policing instead. Evidently, even though I would be dealing with sinners all my life, mine was to be a secular vocation.

With the luck of the Irish, the Murphys happened to have chosen for their lives' work two of our more embattled institutions: the Church and the state's domestic army, the police, or, as it were, the red and the black of America. This was certainly not by design. My sisters became nuns for the usual reason—religious conviction. The men in the family chose policing for the usual reason—it was a good steady job that was a tiny bit out of the ordinary. It was out of such convention that the Murphys one day awoke to find themselves squarely involved in America's institutional crises.

In my own case, the irony *really* came full circle. Policing became my career for the most middle-class reason of all. When I came out of the Navy in 1945, I had, besides a few ribbons and rosy memories as a Navy fly-boy, a beautiful, intelligent wife, one child, and another on the way. I needed a good-paying job. With two brothers to show me the ropes, the Police Department became my womb, and against all the frantic unemployment of the immediate postwar months, I climbed gratefully into the warmth; I had passed the entrance exam, and the N.Y.P.D. welcomed yet another Murphy to the fold. However, from then on it was all downhill for this Murphy as far as convention was concerned, for reasons which are still not entirely clear to me. In any event, by 1973, when I retired from policing at the acme of the industry—the Police Commissionership of the City of New York—I took to the presidency of the Police Foundation (my new job) a reputation as a reformer, as a bit of a maverick, even as something of a radical intellectual on the subject of American policing. *Something* had happened.

Something had happened, however, not only to me but to American policing. When my father was a cop in the 1930s, though no polls were being taken it was safe to assume that policing was one of the more respected occupations in America. Of course, it was never the same here as in England, where (even today, according to the most recent public opinion poll) the bobby remains England's *most* respected figure. But neither was it ever like the situation in Soviet Russia, where, though no polls have of course been undertaken, it may safely be assumed that to the average Soviet citizen on the street the Communist cop is hardly a figure of affection, admiration, and reassurance. But at some point between the mid-thirties and the mid-seventies the American cop, on the gradation of respect and trust, moved away from the British end of the scale and began to move in the direction of the Russian extreme. Why this has happened is a great, troubling question.

Against all sorts of profound and disquieting developments in American policing, I found myself moving ever more rapidly toward the front lines of the crisis. The movement was almost dreamlike, the product not of rational calculation or even Machiavellian "career development" but of a kind of tug and pull of the spirit. Like the state of American policing itself, there seemed to be no time for settling down, no period of prolonged quiescence—especially in the decade of the 1960s, when a great many things seemed to be happening not only in my life but in the violent sea of American society at large, with American police departments bobbing in the water like buoys desperately trying to remain anchored in place.

In that decade, overflowing into the 1970s, I became the head, almost sequentially, of four different American police departments; the first head of a new division of the U.S. Justice Department—the Law Enforcement Assistance Administration—concerned with helping police departments rise to their occasions; and the head of the most significant and serious research institute for policing in America, the Police Foundation in Washington. In that decade I was to supervise one police department that was sitting atop a potential racial holocaust with all the unconcern of Italian villagers living on the side of a suddenly active volcano; one police department practically burnt out by the horrors of perhaps the most terrible urban riot in our history; and two police departments devastated and demoralized by outside corruption investigations of major consequence. In that decade I was to witness some of the oddest incidents: the Houdini-like disappearance of a virtual fortune in narcotics from a supposedly impenetrable police storage sanctuary; the canonization of a young, obscure cop named Frank Serpico; the fall into disgrace of a police department once widely regarded as perhaps the finest in the world—the department of my father. In that decade I was to witness the incredible growth in crime across the nation, and the equally inexplicable failure of government to do much about it except to put out more cops, in the manner of the English novelist Evelyn Waugh's stinging description of a certain kind of patriotism as putting out more flags. And in this decade I also witnessed time and again routine incidents of incredible police bravery and sacrifice.

In this period of time for American policing, which in a way is what my book is mostly about, I took positions often at odds with the American police establishment. I did not think then that more cops were the answer to the rise in crime, and I do not think so now. I did not then, and do not now, believe that a repressive law-and-order approach to crime was any answer at all to what we faced.

When I hear stories about how much money a cop made shaking down a narcotics dealer, or bluffing a nightclub owner out of a cut of the night's take, I do not chortle; I can get sick to my stomach. When a small West Coast police department—a dozen officers strong —gets federal money for a mini-SWAT team complete with high-powered rifles, night-scopes, and the works, when it can't even inspire its young teenagers with time on their hands to spend it on anything but local burglaries, one questions priorities.

I am not by nature a rebel, much less a radical. I am as conventional as the next person. As a youngster I went to Catholic school— St. Ephrem's in Fort Hamilton, Brooklyn—where the nuns drummed a very conventional morality into me. I went to St. John's College—

another Catholic institution—and majored in mathematics, not the most socially "relevant" subject matter. I went to graduate school for my master's in public administration, not exactly the intellectual pursuit of a revolutionary. In the U.S. Navy I was the good sailor, got my wings, spent the war towing targets for gunnery practice—and loved every minute of it. I am speaking frankly when I say that I came out of the Navy in 1945 and into policing not to reform the profession but to bring home a regular paycheck.

But something happened.

Looking back, maybe there was something in the Murphy blood. I remember once—I was barely a teenager—my father coming home from work a little later than usual for dinner, the big daily occasion in the Murphy home. He came through the door a little unsteady, and we could see right away that he was injured. His face had spots of dried blood from cuts and scrapes. After he took off his police jacket, we could see that he had rolled up his sleeves, and that his arms were covered with scratches and bruises. My mother started but did not say a word; she walked directly, stoically, into the bathroom to run the wash water in the sink. My father, without saying a word to us, followed her in. Everyone wanted to help him, but we were all too stunned to move. Five minutes later our parents emerged, my father all cleaned up and wearing a nice new shirt. Then they sat us all down for dinner as if nothing had happened. Later we found out that our father had been summoned to emergency riot duty at Union Square, where a Red rally had gotten out of hand; but during dinner not a word was said about what must have been a very ugly experience. What was remarkable was not so much that my father did not want to talk about it but that we all knew he wouldn't, and that, without being told, everyone knew enough not to cross that line.

My mother was another enigma. I knew she was an intelligent woman, but there must have been a lot of things about her I did not know. One day I saw her collecting some loose change from the neighborhood women. Later I was to discover that this was something she had been doing regularly for years, but at first, since it was the midst of the Depression, I was puzzled to see her begging off others. After all, my father brought home sixty dollars a week as a police officer, and during those times, with so many people out of work, this was the next best thing to being a millionaire. Finally I got up the nerve to ask her about it, and she smiled. Then a few days later she told me what she was really up to. "It's for the Friends of Irish Freedom," she said, and then spoke in great detail about the revolutionary struggle of the Irish against the English across the sea, explaining compassionately about the need to help all oppressed people in the world, not only your own blood. I was impressed, moved, and a bit in awe of my mother. There was obviously a lot more there than had met the eye, especially her own son's.

I appreciated these incidents even more in later years, in the heat of battles as a police officer and as a police commissioner. They helped me, as a kind of protective emotional facing, to cope with a sense of personal limitation and inadequacy—feelings, I believe, common in my field, and as much the product of the incredible emotional demands of the job as of anything else (such as, arguably, severe deficiencies in the general caliber of the practitioners of policing). Stoicism and humanitarianism—about oneself, in the former case, and about others, in the latter—turn out to be not exactly a bad combination of attitudes for the American police officer. The combination can prove especially beneficial to the head of police.

Police chiefs, in truth, tend to be terribly unworldly men, with a literal (not a sophisticated) conservatism in their politics, and a deep-seated insecurity in their attitudes about themselves and about policing. This conservatism and insecurity manifest themselves, for instance, in the duality of a police chief's public toughness, over against his private phoniness. Put most chiefs in a ghetto or otherwise disadvantaged neighborhood, and they'll do their tough-guy act. But place most of these same individuals in the mayor's office or with the power politicians, and the tough guy turns out to be Casper Milquetoast. What we have here is a pathetic spectacle, and those of us in the police world know that the insecurity and weakness of the nation's police chiefs is one major reason why police departments are so readily (a) compromised, (b) corrupted, and therefore (c) controlled by the politicians. The police chiefs do not, cannot, and seemingly will not stand up to the political establishments in their communities. A tiger in the street, bullying the troops and the other unfortunates, the chief is a lamb in the major leagues, cowering and simpering like a court jester in the halls of the mighty.

This generalization may appear awfully harsh, but to know as many different police chiefs around the country as I do is to know what a rough approximation of the truth this is. It is also to understand the factors of conditioning that have produced a nation with a dangerously weak executive police corps. This understanding leads (as I hope it will lead you) to sympathy, even compassion, as in a situation where events are beyond men's control; but also, and most importantly, it leads to alarm. For in the performance of American policing a great deal more is at stake than the public reputations of police chiefs. The failure of American policing at the top is responsible for the failure of American policing at the bottom, at the level of most intimate contact with both the good and the bad of society.

The American police chief without a sense of inner stoicism or outwardly directed humanitarianism does not measure up to the situation in which he has been placed. A police officer all his life, he has, in the school of the street and of hard knocks, been trained to be a police officer, but not to be a police chief—which is to say the head of a difficult, complex, and sometimes huge bureaucracy; a community leader; even a moral symbol. Most of all, he is not prepared for the political community, whose mores and morals are alien to the paramilitary traditions of policing. In this circumstance, the police chief is not so much in over his head as he is out of his element. In the larger community, aside from the immediate political establishment, the chief or commissioner evokes a variety of conflicting emotions, from a certain bemused incredulity to visceral dislike, especially from the minority community, which seldom feels emanating from the police commissioner that overwhelming sense of cooperation and that cowering and simpering that the political establishment usually detects.

Yet a certain distancing from the political establishment and a genuine sympathy for those far removed from the strings of power are precisely those ingredients that can help keep a police chief, and the department, off the ropes, away from the knockout punch of serious corruption on the one hand and a devastating alienation from whole segments of the community on the other. For one does not always observe a police department relatively free of serious corruption that is also under the thumb of the politicians, or a community with a P.D.

insensitive to minority rights and sensibilities that does not face the enervating threat of civil disorder.

"Pat, I'm just trying to survive," a troubled police chief from a Western department told me in confidence soon after I went to the Police Foundation a few years ago; and I understood. What I did not understand then, however, was the extent of the trouble. For in the months and years to follow, commissioners, police chiefs, sheriffs, and what have you from every part of the country would in the privacy of my office echo the same thing: "I'm just trying to survive."

The vast majority of police officers in the United States progress through an entire career within the confines of a single police department. On the whole, there is virtually no lateral mobility in American policing. Even a police officer in a major metropolitan department tends to remain as provincial in his understanding of things beyond his own horizon as a forest ranger. As a prisoner of limited experience, he has little opportunity to see beyond the cell of his own life. His comprehension of law enforcement challenges may possibly not have advanced beyond a marshal's in Dodge City; certainly few chiefs will have been tutored in such basics as the management of government institutions. And yet it is largely out of this pool of talent that selection is made for the administration of American policing.

American policing, as an interrelated set of institutions, cannot possibly wipe out crime, because the causes of the phenomenon are huge, profound, and possibly beyond the capacity of any set of democratic institutions to eliminate. The occasionally voiced proposition that placing a cop on every street corner in America would eradicate crime is demonstrably false, for a number of reasons. Among them is the fact that street crime is but a small part of the entire crime picture; another consideration is that the cost would bankrupt governmental treasuries. The criterion by which we hold our police forces and our police officers accountable, then, is related not to the elimination of crime, which in a democracy is perhaps both a technical and philosophical impossibility, but to the improvement of the police service, which essentially involves the question of whether the citizen is getting his money's worth from the policing institutions his tax dollars are supporting.

It is on this interface—the performance versus the cost—that American policing is most vulnerable to fair and important criticism. There are about seventeen thousand police departments in the United States. There are about 500,000 sworn law enforcement officers. The annual cost runs to at least $10 billion, and possibly a good deal more. What we have is a numerically huge and financially costly industry: the business of policing.

Future outlays for policing should *not* be directly contingent upon crime reduction, but should be contingent upon the proper and efficient utilization of the resources we have made available to our police agencies. We cannot insist that an extra cop mean an extra point of decline in the rate of crime, but we can and should demand that that extra cop not spend our eight hours of tax monies in corrupt activity, or sleeping, or otherwise in a way utterly unrelated to the provision of desperately needed police service. The police can hardly be held responsible for the root causes of crime, which extend to the totality of social wrongs and economic discontinuities in our society; but they can and should be held accountable as public contributors to the greater good. We do not, for example, demand that the medical profession as a condition of its minimum performance eradicate all disease (we know, intuitively, that this is simply impossible); but we do have a right to expect that doctors will so manage their services as to contribute to the improvement, over time, in the system of disease control. And this is what we must ask of our police: that they so manage their affairs (and our money) that the net result is a more efficient, more *helpful* system of crime control.

Thus, the quality of the management of our ten-billion-dollar, half-million-officer-strong domestic army is quite central to the matter of public safety. Can we say, at the very least, that American policing at most levels has utilized to the best and most efficient advantage those monies which we have given for its purposes?

It was sometime in early 1946 when I found the answer to that question. I was walking a beat in Brooklyn, the classic rookie cop. I was thinking back to a year ago, when I was a lieutenant in the Navy, about the military life, about all those Catch-22s in the service that all the men used to make such fun of. I also realized that perhaps the experience of having been a military officer, which included a real and gratifying taste of command, made it easier for me to accept a police career once I became a civilian. Perhaps I was even looking in civilian life for something similar to what I had enjoyed as a Navy pilot. But as you will see in the next chapter, those initial months as an American police officer passed over me like waves of a bad dream, and in one clear and simplistic flash, walking that Brooklyn beat, I thought I could see how America could win two world wars abroad, yet lose battle after battle at home in the struggle against crime. I suddenly realized how unfair the comparison between the military and the domestic police had been to the Navy: the Catch-22s and other instances of irrationality and insanity which I found in the Navy were but minor irritants compared to the wholesale inefficiency, inept management, and sometimes maddening corruption that I was to find in the New York Police Department, and then later in police departments elsewhere. Of course, as I grew older and more shrewd, I began to perceive added dimensions to the problem, but I never lost sight of that original flash of truth, that compared to police departments our armed forces are pretty well managed, and that in that comparison somewhere lies the reason why, in the struggle against crime, we have become such losers.

As you will see, something *has* happened to the equanimity and pleasure with which I used to view my father's profession. To put matters bluntly, I now *know* from experience, but there are not that many people in America who do. Partly this is because policing has been almost a clandestine activity; the public has just not been permitted to know what has been going on. But perhaps an even more important reason for the state of our ignorance is that for too long we have simply taken our police forces for granted or romanticized them beyond recognition in our television and movies; and this may be because some of us do not take our cops seriously. Like the orangutan in the city zoo, the American police officer, with his sirens and flashing lights, .38 Police Special, official shield, and quaint way of talking (e.g., "poip-a-trait-uh"), is viewed by some as a spectacle of entertainment. Whereas, in truth, the police officer, in his mission to help secure observance of the law, is in fact, as the noted Scottish scholar

Charles Reith has put it, "the primary essential to the existence of all communities."*

Yet another reason for the current state of policing (and for our failure to take it seriously) is that federal and state governments, evidenced by their behavior, themselves do not take the problem seriously. The states have not, as they should, coordinated policing within their respective boundaries as an antidote to the decentralized chaos which makes law enforcement more a matter of chance than the functioning of a logical system. By adopting what is virtually a laissez-faire attitude toward our seventeen thousand police departments, the states have managed to do little more than witness the deepening chaos. The federal government has also neglected the problem, perhaps fearing to raise the specter of a national police force. But when it hasn't been inept, its involvement has been pernicious and destructive. Federal law enforcement institutions like the Federal Bureau of Investigation and the U.S. Law Enforcement Assistance Administration—potentially, in my view, key elements of the overall answer—have more often than not been part of the problem. But without proper overall guidance and example at the federal level, and detailed standards and planning at the state level, policing at the local level simply has no chance at all; and in the war on crime, not only will more battles be lost but in the hasty retreat from the front lines of our streets and our communities the very style of our lives may be on the line.

But a final thought to be considered comes even closer to home. It

---

* Reith, in his classic and ground-breaking study *The Blind Eye of History,* was livid about the failure of scholars, of all people, to understand the profound role played throughout history by the police. "On the shelves of the world's libraries," he wrote, "there are untold thousands of books on the subject of laws, to the compiling of which untold thousands of able writers have devoted their lives and energies throughout the ages. Laws certainly deserve their place in the record of what mattered . . . but of infinitely greater importance to mankind is the record by which rulers and governments have secured observance of their laws, because, if they are not observed, the most perfect laws which the wit of man can devise are useless, and the rulers and governments are impotent. . . . On the shelves of the world's libraries, along with the miles of books in which the history of laws and law-making has been recorded, one can search in vain for a single volume which supplies even an outline of the history of means of securing law-observance." One of the most heartening developments in recent years concerning American policing has been the rise of a new scholarship on the subject—especially in our universities.

concerns the citizen's appropriate demands on his police. The question even goes beyond the matter of asking cops to eliminate crime; it goes to a deeper understanding of what police do, what they should do, and what they cannot do.

On the simplest level, it involves understanding the sheer mechanics of policing, and the mores and styles of the police world. It involves being taken on a tour of headquarters, and sitting behind the cluttered desk of the police commissioner. It takes in a clear and unsentimental examination of the terrible problem of police corruption, and the even more difficult and essential problem of managing police departments. It means looking at the whole problem of crime from the level of the lowliest beat officer to the heights of the most powerful police commissioner.

But, more than this, it involves a better understanding of the role of the police in the context of our lives. Do we ask too much of our police, or too little—or some of both? Do we ask them simply to be keepers of our gates, or also custodians of our morals? What are the offensive and societally destructive behaviors which we ask them to regulate, and which ones are susceptible to actual regulation?

In short, as we look at our police, do we see the red or the black? Do we see them for what they are or should be—professionals providing a vital public service? Like my mother, who wanted me to be a priest, can we be satisfied to permit them to be just cops? For if we ask them to do too much, in the confusion of what they are we may find that they are doing too little.

Chapter Two

Toward a New Mode

The Murphys were quite a close family, and the supper conversation around our dining table was often the centerpiece of the day for all of us. But neither my father nor my two older brothers ever talked much at these intimate daily gatherings about their work as New York cops. When I became a rookie patrol officer in 1945, I walked into the Police Department utterly naive about the job and, indeed, was expecting something entirely different. The reluctance of my father and brothers to talk about "the job," I suddenly understood after about five days on the force, was painfully understandable.

My first precinct stationhouse, in Brooklyn, turned out to be run according to rules we had not been taught at the Police Academy. One rule seemed to be that superior officers could be drunk at will. Another rule seemed to be that liquor bottles, once empty, had to remain in place and could not be collected or hidden out of sight. A third rule seemed to be that sergeants, especially, could be obnoxious drunks, giving no quarter of peace and tranquillity to anyone, and could be doubly rough on the rookies, who, so inappropriately prepared for life in a precinct by the Police Academy, could be kept on the defensive for months. In short, the one thing that our pre-beat training had not prepared us for was that, behind those precinct doors, police operations came close to being a fraud.

The top management personnel of the precinct, with certain notable and heroic exceptions, were known among the rookies as the walking stoned. There was one lieutenant who was particularly obnoxious, and there was one sergeant who even more than the rest of us hated him dearly. Time and again this sergeant would pull some

31

merciless prank on the drunk lieutenant, such as calling him just before the end of a tour to report "a really big dice game, Lou. I'm down here on Sackett Street, and if you wanna get in on it, you'd better hurry up." Though dying to get to a bar, the lieutenant could hardly pass up the possibility of a "big score." (The sergeant was saying that the gamblers were heavy and could be shaken down.) Of course, the incident was entirely fictitious, and when he arrived at the scene, huffing and puffing, the lieutenant would discover to his chagrin, in the absence of either gamblers or police officers, that once again he had been taken by the sergeant. But such was the lieutenant's greed and cupidity that this would happen over and over again.

This was the esprit de corps of the precinct. Worse still, however, was the degree to which hypocrisy was practically institutionalized. This, for me, was the most difficult feature of precinct life to accept with total equanimity. The hypocrisy was built into the very rules of procedure by which precinct life was regulated. The hypocrisy was the differential between what we all were supposed to be doing and what in fact we were up to.

For example, take the police signal box system. Its official purpose was to maintain a management check on the movement of officers out on patrol. Each precinct had a large number of call boxes that were laid out in the pattern of an electronic grid, more or less in a logical schematic pattern across the territory of the precinct. However, there was a hitch in the scheme's logic, which required all officers to phone the precinct switchboard once an hour, the line on which the call was received identifying the caller's location.

The hitch was that there might be two to four boxes on the same line. One learned this beat-the-system fact on the first day. "Kid," one veteran explained, "you can call in on any one of these three boxes, and for all they know at the switchboard, you could be at any one of the three locations. They're all on the same line. You can call up and say, 'This is Murphy on Box Four,' and since Four is connected to Six and Eight, be at either place." What the experienced hand was saying was that Murphy could be playing poker in a "coop" (sleeping or loafing location kept by officers) near Box Four, but could call in and give the impression that he was blocks away. An hour later, to give the impression that he was on the move, he could call back from the same box and give a different location entirely. Yet the system was designed, and publicized, as a management control measure to insure constant movement; this was the great police omnipresence.

In some precincts, one got the distinct impression that just about the only person working hard was the switchboard officer writing up the daily sheet on the phone call-ins from the boxes. There were ground rules to the institutionalized joke, of course; the game had to be played according to a certain protocol. It was permissible to ask a fellow patrol officer to put in a call for you if you were sound asleep, but it was not permissible to ask a sergeant for the same favor. There was, after all, a certain pecking order, and it was necessary to beware of the avenging sergeant, who, after all, knew the weakness of the call-in control system as well as anyone. "This is Murphy on Box Four," you might say one night, standing in front of Box Six. But instead of the regular switchboard officer, a sergeant on the rampage might answer instead, "Did you get that guy? Was it you who got him?" You'd reply, flustered, "What guy?" The trap now snapped shut: "That dead body leaning on Box Four." Well, you were caught.

But with few exceptions the official regulation about reporting "telephonically" was easily circumvented; and the call-back system was a big part of the daily routine of the patrol officer. But, then again, most of the regulations and rules added up to considerably less than met the eye.

After a few weeks on the beat, I began to wonder whether most of the rules and regulations hadn't been designed merely as a device to insulate Headquarters from embarrassment. There seemed to be no other possible reason; it was as though the cardinal concern was not proper management but public relations. Above all, don't embarrass the Commissioner!

There were a great many rules and regulations, so many that in their abundance one lost respect for many of them. Ten commandments would have been more than enough; but in the N.Y.P.D., as in most police departments, I was later to learn, Headquarters seemed to have felt that there was safety in numbers. The rules were designed not so much for quality control of the product—the policing of

America—but for the protection of the higher-ups, to enhance their leverage vis-à-vis the lower ranks in the event of public embarrassment, e.g., an explosive newspaper story. In this event, Headquarters could literally throw the book at a few hapless scapegoats and wash its hands of the whole mess; it could invoke rules 3012, 3013, and so on—rules which in the ordinary course of business had been discarded or hidden from view for years—to hang the miscreants.

It seemed to me that these rules, phony and demoralizing in the way in which they were invoked, were weapons for the pleasure of the "shooflies," the officers of the Internal Affairs operation with primary responsibility for integrity control. Internal Affairs applied these rules selectively (by definition, there were too many of them to be applied uniformly and routinely), as a Headquarters hedge against the worst forms of corruption. The implicit message to the lower rungs was to keep the corruption down or Headquarters would swoop down on the noisy ones and conduct some public hangings. As a corruption control method, the system was not without certain advantages; but weighed against the disrespect and cynicism engendered for the operational rules of the department, the system was far too costly. Whatever it might have been doing to counteract corrupt cops, it was also creating ever more cynical cops.

Cynicism, the unhealthy kind, was the system's most enervating by-product. In my era as a beat cop (I suspect this observation will prove equally applicable today for many police officers), commonly the most ballyhoed anti-corruption shakeups tended to elicit great derision from the troops rather than appropriate notice and concern. "Biggest Shakeup in the History of the Department"—the headline seemed to occur annually—was all too often an exercise in cosmetology, almost an elaborate charade in which, for instance, plainclothes squad A would be transferred to territory B (with the reverse maneuver executed, group B to turf A). Necessarily, a handful of officers in each group might be transferred out of plainclothes entirely as a gesture of sincerity. But the net impact was largely similar. Indeed, on several occasions word would get around that representatives from each of the transferred divisions had secretly met in some hotel room to exchange the "pads" (the rosters of businessmen and organized crime figures involved in illegal enterprises and therefore making contributions).

At the Police Academy, where recruits were trained, the picture painted for us was quite different. There were, one read in the holy (and wholly irrelevant) texts, basically five essential functions of the modern police officer. They dealt with the ability to handle ambiguous situations, challenges to one's manhood and self-respect, the physical capacity to restrain persons, the comprehension of the relevant legal concepts in illegal situations, and the acceptance of responsibility for one's own actions. At the center of these precepts was the assumption that the police officer's primary job was to deal with crime. He was, according to the ritual, a crime fighter.

What we were not told at the Police Academy—and what most trainees in the country do not find out until much later—was that very little of what we did had an intimate connection to crime or crime prevention. In the vast majority of police agencies in the United States, crime—the burglaries, robberies, homicides, larcenies, and so forth—constituted perhaps as little as 10 percent of the police officer's daily regimen, and perhaps even a smaller proportion than that. "Uniformed police in large urban areas," according to a study by Professor Gordon Misner, "typically spend less than three percent of their working time" dealing with crime and criminal enforcement duties. Instead, the study suggested, the patrol officer spends most of his time with public service–type activity, including everything from helping tenants without heat to intervening in family quarrels. There is nothing wrong with such responsibilities; they are neither demeaning nor unnecessary. But the young police officer does not receive either warning or training before he is thrown into the swim; he is given a textbook education, a .38 Police Special, a badge, a pension system, a prayer, and is then sent off.

Management's contribution, generally, is to make the officer's task on the street as difficult as possible. Besides its proliferation of rules and regulations, management was often involved in seemingly point-less manipulations of officers. In addition to the periodic plainclothes rotation, conducted for the sake of appearances, there was a man-power deployment system at the precinct level that seemed designed to maximize confusion. When I first came into the department, patrol officers were scheduled to work six tours a week (a tour is an eight-hour shift), but the sergeants were slotted for five tours and the lieu-tenants four. The effect was like dividing your army up into three parts and having them march in different directions; for the soldier on the street the impact was disorienting, because it removed from his life the principle of a steady supervisor. The boss was not a single individual but an incoherent system, seemingly organized for maximum feasible confusion.

Without steady personalized supervision, the young officer is left to his own devices, cast out into the sea without even so much as a life line of his own. So he bobs, improvises, does as best he can under very difficult circumstances. He is forced into constant contact with the community, and he takes refuge, characteristically, in the sanctuary of cynicism and the cruiser car or, worse yet, the coop. He is not prepared for the emotional demands of dealing for eight hours straight with people with different (and often unpleasant) sorts of trouble. And management is no help. Rather than encourage him to meet the enormous challenge of dealing with non-criminal problems, which constitute the greatest portion of his work, management rewards only heroism. Police officers who perform meritorious peace-keeping and community-service work have to find in their virtue its own reward; but sometimes, against the crushing demands of the job, virtue is not enough of a reward. Outside reinforcement would help. Without it, the patrol officer is compelled to devote most of his time to work for which the department offers no positive reinforcement. In this omission, management seemingly fails to recognize the actual content of the average police officer's work.

The lack of managerial concern for the actual content of the work of the police officer on the street or in the patrol car perhaps helps account for the tremendous boredom on the job, whether in New York or anywhere else. The constant draining, boring tours of duty, perhaps more than anything else, surprised and then depressed me about the job. I could imagine in the back of my own mind police officers turning to cooping or corruption at least in part as a relief against the waves of boredom that wash over one in the course of a tour. I remember my own first tours vividly, when I was wide-eyed with every expectation of immediate excitement and heroism. My beat was in the Red Hook section of Brooklyn, a tough neighborhood populated largely though not exclusively by Italian-Americans, and my job, my sergeant had said, was just to walk and stay out of trouble. And so I walked, endlessly, pointlessly, up and down streets, trying to stay clear of trouble, minding my own business, leaving crime prevention and investigatorial entrepreneurship to the "brains department," as the sergeant had put it—the famed Detective Bureau.

The Patrol Bureau, it was now clearly understood, could have the scraps off the Detective Bureau's table—the sick calls, the cats on roofs, the drunks, the family fights—but the heady stuff was off limits, and the Detective Bureau did not look kindly on investigative entrepreneurship by a street cop. This was a clear violation of its franchise, and the uniformed officer intruding on its preserve risked an unofficial (or even official) reprimand, or worse yet, perhaps a transfer to an undesirable post. The Detective Bureau was powerful enough—and in most municipal police departments in the country it is a major power indeed—that the game had to be played according to its rules.

Occasionally the boredom of routine patrolling—up and down the streets, showing the night-stick, creating some sort of presence—was relieved by the necessity to make an arrest; not even the famed Detective Bureau could handle it all. Indeed, I was to learn that for all its aggressiveness about monopolizing interesting cases the Detective Bureau actually made a very small percentage of the department's total arrests. This stunning and unexpected truth was largely attributable to the high correlation between citizen complaints and arrests, and the low correlation between entrepreneurial investigations and ultimate arrest. In department after department, throughout the United States, studies showed that in any one year the great bulk of the arrests were being made by patrol officers in response to civilian complaints or tips. In the Washington, D.C., Police Department one year, according to a survey, 87 percent of all arrests were made by officers of the patrol division. Analyzing data from four high-crime precincts in Washington, researchers concluded that most complaints leading to ultimate arrest originated in citizen calls to police. At the same time, the researchers found, very few criminal cases leading to possible arrests arose from non-complaint entrepreneurship. In other words, in most departments, in most instances, it is the citizens who are "cracking" cases, and it is the common patrol officer, perhaps because of his relative proximity, who is the primary recipient of this intelligence information.

These lessons were clear to me, as one suspects they are to most officers, after a few weeks on the beat. It was then, in an effort to overcome the dispiritment, boredom, and cynicism, that I began to maneuver a bit, not in such a dramatic way as to attract the attention of superiors or the Detective Bureau, but enough to keep my own senses on the alert, and to satisfy myself that some portion of my job was indeed worthwhile.

Perhaps my primary problem was overcoming the community's understandable suspicions about me. In a beat that was almost exclusively Italian-American, my uniform and Murphy face made me as inconspicuous and acceptable as a white narcotics undercover cop in a Harlem after-hours club. I felt irrelevant, alone, absurd. But the hardest part, which was breaking the ice, became ingenuously simple in the implementation of a suggestion by Betty, my wife. The suggestion was to go around and begin to collect some recipes for Italian cooking from the good ladies of the neighborhood.

That such an otherwise inconsequential suggestion might actually prove to have a profound effect on my ability to relate to the community was at the time unpredictable; but the fact was that, in the process of introducing myself and explaining my wife's desire to expand her culinary repertoire, the residents of the community began to perceive me not as an extension of City Hall, which long ago they had given up fighting, but as a possible ally in their own private war on crime and fear of crime. The assumption—which white cops sometimes make about black neighborhoods, or Irish cops about Italian neighborhoods—that a community is hopelessly crime-ridden turns out on further examination to be a terrible, slanderous falsehood. On the contrary, the vast majority of residents of *any* community, black, white, or brown, will turn out to be not only law-abiding but also possibly law-assisting. My job, the job of any patrol officer, is to enlist the law-abiding allies in the struggle against crime and criminals. It is my job to make friends with my natural allies.

The recipe collecting led to other contacts with the community. Spending time at the school crossings talking to teachers, parents, and students. Kibitzing with the old men in the parks. Playing a game or two of checkers with the local masters at the social clubs. Sitting on a park bench now and then to talk to the older people who with time on their hands could become valuable, trusted sentries.

Before long I began to see that intimacy between a patrol officer and the residents of the territory under patrol was a necessary part of the social contract which permitted police officers the substantial authority and responsibility they possessed. The police department that was isolated from and basically indifferent to the citizens for whom its service was designed would necessarily become a remote, abstract organization, with headquarters moving men and equipment around like Hitler and his high command long after their war had been lost.

The alienation of the patrol officer not only from his work but also from the community in which he worked was further troubling when one considered the mathematics of modern police departments. In most P.D.s, the patrol bureau accounted for from 40 to 60 percent of the total manpower. Detectives—who received much of the credit and publicity from the press for cracking cases, when it was often citizen complaints in combination with patrol officer follow-up that was responsible—by comparison accounted for perhaps a total of 50,000 officers out of the nation's 500,000 sworn police officers. Thus, leaving to the "brains department" primary authority for crime-prevention entrepreneurship was tantamount to tying a police department's hands not with fussy, restrictive court orders concocted by soft-headed jurists with liberal blood coursing in their blue veins but with inept management policies designed haphazardly by otherwise "tough-minded" police administrators.

In some police departments, the low priority accorded by the bosses to contact between patrol officers and residents is cloaked in the virtue of a formal management philosophy—known colloquially in police circles as "stranger policing." Until recently, when some changes were made, stranger policing was the philosophy of the Los Angeles Police Department. (The caricature was television's cop Sergeant Friday, who made a career for himself and a name for the L.A.P.D. by saying "Just the facts ma'am" at least five times per show.) The essential feature of stranger policing is aloofness and a properly distant posture between patrol officers and citizens, as if what is involved is not so much a community police service as the occupation of conquered territory by an alien army. Under stranger policing, for instance, it is permissible for officers to hide in their radio cars with windows rolled up, communicating not with the community but only with each other, the dispatchers at headquarters, and their own private thoughts. In this "philosophy" of policing, the community—the law *abiders*—hardly get a wave from a passing car. I remember once, many years removed from being a beat cop, meeting with Mayor Tom Bradley of Los Angeles in his office. Others in the room included some of the top brass of the L.A.P.D. Bradley, a former L.A.P.D. lieutenant, had just returned from a trip to New York and had noticed, he was telling us, how friendly New York cops seemed to be, at least by comparison to the aloof, Kaiser-like L.A. police. "Do you think," he asked the police brass in the room, with a twinkle in his eye, "that at the academy we could begin to teach our police officers how to smile?"

The reliance on the radio car is, indeed, not only a characteristic of stranger policing but, sadly, a measure of American policing's general infatuation with technological strategies for coping with endlessly complex human and social problems. Motorized patrol, like computers and other technological innovations, is often substituted for precise analysis by management, and it is a very poor substitute.

A study of the Miami Police Department shows the dimensions and character of the problem, which is that to a considerable extent the overuse of the patrol car inhibits good policing, especially of neighborhoods. From officers in a patrol car, the study revealed, the average number of police-citizen contacts over an eight-hour shift was a dismal 4.4. In numerical hours, simple, uneventful no-thought cruising in patrol cars occupied at least 3.6 hours of every eight-hour shift—and quite possibly, the researchers suggested, well over half the tour. These findings suggested that, as infrequent as police-citizen contacts tend to be among officers on foot patrol, contact from officers in cruisers is even less frequent. The implications are quite disturbing, in my view, because, almost as an article of blind faith, police administrators around the country believe in the cruiser—the warboat of their armada in the unfriendly sea of society.

Appropriately, the cruiser car is permitted by police administrators to be considered a more desirable assignment than a street beat. It took me, as a young officer, quite some time to latch onto a radio car.

(It was probably not just a locker-room sea story, the belief that when necessary one could buy one's way into a cruiser car.) But it didn't take me long to realize that to police a neighborhood from a patrol car was a losing proposition—even more of an abstraction than walking up and down streets like a mechanical toy soldier. Worse yet, to be in a cruiser car was like trying to relate to an alien society from behind the windows of a low-hovering flying saucer.

The patrol car has therefore turned out to be in some respects quite counterproductive. (Obviously, its abolition entirely is not realistic, since a department needs mobility.) A study of the Chicago Police Department showed that cars tend to be in service only 15 percent of the time, for various reasons. One was that, in some respects, cruisers tend to break down, go out on "sick leave," more frequently than the human machines, the cops. But this, according to the study, was only one curious aspect of cruiser "behavior"; another was the odd behavior of those cars that were in service. In one period under study in Chicago, cruiser cars handled fewer than one-third of all criminal incidents in their own beat; and only a little more than one-fourth of all criminal incidents *originating from dispatches* were handled by patrol-car officers within their own beat. The proportion of *noncriminal* incidents was one-fifth—even smaller. Based on the data of the Chicago study, the conclusion seemed inescapable that even with patrol cars assigned to specific beats, officers tended not to deal with the problems of their turf but more likely with the problems outside their turf.

It is worth noting why this phenomenon occurs, since in the examination we can see more clearly what really goes on out there on the streets. Because of their mobility, it seems, beat cars frequently are asked to handle calls outside their beat. This is understandable, and perhaps inevitable. But once a car is on a call outside its beat, it tends to stay there, because the probability increases that the next call it will handle will also be outside its beat.

This chain-reaction effect is evidently quite familiar to students of systems analysis, but it has rarely caught the attention of police managers. It is still an unexamined axiom of traditional police management that officers in a beat car will necessarily spend more time answering calls within the territory assigned by the high command than elsewhere. But the truth is that a system with a centralized command over a dispersed force makes this a pipe dream.* Therefore, from all evidence, the overreliance on the cruiser car contributes to the breakdown in America of the territorial principle of policing.

Of course, the value of the cruiser car in providing a more rapid response to emergencies than an officer on foot possibly could is undeniable. It probably outweighs the reduction in time spent within an assigned beat. However, the long-range goal should be to get the best of both worlds, and the beginning of wisdom here is for officers in cars to do much less routine cruising—the so-called preventive patrol, which has been assumed to be productive but which as we shall see is not—and to use the time out of the cars in a critical interaction with the citizens whom the police are supposed to be protecting.

An important variation on uniformed police is the so-called plainclothes cop or vice-squad officer. This is a regular police officer, not a detective, who is taken out of uniform and put on the street in "plain" or street clothes for special assignment. That assignment usually concerns gambling, prostitution, and other vices, and plainclothes assignment, after only a few short months on patrol, was *my* next assignment.

The idea behind vice-squad or plainclothes work is to utilize the patrol officer in non-uniformed investigatory roles. In the New York Police Department, plainclothes assignment was considered a step up from what was known as being "in the bag" (police slang for the traditional blue uniform). The honest, dedicated police officer, without the giveaway of the paramilitary uniform, could now swim in the criminal sea in the exercise of his duty to snare some big fish. This was the theoretical idea behind the plainclothes modification of uniformed police protection. But to the corruption-prone police officer, plainclothes assignment was an opportunity to insinuate himself into

---

* Cars are indispensable but overrelied on. The rapid-response emphasis has neglected the need for citizen participation in crime control. Five or ten officers are required, depending on whether a one-officer or two-officer car system is used, to man a beat twenty-four hours a day, seven days a week. One officer on a beat should be relieved entirely of rapid-response car duty and assigned to the critical function of working closely with the community in the territory of the beat.

the environment of the underworld not to perform his sworn duty but to make a financial killing.*

A standard joke in my era as a young officer revolved around the exploits of the famed "Connecticut Squire." A corruption investigation had uncovered the existence of a New York plainclothes officer who had acquired, without any other visible means of support than his paycheck, an astonishing portfolio of New England real estate. In locker-room banter, the question of one officer to another about the plainclothes officer would be the cynical line "How many houses in Connecticut has he bought?"

This sort of black humor illustrates vividly and sadly the ethical atmosphere of plainclothes work. It was understood, of course, that impressive personal acquisitions were not accumulated out of the residue of the weekly paycheck. Indeed, it was more commonly assumed that those who *sought out* plainclothes assignment may possibly have not been acting out of the highest ethical motives. There was always with plainclothes assignment a very uncomfortable air of uncertainty.

My own attitude about the sudden, unexpected assignment to plainclothes was not ambiguous. I did not want any part of it. I was happy on the street. The old men playing checkers and the wonderfully warm Italian women with the recipes had become like extensions of the Murphy family, friends as well as citizens to protect, and I felt that in moving over to plainclothes I was abandoning them.

---

* A newer variation on the "out-of-the-bag" service involves what in New York and in some other places is known as the "anti-crime" or "decoy" cop. The officer will dress up as a derelict, a rabbi, even an old lady, in an effort to attract the criminal away from less-capable victims. We tried the anti-crime concept early in my administration in New York and before long found that the anti-crime cops were making tremendous arrests—both in number and in quality. And the arrests were leading to convictions in court (the essence of anti-crime work is that the victim is usually a cop in disguise, and so the evidence in court is invariably gripping and credible). The program was a big success. But when I first proposed the idea in New York, the general reaction in the High Command was alarm that I'd be taking cops out of uniform. Dozens of objections to the idea were raised in the police bureaucracy. So I suggested we put the anti-crime program entirely on a volunteer basis. The response in the precincts was overwhelming: cops were standing in line to apply. They know only too well the limitations of the uniform, and real cops want to do *real* police work.

A further problem for me was the nature of the laws I would be asked to enforce. Whether because of my Irish background or whatever, I am unable to regard gambling as a mortal sin; I also felt, somewhat intuitively, that gambling enforcement is demeaning and quite possibly beneath the dignity of the police. And, as a practical matter, the law against gambling was utterly impossible to enforce, even by the most professional, assiduous police action. The victims, so-called, of this "crime" are supremely unaware of the alleged injustice being perpetrated on them (this feeling holds even when the gambler loses!), and so therefore rarely if ever feel motivated to make a complaint to the police; accordingly, since civilian complaints are the backbone of any successful enforcement program, gambling enforcement is severely crippled. Indeed, without substantial community support for gambling laws, police are not going to be effective —and are, again, caught in the ethical no man's land of American society, between what we say we are, and what we really are when the spotlight of the pulpit is not directly on us.

In this environment of ethical ambiguity, it was possible for the police officer to be highly ineffective and to make money at the same time. The police, allowed to operate in an area of minor concern to the community, could permit gamblers and bookmakers to live their own lives without serious police interference—for an appropriate fee. To the bookmaker or gambling combine, paying off the plainclothes or vice squad in his territory was a small price to pay compared to the cost of lawyers, et cetera. Indeed, the plainclothes payoff was practically nothing more than a routine business expense.

Once the system of corruption was established, the officer in vice or plainclothes did not have to seek out the graft; it was the underworld that sought him out to make its payment. What was involved was not so much extortion as co-optation; it was the system that was corrupt— and plainclothes corruption was just one dark corner of the system.

At the time I was a rookie picking up my transfer orders, I did not fully understand the systemic nature of the corruption. All I possessed was a deep-seated sense that all was not right in plainclothes work. The transfer was deeply, agonizingly troubling. As a practical matter, it was also, I felt, dangerous. Rookies remained on probation for six months, and barely half that had run out. I was still on trial, so to speak, and the prospect of being thrown into the snake pit worried me—and my wife, Betty, now with the second child—no end. I wanted above all to remain in the department, but on honorable terms. Was this possible in plainclothes?

At this time, some four hundred officers were assigned to plain-clothes work. My partner in this new assignment was a twenty-year veteran of the department—and of plainclothes work. The immediate reverberations were not pleasant: Could this rookie Murphy be trusted or was he a troublemaker?

An elaborate and alarmingly subtle ritual was thus commenced, and I was left feeling like a rookie China watcher—in awe and wonder at the endlessly mysterious movements behind the silk screen of deception. Even in this era when corruption reached high into the ranks of the top brass (as the famous Gross gambling scandal of the 1950s revealed, when several high-ranking commanders were convicted of criminal charges or dismissed from the department), one learned the facts of life only by reading between the lines. Not a single word about the system of graft was mentioned directly, especially in front of a suspect rookie like myself. Even if I had been wired, i.e., had been carrying a concealed recording device, nothing that was said in front of me would have been material to an indictable offense.

But it took only a few days of reading between the lines to see that there was more there than met the eye. And, astonishingly, manage-ment policy from on high seemed only to reinforce rather than counteract the corrupt patterns. Management policy demanded as a condition of employment for plainclothes a minimum quota of gambling arrests each month. This monthly quota put pressure on the officers to produce. What was telling about this quota system was a built-in hitch in the logic; by setting the numerical quota sufficiently high, management was precluding the probability of developing major cases against the higher-ups in the gambling underworld, the people who were actually running the lucrative illicit business. Cases against the bigger fish simply take a great deal more time to develop than those against the street-level runner or betting clerk. But man-agement seemingly had no concern for quality—no quality control, only *quantity* control. The idea under conveyance was not effective law enforcement but a numbers game, the quota system.

The plainclothes officer, even if he were disposed to the most honest, uncompromising pattern of law enforcement, was therefore left with this insane Catch-22. To have a real impact on the problem, it was necessary to attack the higher-ups, not just the functionaries. As an investigator, you had to let your line go out far and deep and wait with great patience for the big one to begin nibbling at the bait; you could not jerk your line out of the water every five minutes. But under the pressure of having to produce a monthly arrest "body count," there was no time to go on a fishing expedition, as management would put it; therefore, nose to the grindstone, turn out those arrests so Headquarters can look good and everyone can be happy.

I was in plainclothes work for two full weeks when I began to develop severe anxieties; Betty was perhaps finding me even more difficult to live with than usual. Partly at her suggestion, I decided to ask for a transfer. So I went to my lieutenant, the supervising officer, to request a transfer back into "the bag."

Probably I will never forget that expression on the lieutenant's face. First "I didn't hear you right" astonishment. Then "I heard you right but I still don't believe it" incredulity. And finally "Just to be sure, would you repeat it" sarcasm.

I did.

The problem was that hardly anyone ever requested transfer out of plainclothes; indeed in some circles the effort to land a choice vice assignment consumed the constant energies of scheming men.

The lieutenant kept looking at me, now with evident concern for my sanity. "But why?" he said, after a long wait. Trying not to seem nervous, I gave him my answer. For days I had been working on a satisfactory answer, for I knew I could not blithely say that I did not want any part of possible corruption; this sort of response would create all too many problems for the lieutenant, who I knew had the power to create even more difficult problems for me. What I needed was something that would not fail the test of plausibility; the appeal to sainthood always lacked a certain credibility in a police department. It was necessary to offer something closer to the limbo of the lieutenant's own experiences as a seasoned cop, to avoid trouble for all concerned. So I gave him my cover story: "There's the sergeants' exam coming up, Lou. I need time to cram."

The answer, as I had anticipated, was satisfactory. The tension went out of his face. As the British philosopher David Hume once put it in defining the idea of an explanation as that point where the restless mind comes to rest, the lieutenant had ceased to worry. My explanation implied that back in the precinct I would be able to "steal time." This meant that I would be stealing time from the taxpayers by studying in some coop, taking time from my intellectual pursuits only to make the phone calls in on the box. This explanation for the transfer request thus coincided neatly with an old saying in the department: "The job's only good for time or money." Translation: The occupation offers two main opportunities. One is to graft, the other is to pick up your check without having really done your job.

In short order I was back in uniform. Then a year later I landed an assignment in the Emergency Service Division, a branch of the Police Department devoted entirely to such life-and-death situations as the jumper (whose remains must be removed from under a subway train), the would-be jumper (the suicidal person ready to leap off a bridge), the coronary, the troubled or endangered person. This was, in my view, very satisfying work, and for the period of the four years I was thus assigned I was as happy as I had ever been in law enforcement.

Looking back on the plainclothes incident, however, I have to wonder if I handled it as well as I might. Should I have resigned from the department? (It is a real question now, though it was an academic question then, because I had not only a wife but a growing family to support.) Or, like an early version of Frank Serpico, the famous anticorruption cop of the late 1960s, should I have gone to some crusading newspaperman to launch an expose?

These remain difficult, troubling questions, but in view of the fact that (a) I had no real hard evidence of wrongdoing and (b) knew of no crusading reporters to go to, I probably wound up doing the right thing, because rather than dismiss the weight of the incident from my mind with a shrug, I went to see the Police Commissioner.

I took advantage of a departmental rule rarely invoked: Any officer can request an audience with the P.C.

I went into the Commissioner's office determined to tell my story. And I did. I also told the Commissioner that in the event of a departmental investigation, I volunteered my services in any way that might help.

The Commissioner looked out over his desk with cold politeness. He was an austere man but, I hoped, an honest one. The Commissioner took his time in responding to my allegations and my suggestion that an investigation be undertaken but finally said, "Thank you for bringing this incident to my attention, officer. You can be sure it will be given my every attention. And you'll be hearing from me."

But I never did hear from him again.

The constant uphill struggle against naiveté and frustration continued as I made my way up the ranks. I became a sergeant in 1948, a lieutenant in 1953.

As a sergeant I was assigned to a park precinct, on the face of it not an especially welcome development. The other sergeant assigned with me was a man named Sydney Cooper, later to become one of the department's most feared corruption fighters (and who under my administration of the N.Y.P.D. from 1970–73 became an utterly valuable high-ranking officer). Looking back at the two of us in the Prospect Park precinct—in the N.Y.P.D. a park precinct was known as a "squirrel" precinct—I have to laugh. What an odd couple! What kind of "hook" (political pull) did these two guys have to land a plum like a squirrel precinct?

Actually, the park precinct assignment was a short one. I was soon dispatched to the Police Academy. By 1952 I was permanently assigned to the Academy as an instructor. *That* was a good assignment, providing a great deal of satisfaction. In 1954 a reform police commissioner, Francis Adams, came in with Mayor Robert Wagner. I became Training Officer at the Academy (in charge of training programs), and in that role edged closer to the power and the changes. A number of worthwhile reforms were tried—tighter investigations of recruit candidates, better training, breaking up the long entrenched plainclothes cliques, elimination of political influence in promotions above captain. All in all, it was a time of optimism.

Only after some years of floundering around was it clear that the honest reform commissioners under Wagner were not going far enough. They did not grasp the depth and complexity of the problems in organization and management of a large police bureaucracy. They did not understand how to hold ranking officers accountable for integrity and productivity. To attack corruption they over-relied on an overcentralized headquarters watchdog system.

But in my own limited sphere, I felt I was contributing. With the advantage of a college education and a little luck landing my job at the Police Academy, I was picked by a new reform commissioner's staff for certain Headquarters assignments, including commanding officer of the Inspection Squad. I was even permitted to visit a few other departments around the country and take notes (this latter perquisite at my request). In short order my Gulliver's Travels became a sort of standing joke around Headquarters, as if the very idea of looking to other police forces for ideas about policing and management was instantly hilarious. "Doesn't he know that this is the greatest police force in the world? He can't learn anything from those cow-town departments."

The attempt at humor and the put-down revealed that more than New York's well-known penchant for arrogance and smugness was at work; it also revealed an unnecesesary ignorance of what was happening in the larger area of American policing. For I learned that in a number of important ways the N.Y.P.D. was not above improvement and reform, indeed that in some respects we were perhaps an unforgivably backward department.

Perhaps most revealing in this regard was my 1957 visit to the West Coast to study Chief William Parker's great Los Angeles Police Department. For it was then in 1957—and perhaps still is today—the best-managed big-city police department in the country. Although I had then and retain today certain serious reservations about some of the principal operating assumptions of management, within those assumptions—that is, under the goals which it assigned to itself—the L.A.P.D. was a successful police bureaucracy. In 1957 it was so far ahead of its time, and the N.Y.P.D., in grafting modern management methods onto the daily routine of police work that its operations seemed to come out of a different police tradition entirely.* Which was exactly the case; for many of the West Coast departments under

* On a superficial level, the L.A.P.D. even *looked* better than the N.Y.P.D., the officers smartly turned out, the deportment more clearly official, if somewhat severe, the condition of the physical plant clean and efficient-looking. This was one case in which there was even more than met the eye, however.

examination were otherwise more advanced, down to such seemingly trivial (but actually quite significant) items as the use of modern business forms to record arrests rather than the clumsy old-fashioned blotter system.

On that West Coast swing I visited the Berkeley P.D., long one of the most reform-minded, and it was going through yet another re-vamping. Even the Oakland P.D. was undergoing internal improve-ment. But when I got to San Francisco, I recognized home. Here was an old-fashioned poorly managed East Coast–style police department; it stood out like a sore thumb compared to the L.A.P.D. (In recent months, under the progressive Police Chief Charles Gain, the S.F.P.D. has been put through some reforms, but internal resistance to change has been severe.)

But perhaps the comparative police administration visit that got the biggest laugh at Headquarters was the one to Philadelphia. The Philadelphia P.D. is widely considered to be one of the more troubling big-city departments in the country. No serious effort at corruption reform has been successful, and few attempts have even been tried. In the early 1970s, when a special anti-corruption prose-cutor was named to clean up the situation, the management of the Philadelphia P.D. refused to cooperate,* and ultimately the special prosecutor was fired. But for all this, the Philadelphia P.D. remains not without value to students of police management. Even a simple little thing like pinning mug shots of known criminals in the precinct patrol cars as an aide to surveillance and arrests could have been copied by the N.Y.P.D.—but, I am sorry to say, was not. In addition, the Philadelphia P.D. was later, and remains today, far ahead of most departments in the recruitment of black officers—a necessary task for which the N.Y. City civil service system, for all its liberal attitudes and so forth, has set a sorry example.

I returned home from the trip disheartened, and then cheered. I had for the past several months been reviewing in my mind the pos-sibility of leaving the department—maybe trying out a new career as a teacher. (Finally, I had finished my senior year of college, and went on to graduate school for a master's in public administration; a

---

* Compare the reaction in New York to the Knapp Commission, which was investigating alleged police corruption, Chapter Seven.

little more work and a Ph.D. was within reach.) But upon my return, after a long talk with Betty, I realized that, in a way, I was hooked.

It was the trip to the Coast that hooked me. When I saw firsthand that things could be better, I wanted to make them better. I had grand visions of reforming police departments, reducing corruption, improving police protection, attacking crime, making policing into a profession rather than a bad joke, making the cop one of society's most respected professionals (as he still is, according to recent surveys, in England). Obviously I was deluded by visions of grandeur; as a mathematics major in college, I knew well the odds against ever being in a position to do much about anything. But in 1957 I did not know what fate would have in store for me, and the dreamer in me overcame the hard-boiled odds maker. So I decided to continue in the tradition of my father and my older brothers, to forget the odds.

In my time as a young officer the conditions on the street and in the country at large were not what they are today. There were simply fewer muggings, fewer murders, fewer assaults (not to mention *lethal* assaults) on police officers. It was still a dangerous occupation, but the level of danger—perceived and real—did not begin to approach that of today's crisis in crime. At times a police officer of the 1940s and '50s could feel as if the only thing standing in the way of his performance as a crime fighter was the organization of his job and the policies of management. Compared to those internal problems, the "criminal element"—that abstract catch-all phrase—sometimes seemed to be but a minor nuisance.

These obstacles seemed to me to be real rather than imagined— more than street-cop grousing was involved—and as much the product of uncaring management as inept management. I can remember all the attention lavished on detective work, corruption programs, public relations, and so on, as if all the basic questions and problems of the patrol officer had long ago been considered and solved. And yet anyone on the level of the street, in the precincts, in the neighborhoods, out on patrol, knew this was not the case.

The young officer can become somewhat frustrated with his role as the forgotten man of American policing. Consider, after all, what he is called upon to do in the ordinary course of business. The average police officer is asked to identify the "bad guys" and to separate them when appropriate from the "good guys," and then to make himself available for court proceedings. The police officer is asked to reduce the opportunities for crime to occur, while at the same time observing (indeed, protecting) constitutional guarantees to a tee. The regular, normal everyday cop is asked to aid individuals in danger of harm, and to assist those who cannot for the moment care for themselves. He is asked to identify problems and situations that may be potentially serious ones for law enforcement or government, while creating and maintaining a feeling of community security as a continuum. The patrol officer is asked to intervene in domestic conflicts, such as a family fight, a lover's quarrel, or a street scene, while promoting and maintaining civil order with traffic laws and the like. Last but not least, the normal non-special, non-brass officer, as part of the larger organization, is required to provide service on a twenty-four-hour basis, seven days a week. He and his organization are as visible as a public zoo and, like a hospital, never close down.

We ignore this governmental figure at our peril. We shove him to the side for the consideration of more "important" issues without realizing how important he is. We have given the officer, perhaps without realizing the full extent of the transaction, the power to make more consequential decisions in the course of an average week than many people make in the course of their lifetimes. And we have given him tools to do the job, from the power to make an arrest, to the power to carry a gun.

These powers are part of the unexamined daily life of the American police officer. But the style and the extent of the use of these powers are not uniform from state to state, city to city, or even, in many governmental jurisdictions, from officer to officer. To illustrate on a general level, a study some years ago compared police "discretion" (to investigate, to arrest) from city to city. Among other findings, the study showed that in New Orleans a suspect's chances of being searched by a police officer *without* reasonable grounds were quite high—higher, certainly, than in Boston, Chicago, or Washington, D.C. Similar discrepancies in the practice of American law enforcement abound. For example, in some American cities it is virtually impossible to be arrested for possession of small amounts of marijuana, whereas in other jurisdictions such an arrest might make the local paper.

Whether or not these legal and policy inconsistencies are desirable is not, for the moment, my point. Rather, I am more concerned about the failure of American policing to examine with more systematic introspection than it has exactly what *it* is about, especially at the level of policing that the citizen is most likely to encounter in the ordinary course of events: the patrol officer. But such self-examination has not been forthcoming. For example, if one were to ask one's local police authorities about the troubling discretion problem, ask what laws were more rigorously enforced by patrol officers and which ones were accorded a lower enforcement priority, chances are the answer would come back something like "We enforce all the laws equally." This of course is nonsense. To make such a silly statement is to suggest that higher levels of American policing are ignorant of the larger problems they are supposed to be managing, or are covering up.

Chapter Three

On-the-Job Training

In the early 1960s I became a police chief. Elliot Lombard called to sound me out about the suddenly vacant post in Syracuse, New York. Elliot, a good friend, was an aide to then New York Governor Nelson Rockefeller. Syracuse is a medium-sized city in beautiful upper New York State; its police force had been hit hard by a state investigation report, and the incumbent Chief, under the circumstances, was forced to resign. The Governor's aide said on the phone that the job would probably be mine if I wanted it.

By this time I had been in the New York Police Department for seventeen years. I was now a captain, in command of the sensitive Inspection Squad, operated out of Headquarters. I was on good terms with the incumbent Police Commissioner, but it seemed obvious that, at best, progress toward a really high position in such a large department would be slow (I was now forty-two years of age) if I stayed in the department. In addition, with an acquired taste for travel and a new sense of the importance of avoiding the inherent provincialism of remaining the prisoner of one department, I was as game as I ever would be for leaving the Big Apple.

There was, of course, another factor at work. Ego. Up to now I was not a top cop. Despite important assignments from Headquarters, I was an unknown soldier in our "domestic" armed forces. In the police world, power is highly concentrated in the position of chief—and possibly in a few top brass. This meant that unless you were a high-ranking boss, basically you were nothing. In view of my growing ambition to be associated with a reform movement in American policing, I knew I could not accomplish much without taking a few chances. If policing were, indeed, dominated by the top bosses, it was perhaps time for me to try my hand at being a top boss.

After securing a formal leave of absence from the Police Commissioner, who assured me that the welcome mat would always be out if I decided to return from the hinterlands, I accepted the offer of Mayor William Walsh—evidently a fine, decent human being. I was ready to take on the job of Chief of Police.

Syracuse, I knew, would represent a challenge entirely different from anything I had experienced. The crime problem in a medium-sized city might not come close to New York's, or even to one rough precinct in New York, and the size of the force might be barely one-sixtieth of the N.Y.P.D.'s; but none of these factors would be, I knew, as significant as the difference in the job—being Chief of Police.

In the United States there is no police chief school to prepare one for the job. There is the F.B.I. Academy in Washington, which I graduated from in 1957; but it was really little help, and, in many respects, as I hope to demonstrate in the following chapter, is quite inadequate across-the-board. The only schooling available, it turns out, is on-the-job training. This gap in America's police educational system probably adds not only to the crime-control problem (on the assumption that the policing service like the health service or the legal service is important enough to warrant educational requirements for its licensed practitioners, in the absence of which the level of service would be less than it should be) but also to the nationwide police chief crisis, a crisis in confidence in the visible heads of our police agencies.

In an American community almost no one is a more visible public figure than the police chief (or, by other names, the commissioner, or sheriff, or public safety director). He is, it became clear in the course of my career, either villain or savior not only in the constant drama of a community's concern about crime per se, but also in the shifting morality play of American life, in the unfolding of which ethical guidance is deemed a proper and important role for law enforcement. That is, the police chief can be viewed not only as the community's chief law enforcement officer but also as the custodian of the community's morals. In the civil religion of local government, the police chief may become something akin to a secular pastor.

This semi-ecclesiastical dimension to the chief's job arises in part from the perception of behavior which arguably may be nothing more than a question of bad taste (pornography, certain forms of gambling, drug use) as clearly and offensively criminal in the strictest moral sense. In this perception, the police chief becomes the focal point not only of a community's sense of physical security but even of its spiritual well-being.

For this positioning of the police chief in a community's hierarchy of values and expectations, no one could be adequately prepared, intellectually or emotionally. The challenge is heightened when one assumes a job vacated suddenly in the wake of a corruption exposé. Revelations of wrongdoing in a police bureaucracy can shake a community to its core. They tend to be very troubling because they involve a violation of a sacred trust. Police are sworn with the power of arrest and of the gun not to break the law but to enforce it. A reversal of role can be as psychologically disorienting to the citizens of the community as it is exciting and newsworthy to the media. In this situation the new reform chief walks into a serious and difficult job with the expectation of encountering a great deal of ugliness. In my own case, having sensed many kinds of corruption in New York, and having been teased by colleagues about the demoralized condition of a non-metropolitan upstate city like Syracuse, I came to it fully prepared to have all my prejudices confirmed.

In part, expectations were stimulated by the news, which had even made the New York City press. A state investigation commission had issued a report detailing evidence of corruption in the Syracuse P.D.; in the wake of scandal, the Police Chief had had to resign. On the day of my appointment by Syracuse Mayor Walsh, a newspaper story summed up the situation with these words:

A veteran New York City police captain will take command of Syracuse's scandal-rocked police department. . . . The department is still wobbling from the wallop it received from testimony last month during a public hearing at the State Crime Commission. The hearing disclosed links between some police officers and local rackets bosses. It disclosed that some officers received payoffs, protection money, and favors, in return for which they allowed prostitution, gambling and narcotics to flourish.

At a farewell party for me at a restaurant near Headquarters in New York the day before flying to Syracuse, the big joke was whether poor Murphy would be able to get out of town without getting indicted. "You know those upstate towns," said one colleague. "They're not like the N.Y.P.D. It's Sodom and Gomorrah North up there."

The joking, while well-intentioned, had a chilling effect on me, perhaps because I did not share my colleague's belief that whatever the N.Y.P.D.'s corruption problem, other cities were worse. On the contrary, I perceived the corruption and management problems of the nation's "finest" department to be far more consequential and troubling than the top management had been able to identify and deal with. In part my belief arose out of the brief plainclothes experience, which I mentioned in the last chapter. It arose too out of some generalized impressions I was able to draw as the commanding officer of the Inspection Squad, a Headquarters-based terrorist unit that was designed (poorly, in fact) to cope with a variety of Headquarters dissatisfactions with the lower ranks. My big overriding concern about police departments, whether the N.Y.P.D. or the Syracuse P.D. or the Podunk P.D., would inevitably center on possible links between organized crime operators and police officers charged with enforcement of "moral" crime, i.e., gambling and prostitution. In the State Crime Commission censure of the Syracuse P.D., links between gamblers and officers were precisely what had been exposed for inspection.

Let me illustrate my fears with just one incident from my pre-Commissioner New York years which may serve as background. The year was 1961, and I had been assigned from Headquarters on temporary field duty as a staff aide to the beleaguered commanding officer of the Patrol Bureau, Manhattan North, who had a very special assignment: to protect Fidel Castro during his seemingly endless stay in Harlem's Hotel Theresa during the opening of the General Assembly session at the United Nations.

One night during that assignment I was driving home to Brooklyn from Harlem. On this particular night Castro had been rambunctious and quite active, embarking on several impromptu walking tours of Harlem. By the time we had concluded he was not coming out again, we had checked out several assassination threats and numerous crank tips; and we were all dead on our feet.

I started my drive home in the wee hours of the morning, taking Second Avenue downtown. But I had gone only a few blocks when I spotted a big brassy Cadillac—conspicuous at any hour of the day but at three in the morning in black Harlem more than conspicuous: suspicious.

Something turned over in my head, because although I was dog-tired, I just could not resist checking the car out. I was driving an unmarked car, so it was a simple matter to flash past the Cadillac for a quick look inside.

What I saw inside was a major New York organized crime figure, Carmine Tramunti.* I would recognize Tramunti's distinctive mug under any circumstances.

I made a quick circle around the block and followed the Cadillac from a few blocks behind. Suddenly the Cadillac stopped and pulled to the curb. I stopped.

A few minutes passed, and then a marked patrol car from the local precinct appeared out of nowhere and pulled up beside Tramunti, as if by prearrangement. For about a half hour the officers inside the car engaged the organized crime figure in conversation—from all I could tell, friendly, even jovial conversation.

Naturally, this scene struck me as odd. What sort of business could patrol officers in a precinct car have with a person like Tramunti at this hour of the day except, possibly, an arrest?

The next day I verified that the license plates were Tramunti's. Then before reporting for duty outside the Hotel Theresa, I ordered a check to determine the names of the two officers assigned to the precinct car. After an investigation the officers—who were at a loss to explain the conversation—were transferred out of the precinct.

The incident left quite an impression on me. The lesson seemed to warn of the dangers of naiveté regarding organized crime and the Police Department.

On my first night in Syracuse I was lying awake in bed staring at the ceiling, with a million things on my mind, when down the hall came the distinctive sounds of women giggling and carrying on.

* Later to become one of New York's organized crime bosses, the head of an entire syndicate family.

At first I thought nothing of it. I was, after all, in the best hotel in Syracuse, the room selected by the manager at the request of the Mayor, my temporary home until Betty and the children arrived from New York. But as the patter of female feet became more insistent, and worries about the pattern of police corruption in Syracuse more persistent—as the sleepless night wore on, my mind was working overtime on the ugliness I would face tomorrow after being sworn in—I began in my mind to connect the two. So I got up from bed, paced the room, and occasionally glued my ear to the door to catch the action down the hall that more and more seemed highly suspicious.

By daybreak the suspicion had been converted into an inescapable conclusion. Whatever its reputation, the Hotel Syracuse was a hostelry for hookers, and the new Police Chief—nay, the *reform* Chief—had been accommodated in what was nothing more or less than a high-class bordello. With all due apologies to Toulouse-Lautrec, this was not exactly my idea of suitable accommodations. And I knew it would hardly be Betty's!

As I shaved and showered, I vowed that my first official act as Chief would be to raid the hotel and close it down. But was there time? Had I been "set up" by the Syracuse establishment, compromised early, so that, for all the talk about reform, I could be controlled?

My mind was racing like the wheels of a car spun over on its back. I dressed quickly and via the back stairs rushed down to the lobby. I went up to the manager, who was behind the desk, and began to complain bitterly. All my fears ("Murphy, you'll be lucky to get out of that town without being indicted") rose to the surface. As I explained with disgust my distaste for residency in bordellos, and was about to grab the manager by his lapels, I saw a dawning awareness, even amusement, in his eyes; and the combination, quite unexpected (I had expected fear, or at least a slickness), stopped me cold.

"Oh, Chief Murphy," said the manager, now barely restraining a laugh. "That's not a hooker's hall up there on the seventh floor."

"Then what the hell is it?" I countered, still angry, but now puzzled.

"It's girls from Le Moyne."

"What's Le Moyne?"

"The local Jesuit college. They're still building a new dormitory, and while it's under construction, some of the coeds are being put up in the hotel. We thought a most fitting place for the new Police Chief would be the unoccupied end of a floor taken over by a Jesuit college."

I was stunned, then completely overcome by my paranoia and suspiciousness. I started laughing, but held back enough to say finally, "You have my apologies, sir, but do you think, for tonight, I might change my room to a somewhat quieter location. We older folk need a bit more sleep, you know, than these young girls."

"By all means, Chief," said the manager as we engaged in a relieved handshake and a last-minute exchange of jokes.

A few weeks later, my feet now more firmly planted on the ground, I could more happily reflect back on that first night for the very real lesson that it held.

The police mind is by nature a suspicious mind, and by necessity a very quick one. The hotel incident was classically illustrative. You are faced with a situation, you feel you have to act quickly, you jump to a conclusion, and, *sometimes,* you're wrong. Dead wrong. Because of the nature of the police mind (a product largely of the conditioning of training and the street), police power contains inherent potential for misuse. The lesson of the Syracuse "bordello" incident is the very imperative need for police restraint. You often have the power to act on your initial impulse, *but,* whenever possible, that power is best exercised with initial restraint rather than by presumptive action. In cases where it is possible for police power to put a rein on itself, to double-check the reality of the presumption on which the power is to be exercised, this is the course of wisdom. Time and again after I left Syracuse for Washington and Detroit, and in my years as New York's Commissioner, I was to see this lesson replayed—in street incidents escalated by pre-emptive police action, in political incidents worsened by police prejudice, in riot situations made worse by the lack of police restraint.

This was the first lesson of Syracuse: Police power—and in America cops have plenty of it—must be exercised in an atmosphere of caution and restraint. And not only for society's benefit, but also for the police officer's. In the case in point, how would I have looked if I had not bothered to check with the hotel manager and had gone ahead and ordered the Syracuse vice squad to investigate several dozen Jesuit college coeds?

A few weeks after this incident, I had also reached a conclusion about the corruption situation in the Syracuse Police Department. With William H. T. Smith,* a colleague from the N.Y.P.D. who came to Syracuse with me to become First Deputy Chief, I had exhaustively analyzed all the available evidence—and some new material which Bill and I had made available through some tried and true New York techniques of undercover revelation. Our conclusion astonished both of us, but it was undeniable. By New York standards, the Syracuse Police Department was a relatively clean police department. The corruption scandal had been blown out of proportion by the State Crime Commission and the press.

What we found was that those alleged links between local racket bosses and police officers amounted to inconsiderable exchanges of liquor and small change over the holidays—nothing to be proud of, something to be eliminated, but certainly not enough to sink an entire police department.

Syracuse, with a population of several hundred thousand, may not have had a significantly corrupt police department, but it did have a growing crime problem. Like most cities in America—not just New York or Chicago or other colossi—it possessed, or rather was stuck with, a police department which just did not seem to measure up to the problems it was created to solve. The realities of crime appeared to have far outdistanced the law enforcement institutions. In Syracuse in the average year, there might be about ten murders, a handful of armed holdups, and innumerable burglaries, assaults, and family battles. But more than this, the good citizens were victims not so much of the sharp edge of crime as the soft, illusive, psychologically shattering image of crime as a *1984* presence, big brother being not the government omnipresence but rather the crime omnipresence. Nothing in my New York experience, except perhaps those first few years on the street in the late 1940s and early 1950s, adequately prepared me for the jolt (this now is in 1963) of crime on a community's composure and sense of dignity. It was perhaps this emotion

* When I became New York Commissioner, Bill Smith left a high position in H.U.D. in Washington to return home as the number two man in the N.Y.P.D. (When I left Syracuse in 1964, Bill was appointed by the Mayor to replace me.)

more than anything else which made me conclude that the good police chief could profitably devote as much time to dealing with fear and ignorance as with crime and corruption.

An illustration: Early on, an attractive middle-aged female resident of Syracuse was murdered by strangulation in the early hours of the morning in a city park. The local papers played the story on page one for days; it was the most spectacular crime in the early part of my administration, and it had quite a chilling effect on the community (and on me). A crime of this grisly nature inevitably exacts a psychological toll on a community, may indeed even cause a community to alter its habits for the better (giving more attention to the security of the home) and for the worse (refusing to go out at night, hiding behind locked doors).

We had our homicide unit investigate the murder, and its report was on my desk just as I was leaving my office across from City Hall to address a luncheon given by a local women's auxiliary organization. The ladies of Syracuse were understandably agitated about undergoing a similar fate in what now seemed to them an increasingly unsafe city.

In truth, Syracuse's crime rates had not taken off dramatically; but an impression of deterioration had been created that was almost as destructive of the fabric of a community's self-confidence as an actual crime wave might have been. It was to this that a chief could profitably devote his attentions. I spoke to a packed luncheon that afternoon with the homicide report in front of me. I did not reveal the contents of the report, out of respect for the victim, but toward the end of the session one of the ladies asked me what advice I might have for women who might venture out in the terrorized city of Syracuse at night.

I glanced at the report again and decided to reveal the essence of its contents by way of circumlocution. I began this way. When you are out walking the streets at night, try not to walk into strange, totally unfamiliar neighborhoods. If you *are* out walking in an unfamiliar neighborhood and you pass a strange bar, try not to go inside. If you *do* find yourself inside a strange bar in an unfamiliar neighborhood all alone late at night, and a man comes up to you and asks whether he might purchase a drink for you, try to decline gracefully but firmly. If you *do* let this strange man in a strange bar in a totally unfamiliar neighborhood buy you a drink, and then he asks if he can walk you home, by all means decline gracefully and call yourself a cab. If you *do* let him walk you home—this strange man in a strange bar in an unfamiliar neighborhood—and then he asks if he might be permitted inside, by all means graciously decline. But if you do let him inside . . .

I kept watching the eyes of the ladies to see at what point in the story they would get the point. (Of course, some in the audience never did.) In a subtle way, I wished to convey the unusual (for Syracuse) contours of the case (the murdered woman was, literally, a woman of the evening) without actually slandering the woman in her grave, and to explain, as an educator, and extract, as an investigator, the reality of crime from its image. Even the best police department will have its hands full with the reality of crime, but in an age of crime shock as well as future shock, it can hardly deal as well with all people's accumulated pent-up fears; but to this the police chief should properly devote himself in an effort to take some of the pressure off his troops and some of the fear out of the citizenry.

The importance of this task was made clear during my first week in office. This was when I was thrown into the swim. The invitations to speak, the requests for interviews and television appearances, piled up on my desk like Christmas cards. The first week I accepted the invitation to appear on the local *Meet the Press*. It was the first time in my life that I had been on a television talk show, and I thought I would be nervous. To my surprise, I was not. Perhaps having to stand up before large groups as an instructor at the Police Academy had helped, but in truth I think something else (aside from personal ego and ham) was involved in the evident success of the appearance, according to the Mayor, who telephoned his congratulations.

In my view, a police chief ought to be available and visible to the community and to its representatives in the press. Pragmatically, police chiefs must recognize that the press is there and won't go away. Either you're going to avoid it by cowering in a corner, or you can go out and meet reporters and seek out the best possible press for the department. So during that first local *Meet the Press* session I simply answered the questions exactly the way I felt. I did not get tongue-tied in an effort to distinguish the correct "public relations" answer from what I felt to be the truth; and where I did not know the answer I admitted as much and indicated I'd try to find out rather than attempting to bluff through an answer, a tactic that is often as transparent as it is phony. In the end, I felt comfortable in the role of Police Chief as Spokesman on the Public Safety Issue.

But few police chiefs do feel comfortable with the press. For most of them, certainly for virtually all of the small-town chiefs, the effort to meet the press is a harrowing, horrible ordeal. Later, at the Police Foundation in Washington, several small-town chiefs would practically go into therapy in my office, leaving me to put them back together by explaining that appearing in public and talking about crime and police work is part of the job, and that the best approach is to go before the public and tell the truth.

The uneasy relationship between American police chiefs and the media is caused by a number of factors. Only one is pertinent here (it makes more sense for me to relate the others to you in later chapters as the story evolves): the inferiority complex felt by most chiefs, especially those in middle-sized cities and small towns. This inferiority complex is actually a reflection of a host of personality and institutional factors that characterize small-town chiefs and small-town police departments. But the most important of them is the lack of mobility and the insularity of American policing.

Police chiefs are usually home-grown products. They enter the department of their home town, work their way up the ranks by being unobtrusive, cooperative, and perhaps even competent, and reap the reward of their department's top job. Every once in a blue moon a new chief will arrive from another department; this sequence occurs most frequently in the wake of a corruption scandal and the community establishment's perceived need for a chief from outside the department (the Syracuse model). But this sequence occurs all too infrequently indeed; even when a department advertises for a new chief in the police chiefs' trade journal, it is often just for show, the choice having already been made by the establishment for an "insider" who can be "trusted."*

* I have personal knowledge of this. In 1961 Seattle advertised for a new chief. I applied, flew to the West Coast, was interviewed, and told I was the outstanding candidate. But in the end the nod went to an officer from within the ranks of the Seattle P.D. A few months later a city official, on a trip to New York, met with me to apologize. "The selection process was fixed," he said. "The advertising for an outside chief was just window dressing." Often window dressing is exactly what it is; Seattle was no different from many cities.

Not surprisingly, the best chiefs tend to be those rare outsiders who have managed to include mobility in their careers; whereas chiefs who work their way up the ladder without having worked in any other department are often referred to behind their backs as "cops in gold braid"—a derogatory term for the police chief who is all uniform and little substance.

Robert di Grazia, for instance, the current chief of Montgomery County, Maryland, is one of the most courageously outspoken police executives in the United States. Di Grazia had been the Police Commissioner in Boston and a chief of the St. Louis County Police Department (as well as of a small California department) before landing the job as chief of one of the largest suburban counties in the United States. In Boston, his shrewd, cool leadership of the Boston P.D.—theretofore not recognizable as one of the more progressive police agencies—during the tense, widely-reported school busing incident was practically a model of smart police executive behavior.

Another outstanding American chief is Al Andrews, a little-known chief of a little-known police department, the Peoria, Illinois, P.D.

Perhaps even better than di Grazia, Chief Andrews illustrates what is at stake. Andrews, unlike most American chiefs, understands the basic weaknesses and needs in policing, can conceptualize and institutionalize reforms, and is not only articulate but is also willing to speak out. Andrews did not come up through the ranks of one force. He attended the police administration program at Michigan State University (one of the very few decent police administration courses of study in the United States), but rather than enter federal law enforcement work after receiving the baccalaureate degree (the usual career pattern for M.S.U. police administration graduates), he stayed on for advanced work. Andrews, interestingly, has worked in state government in addition to being a chief, which in my view is excellent preparation for the job of being a police chief in America.

In theory the bureaucratic system of working one's way up through the ranks is admirable, in the sense of democratic fairness; but it is awfully limiting to the extent that it is perceived as virtually the only way to produce a police chief. A better system would be one that would not, with rare exceptions, exclude outsiders, and even encourage more mobility. To this end, a national career system for police chiefs (including transferable pensions, comparable health insurance benefits, and all the rest) would be most desirable.

Against the American bureaucratic model, the English system is designed to produce stronger leaders. Before World War Two there was actually a police West Point in England. It was known as Hendon, and it was terribly elitist. The only way one got to head a police department was to be either (a) a Hendon graduate or (b) a commissioned military officer. Since World War Two, however, the tradition has been democratized, the last of the Hendon officers has gone, and police chiefs all come up from the bottom. Comprehensive training and education programs (including long-term university degree programs and the outstanding police college at Bramshill) are strengthening leadership from the sergeant to the chief constable level. A very active system of lateral transfers among the forces for moving the best leaders to the top positions is decidedly better than the American practice of immobility.

After getting used to the new experience of having to deal with the Syracuse press virtually every day (in my eighteen years with the N.Y.P.D. I hadn't been interviewed once by a reporter), I then had to get over the shock of having to deal daily with the city's political community.

Under other circumstances I might possibly have gone under from this pressure, but I was protected from any difficult political problems by Mayor Walsh, the first of the outstanding mayors I was to work with. Walsh gave me good advice: Be friendly, be cordial, be open, but don't let yourself get pushed around by the politicians. Basically, Syracuse was a warm-water political community; there was no pervasive climate of corruption in which the police department floated. Traffic tickets, for instance, weren't being fixed in the Police Chief's office (a very common occurrence in American police departments).

But many chiefs are totally subservient to the local power structure. Not just traffic tickets are being fixed, either. Cases are being quashed; individuals who should be behind bars are not being arrested. There is continuing and impudent political interference, undercutting and demoralizing the entire department, making the chief a private joke among the rank and file.

By many political establishments in America, the police department is seen as an organization of dumb cops with the sole mission of bending to the whims of the power structure. Many departments accordingly suffer the passage of two or three chiefs in the course of a four-year mayoral term, unable either to attract talent or keep it. The main explanation for this unseemly instability is the absence of an actual *profession* of policing, or even of police administration.

In Syracuse, with Mayor Walsh's admirable hands-off policy, we were able to institute some reforms and, I believe, improve the department both in appearance and effectiveness. But where you have a police department which is a pawn of power politics, the people will not get good policing; more often than not they will get a political circus.

Perhaps a more amusing example of circus management of a police department was the case of the Brockton, Massachusetts, P.D. Here we had at one time the spectacle of the department looking for a new chief while five former chiefs were still in the top ranks of the department—as captains! Imagine trying to run a modern corporation by having the former presidents for the last twenty years in positions of power, just waiting to jump on the new president and make his life miserable. Who would want to be chief of a police department like that? But the Brockton P.D. is hardly the only department in the country guilty of Keystone Kops management.

One private joke concerned a small police department in Ohio. The entire force consisted of seven officers. This department persuaded the federal Law Enforcement Assistance Administration to provide it with riot gear. What happened was that the Chief read a newspaper story about all those agitating blacks in nearby Cincinnati and said, "We've got to be prepared." And, incredibly, L.E.A.A. bought the argument!

But Keystone Kops stupidity is not confined to ridiculously small police departments. Many large police departments have in recent years, with considerable justification, developed SWAT's (Special Weapons Attack Teams). Less justified is the spin-off effect on smaller departments, which feel that to be "professional" they have to emulate features of the big-city departments—like a banana republic that feels it can't be considered a member of the family of nations until it possesses an atom bomb. One fourteen-man department in the

San Francisco Bay Area was getting machine-gun training for its own mini-SWAT team. Where was it getting the training? From the great Federal Bureau of Investigation. But, after all, millions of Americans who visit the F.B.I. Headquarters in Washington each year are treated to a demonstration of heavy weapons firing—an unfortunate image to project of democratic law enforcement. The F.B.I. has traditionally been restrained in the *use* of firearms. Too bad it sells itself differently.

In the occupation-army school of policing, minority communities suffer the most repressive policies. Indeed, in a great many American departments there is a built-in policy duality at the patrol level, with one set of policies (usually sophisticated, suburban-style) for the white neighborhoods and another (usually heavy-handed inner-city) for the non-white.

In Syracuse in 1963, relations between the police department and the non-white community were nonexistent. There wasn't a large black population at the time, but it was growing in both size and consciousness. During my administration the leadership was focused at a local university, where one black professor in particular was seeking to bring the black community together. In a good police department, understandably, contacts between the police and minority leaders will be extensive, though at times confidentially maintained. (It is bad for the black activist's image for it to be known that he tips off the police to what is happening in return for certain accommodations.) But in a police department that is behind the times, such contacts will be frowned on, perhaps even thought of as subversive, unnecessary.

At one point I learned (not through department channels, but through my own rapidly increasing contacts in the community) of plans for a protest demonstration by blacks. I mentioned this "intelligence" item to several higher-ups in the department; their reaction was as though I was predicting the return of World War Two. This was traditional police "planning" at its best: ignore a potentially troublesome situation until the last minute and then attempt to solve it by cracking heads, thinking that is further confused and muddled in the case of police-minority relations by the deep-seated racism in many departments.

In the case of a protest demonstration, ideally, the proper procedure is to attempt to anticipate every aspect of the demonstration. That was exactly what we did in this case. We contacted the leaders of the protest and arranged for a discreet, unpublicized ongoing dialogue. To the incredulous black leaders, who were not used to being talked to as adults by police, we explained our "problem." We had no quarrel with the protest, either as an idea or as a political operation; our only concern was that it not get out of hand, triggering bloodshed or wider violence. To this end the Syracuse Police Department would bend over backward to be as cooperative as possible.

Accordingly, we would behave exactly as they wanted us to. Did they want us to arrest all of the protesters, or just the leaders? Did they want to act brutalized while the television cameras were on? Did they want to walk to the van or be carried? What was the preferred sequence? Would the protesters trespass while shouting "police brutality" and "pigs," then get arrested and handcuffed? Or should we make the first move with some seemingly menacing gestures before they trespassed, to provide a plausible motive for the obscenities and scuffling?

In this way we plotted out the entire protest demonstration as carefully as Balanchine choreographing a new *pas de deux*. Best of all, strategies in which protesters are taken into the department's confidence and treated as citizens rather than as ordinary criminals will often work even from a literal police point of view. In this case the protest demonstration unfolded without a wrinkle. No one was seriously (or even marginally) injured; the protesters got their television footage and newspaper ink; and the department got credit for a job well done, the job being simply, classically, importantly—to keep the peace.

People do not really expect these days a great deal from their police departments. They've been disappointed too often, in the case of many communities, to expect miracles or perfection. What they do want is their P.D. to be clean, neat, courteous, and not so stupid. And American policing is improving. Reading over the literature on our police departments written in the 1930s, for instance, gives one a perspective on how far we've come. Constitutional issues of legality, today so much in the forefront of police literature, were deemed totally academic back then, so sadistic and repulsive were some police practices. One study by the famed Wickersham Commission got the title *Our Lawless Police*. Today, the very fact that some police chiefs continue to carp about Supreme Court decisions on criminal procedure at least makes a point about how consequential these rulings are in the police world; only a half century ago such legal niceties would have been dumped by the chief into an overflowing wastebasket.

In point of fact, in the last fifty years policing in America has improved more than judging or prosecuting. The police world has been more willing to change, and to do so expeditiously, than prosecutors and judges. To some extent, of course, progress in policing is perhaps more than anything else a reflection of how far it was necessary to go; but still there are many excellent police departments in the country.

For example, many of the smaller cities in California have pretty good departments. In part, the bright California scene is a legacy of the late August Vollmer, the reform-minded Berkeley chief who virtually invented the police radio car, and introduced the hiring of college graduates as cops. He hired college students as summer interns and then persuaded them by force of example to continue in policing as a career.

Wichita, Kansas, has had a good police department; again, as a consequence of a legacy. In this instance the credit goes to the late O. W. Wilson, who, en route to becoming the great reform chief of the Chicago P.D., stopped off long enough in Wichita to make changes in the department that have endured to this day.

Syracuse, simply put, was a great education. For one thing, besides being identified with an outstanding mayor like Walsh, I was given a sizable, consequential police department to manage—not too large so that I was in over my head, but not so small that I was wading in the kiddie pool.

The question of size is worth further discussion. As I was to learn, Syracuse, for all its Main Street conformism and mainstream typicality, is not a typical American town. Syracuse had a *real* police department. By contrast, a great many American communities are policed by a farcical little collection of untrained individuals who are really nothing more than guards. These genuinely *small* departments (fewer than twenty-five sworn officers), to begin with, tend not to have much of a franchise by and large; with small territory and limited clientele, they do not face much of a crime problem. They don't face alcoholism on any scale, or much family violence; the occasional burglary stands in contrast to the rare mugging or holdup. Some of these departments go an entire year or several years in a row without a murder. Nor do these departments have a minority problem. The chief could be a degenerate racist and last in office for twenty-five years; in Harlem he wouldn't last two minutes.

Additionally, Syracuse presented the challenge of moving against a bureaucracy, with all the attendant problems of internal communication, management, and training. A small department is more easily managed. Take the case of a police department of one hundred officers—for instance, Rick Clement's small New Jersey department. (Clement is the past president of the International Association of Chiefs of Police.) Chief Clement knows every cop in his force. If he has a problem with an officer, he can take care of it in the force's parking lot at four in the morning. At the same time, small departments, alas, are perhaps even less immune to political interference than the larger police agencies. Favoritism for influential citizens is often a notorious hallmark of the more egregious practitioners of a dual standard of justice and law enforcement. One is reminded of the industrialist who contributes heavily to the mayor's campaign and receives special treatment by the police in the handling of a difficult strike (otherwise known as strikebreaking). Or of the bank president's son who steals a car for a joy ride. (Although there's a Cadillac available to him at all times, he's never driven a Porsche.) Or of the "best" kids in town who drink some beer and vandalize the school but who receive "special" treatment. The power elite of a small town is, of course, quite comfortable with its small P.D.—more easily controlled than a distantly headquartered county-wide police department, which might "foolishly" arrest a pillar of the community caught driving drunk, to mention just one example.

But the Syracuse P.D. perhaps exhibited fewer of these typical mannerisms of the smaller police agency than might have been expected. Indeed, in some respects, the Syracuse department contained several features of the sophisticated agency, including the *sine qua non* of the consequential department. This was the specialized unit. In a department of ten or twenty or fifty officers, it is impossible to develop and maintain expertise at the ready. A big-city hostage unit (dealing with problems like those fictionalized in the film *Dog Day Afternoon*) may have ten to twenty officers; compute that down to a small department and the unit simply disappears. Another important area of specialization is homicide. This is a complex, well-developed, and terribly important police function—perhaps the *most* important on the investigatory side of a department. But one doesn't have to go too far down in city and state police departments to where one simply runs out of good homicide investigators. In point of fact, small departments blunder in their homicide investigations all the time. Officers will walk all over the scene of the crime, mess up or even destroy the evidence, and panic. Even simple husband-and-wife murders are botched, and the botch is then covered up.

To be adequately policed, a community needs a department with all these resources; but in the small police department the only function that can be justified on the budget is patrol, and often the patrolling is performed in such a routine, unimaginative manner that little is accomplished. Other public services, such as a crime lab, an adequate communications system, twenty-four-hour response, trained criminal investigators, and expertise in juvenile crime, cannot be provided.

If you provide all these functions with the smallest possible staffing, you arrive at a police department of at least two hundred employees. Interestingly, British experts in this analytical fashion came to a figure of five hundred, but the British can operate in the luxury of having attained the two hundred minimum for all their police forces by the end of World War Two; today they are down to forty-two police forces, the smallest of which has six hundred officers.

The small police departments need not necessarily be abolished, but they should not receive public funds—certainly not county, state or federal funds. The Long Island model is instructive. Here we have a county-wide overlay by the county police, which by national standards is a force well above the norm. However, many of the wealthy little duchies maintain private or public forces of their own. Long Island, in my view, is saved by the county-wide overlay. But in many areas of the country county police are either weak or nonexistent, leaving the policing to a myriad of tiny forces. With this system criminals have every advantage; they can always lose themselves in the cracks. One good sign is that in some areas of the country the county police departments, including many sheriffs' departments, are taking over the tiny forces on a contract policing basis.

In Syracuse, with the proximity to vast rural areas of upstate New York, I had a good glimpse at rural policing and rural crime. Largely the system was centered around the elected sheriff. Unfortunately, the elected sheriff is usually viewed as a throwback to an earlier era and as possibly a hack. In truth, there is a grain of remarkable de Tocqueville–style insight in the *idea* of an elected chief police official; the principle of accountability is taken to its logical conclusion. Unfortunately, the idea is too often burdened with the reality of an inadequate sheriff's unit to carry it off. Still, the sheriff idea is having a renaissance in America, and this is largely to the good. But twenty-five years from now, with (one hopes) consolidated professional police departments, the sheriffs' units will be amalgamated into larger, more professional agencies, and the sheriff with less than two hundred employees will go the way of the dinosaur.

Even with significant consolidations of rural police forces, rural crime will remain a necessarily difficult enforcement problem. Though reported crime in rural areas continues at a level far, far below urban or even suburban crime, there is every reason to suspect that in rural areas the degree of *hidden* crime is astoundingly high. This is disturbing, but possibly unavoidable. Several factors seem to be at work. First is the population-density factor, which accounts for both the lower crime rates (crime tends to increase geometrically against increments in population) and higher hidden crime. We know, for instance, that a great many covered-up or hidden murders occur which in urban areas would likely come to the attention of the authorities. You murder your wife in the city and everyone in your apartment building hears the screams.* But in the country a murder is more easily committed without attracting immediate attention. The possibility of

---

* The so-called Kitty Genovese syndrome is overrated. The term refers to a much publicized crime in New York City during which a young woman was raped and murdered while many people reportedly watched and listened and failed to act, even to the extent of calling police. This was a vicious crime reported with considerable dramatic license, which unfairly implied a callous indifference in New Yorkers.

hiding a murder is further enhanced by the general ineptitude of many rural police. Another factor adding to the degree of hidden crime is ideological. Economic or political crimes that in urban areas would attract notice are more easily covered up in a rural environment—for instance, the exploitation of migrant labor.

In Syracuse the need for the consolidation and improvement of rural police was everywhere evident. For instance, in dealing with burglary—statistically the most rapidly expanding area—rural police were simply unable and too ill-equipped to begin the crime analysis process and the collection of criminal intelligence information which is essential to the orderly procedure of identifying and dealing with repeaters and burglary rings.

Consolidation of many of these tinker-toy departments would inevitably create the minimum conditions for more intelligent police work. In the State of New York, for instance, there might be ten or twenty cities that rightfully and demonstrably require their own departments; but the rest of the state should and could be covered by county departments (with some very sparsely populated counties merging into one regional county police), so that the state would wind up with at most twenty-five or thirty departments where now there are hundreds.

Even with the best of coordination, however, rural crime will remain a major problem, possibly far beyond the scope of police solution. This is because the factors giving rise to this crime remain well beyond the parameters of police power. In dealing with the rural burglary problem there is not much the police can do to combat boredom and rural unemployment, especially among young people, who evidently commit the greatest percentage of these burglaries. Thus, in the area of prevention, the appropriate measures lie not with the police but with the state legislatures and the rural communities themselves. What are the politicians or the community leaders doing to decrease boredom among young people? What are the state legislatures doing about youth unemployment (not to mention about the very necessary consolidation of police, a process which must begin at the state level)?

It seemed to me in Syracuse that it was absurd to expect local police, who often cannot handle even the most elementary murder case, to grapple with larger societal problems which only for convenience's sake can strictly be classified as "criminal" manifestations. Yet if you ask most of these local chiefs whether they can "solve" the burglary problem, or the youth crime problem, they will stoutly insist that they can—just give us more men, more equipment, more money. This, of course, is a totally false solution, and will remain suspect until such time as we police chiefs give better evidence than we have so far that we are able to make far better use of the personnel and material resources that we have. With the consolidation of rural and suburban police departments—which, if seriously undertaken immediately, should begin to make a difference probably by the turn of the century—perhaps we will be in a position to assess more intelligently the clamorous demands for more of the same.

Chapter Four

Tower of Babel

In Syracuse, as Chief, one could begin to see what was wrong with American policing on a grand scale. For all the national and even international contacts built up in New York, it took the unique perspective of being the head of even an otherwise unnoticed department to illuminate the larger landscape. To begin to see it all, it helps to have seen it from the top.

In 1964, when I returned to the N.Y.P.D. after almost two years in Syracuse, as today, American policing remained in a state of unpardonable disarray. Crime was perceived as a local problem, to be solved by local authorities. Cooperation among law enforcement agencies was hardly as common as fierce, often mutually neutralizing competition. The net result was considerable chaos and disharmony in policing.

The Syracuse Police Chief and his department were virtually on their own. The state police might help in some cases, and in the background were the feds—Hoover's great F.B.I., the Bureau of Narcotics, the Treasury men. There was some sharing of information among us, as there is to perhaps a greater extent today, but not enough to brag about. On the whole, the predominant style was what might be called Lone Ranger policing; we were all more or less left to our own devices and resources.

This Lone Ranger complexion on the face of American policing would leave a police chief feeling isolated, a single tree standing in the storm. Later in my career, at the U.S. Department of Justice and at the Police Foundation, I would initiate occasions formal and informal to bring together police chiefs from around the country in an effort to overcome the tremendous isolation, the feeling of being in solitary confinement. But even today there are seventeen thousand heads of police—seventeen thousand chiefs and a half million Indians—all going about tackling the problem of crime, unhappily, in their own fashion. It was not and is not a healthy, rational situation.

Today the profound dimensions of the crime problem are becoming fully evident, and the situation seems much worse than we had thought. Crime is not just keeping pace with the growth in population; it is exceeding that growth in geometric proportions. Crime is not just a problem of the overpopulated, underemployed, ill-housed, and poorly integrated cities (though that is where most of our crime is). It is spilling over into the suburbs, and it is causing trouble even in our pastoral localities, where some of the very same causes of crime in our cities can also be found: youth unemployment, cultural anomie, family disintegration, alcoholism, mental health breakdown, racism, child neglect. Unquestionably, crime is now no longer a local problem; it is national in scope.

And yet, for all this, we still continue to police America in the old manner—with numerous decentralized police agencies scattered all over the place. The blame for this can literally be ascribed to a failure in government, or, rather, of two governments: state and federal.

This is not to say that the ultimate rationality lies in fifty state police forces, or one national federal police. On the contrary. We are eons of evolutionary progress away from that extreme of coordination, even if it were desirable; and it is neither desirable nor necessary. We do not require fifty state-wide police agencies as a substitute for the myriad police forces within a state; indeed, under my concept of consolidation, strong regional and county-wide police departments would obviate the need for a strong state police. But we do need the state to coordinate the police activities within its boundaries. Nor do we need one all-powerful Orwellian national police in place of the circus we now call the American police service; indeed, under the plan being proposed here, a network of stronger, less incompetent regional, county, and city police, supported by state coordination and standards, would help create an atmosphere in which any perceived need for a national police force would wane. But still we do require broader, more discriminating and intelligent federal participation in American policing. Since crime is now a national problem, the solution can no longer be sought solely at the local or even state level.

At the state level what you find, besides corruption, is incompetence and neglect. Perhaps the only significant contribution of the states to policing has been the highway patrol. (Though it is sometimes called something else, it is usually nothing much more than this.) The states have not coordinated, shaped, set minimum standards for, or otherwise had an ameliorative effect on the art of policing; in their abnegation of responsibility, they have contributed to the chaos of American policing. You can, for instance, drive through any number of states in your car, from one end to the other, and intersect literally hundreds of different law enforcement jurisdictions, some more or less hilarious, incompetent, uncaring, frivolous, and corrupt than others. You may legally do something in one jurisdiction which may be quite illegal in another; you may even by chance pass through the territory of an utterly honest, decent, hard-working, dedicated police department, surrounded on all sides by incompetent, uncaring, frivolous, and corrupt police departments. But this is the great American police network: a net full of holes and tears and weak lines, through which crime and criminals pass as easily as water through a sieve.

What the states might do—develop overall state coordination of policing, perhaps in the form of a powerful state crime coordinator—cannot take place, however, without more positive encouragement from the federal government. The states cannot do it alone, because primarily they do not have the money or, often, the imagination.

The federal government might have demonstrated more talent, in the areas of both money and initiative, but its contribution on the whole has been either inadequate and misconceived, or heavy-handed and malevolent. In the former category, the key error has been in the assumption that policing is primarily a matter of concern to local governments. In my view, as with education, welfare, and unemployment, policing is a national problem, too large and complicated to be left out of the federal arena; the role of the national government must increase drastically.

For instance, the U.S. Law Enforcement Assistance Administration,* which has suffered growing criticism from both Congress and law enforcement authorities and experts in recent years, must not be abandoned. This grant-making unit of the U.S. Justice Department offers exactly the sort of leverage the federal government must have to help shape—and shape up—the police service across the country. L.E.A.A., however, should be understood by all concerned as not a political pork barrel machine for municipalities and localities deemed worthy of White House political affection but as a mechanism of federal power for shaping our future.

L.E.A.A. has gotten into trouble because of its granting of funds for sophisticated, expensive technological gimmicks to police departments that hadn't the slightest idea of how to use them, but this has become an overworked criticism that has tended to obscure a more fundamental problem. This is that the L.E.A.A. system of granting money has been essentially misconceived, based as it has been not on the incidence of crime but on the random quantity of population. Under the L.E.A.A. formula, places like Montana and North Dakota, with all their cattle rustling, receive money at the same rate as Los Angeles, Detroit, or New York. It is this grant-allocation system that has produced, among other undesirable things, the specter of fancy, costly equipment going to small forces that cannot possibly use it. In truth, some L.E.A.A. money has practically been forced on localities that faced only minor and comparatively simple crime problems. But most consequentially of all, the system has produced tremendous inequities. Vast troubled metropolitan areas face tremendous, complicated crime problems, problems that have grown *geometrically* (not linearly) with population; and they are faced with a federal program that treats all jurisdictions according to a simple-minded population formula. In essence, as I see it, why should the federal government give unemployment money to people who have jobs? But this is

---

* In 1968 President Johnson signed legislation creating the new federal agency and nominated me to become its first administrator. I was behind my desk for several months as acting administrator, waiting for Senate confirmation, which, in the circumstances of Humphrey's defeat by Richard Nixon in the Presidential election, understandably never came. Obviously, I was not Nixon's kind of police chief.

At this writing, the Carter administration has been thinking of reorganizing L.E.A.A. But whatever we call it, and however it is organized, something like L.E.A.A. is desperately needed at the federal level.

exactly what L.E.A.A. has been doing in granting funds to states and localities with relatively little crime.

The task for L.E.A.A. is to modernize American policing by helping establish standards of performance and mechanisms of consolidation—consummation of which will be rewarded with federal dollars.* The justification for L.E.A.A. is not, as previously advertised, the "reduction" of crime, but rather the improvement of policing. L.E.A.A. is not a police agency which catches criminals but, ideally, a kind of regulatory agency over the American policing industry; and any regulation it provides should be accomplished not by the negative, punitive sanctions of agencies like the Securities and Exchange Commission (which acts against egregious misconduct by American business) but by positive, reinforcing policies and programs that will give American policing a lift, a new look, and a new future.

Perhaps the most significant contribution, in the long run, of L.E.A.A. is its support of research. This of course is a logical role for the federal government. Police departments have not supported, or even sought, research; they have willingly accepted traditional assumptions which have never been tested. Neither have state or local governments given much support to genuine research into police policies and methods. Academics have not had the financial resources to probe the many issues requiring thorough inquiry.

The federal government has begun to fill a critical void by supporting research. Interestingly, its concerns have hovered in the same general area as the Police Foundation's. As a result of the two institutions following different but parallel policies, basic assumptions are being challenged. The effectiveness of patrol is now no longer taken for granted. The productivity of detectives and the value of rapid police appearance at crime scenes (see Chapter Nine) are now being questioned. It is in this way that basic research, long relegated by the police mentality to the stuffy corners of dusty libraries, can prove a powerful force in bringing about reform and needed change.

Finally, L.E.A.A. is valuable for its leadership role in helping us understand how the various components of the complicated and

---

* For instance, in some areas of the country, county police forces have taken over local policing responsibilities from a local government on a contract basis. This is the sort of movement L.E.A.A. could, and should, reward with financial assistance.

often poorly coordinated criminal justice system work—or should work. After all, the courts, correctional system, and prosecution offices are as germane to the crime control effort as the police, even if they do not ordinarily receive the same attention or equivalent level of funding. Projects designed to improve the working relationship among these various agencies, which so often work very poorly indeed together, are as worthwhile as anything L.E.A.A. could undertake. L.E.A.A., which has to its credit developed information systems necessary to accomplish coordination (What's the mix of cases the police are plugging into the system? What's the mix of cases that the courts are handling and prosecutors trying?), should do as much in this area as it possibly can. The main problem of the criminal justice system in the United States is, simply, that it is not a system.

On the heavy-handed and malevolent side of federal involvement in law enforcement, we have the great Federal Bureau of Investigation.

The F.B.I. merits a special section of its own in this discussion of the Tower of Babel effect on the American police service because of its special powers and its prodigious behind-the-scenes influence. The Bureau has even had an effect on my own career, having identified me in the mid-1950s as a police careerist and having accepted me into its prestigious three-month course at the Bureau's National Academy outside Washington. More than even my baccalaureate and master's degrees, the certification of graduation from the F.B.I. Academy served to enhance my credentials in the eyes of press, public, and even mayors. In truth, certification meant rather nothing at all, except that the experience served as a vehicle for explaining and exposing the behind-the-scenes relationship between the Federal Bureau of Investigation, under J. Edgar Hoover, and the American police service.

It is not generally well known, but the relationship, historically, between the Federal Bureau of Investigation and state and local law enforcement agencies has been one of menace and mutual distrust. The origin of this strange and unproductive relationship is easily and precisely pinpointed: the rise to power of J. Edgar Hoover.

In 1927, to reach back into history a bit, the F.B.I. was a limp, inconsequential, virtually unknown federal agency, and young Director Hoover was a small fish in a very big pond. But before too long,

Hoover became a major political power in Washington and a media celebrity. In large measure as the result of clever exploitation of the national fascination with notorious criminals like John Dillinger and Pretty Boy Floyd, Hoover overnight built up a public relations image for the Bureau which rapidly outdistanced the reality. In short order, Congressmen stepped over themselves in an effort to create new jurisdictions for the Bureau and to vote with unanimity vast new appropriations for what only a few years before had been a minor agency with a minor mandate.

Hoover, the gangster killer, thereupon maneuvered himself into the position where the Bureau could pick and choose from among those assignments Congress had lying around. In the fashion of a consummate poker player, with a consummate poker face, Hoover had the instinct for knowing when to lay down a heavy bet and when to fold. Assiduously avoiding such difficult law enforcement assignments as organized crime, narcotics trafficking, and street crime, Hoover put his money on such easy winners as kidnapping, where the criminals were usually dumb and clumsy and the crime was susceptible to solution within a short period of time. In addition, Hoover so organized the Bureau that when a major kidnapping incident broke, enormous manpower (far greater than anything a local police department could match) would be thrown into the case. In essence, when Hoover believed he could win, he would wager big. Largely on the strength of the Bureau's undeniable but cheap* victories on the kidnapping battlefield, Hoover further induced Congress to give the Bureau all that it asked; this was the continuing process by which Hoover became a national political power and personality.†

In reality, the F.B.I. then was more a product of a personality than

---

* Kidnapping cases have about an 80 to 90 percent solution rate, far in excess of the solution rate for most other crimes. This high rate applies not because of F.B.I. involvement but because of the nature of the crime, which requires the perpetrators to reappear to claim their ransom. This, in essence, means that the criminals set their own trap.

† The rise to power and fame may also have been enhanced by a continuing process of data collection, the data in question concerning the private lives of such public people as Congressmen, Senators, and perhaps even Presidents. It is widely assumed in law enforcement circles that Hoover, through the Bureau's well-known techniques of surveillance (electronic and otherwise), collected private files on the private sexual practices of key political personalities in Washington. He used these files the way a poker player might show that ace in the hole.

anything else. It came together not out of a coherent crime control plan at the federal level but out of a spectacular public relations campaign and some equally spectacular inside political maneuvering. Even today there is no coherent policy—no carefully considered set of guidelines—on the vital question of the F.B.I.'s role in crime control; and there are no answers to such important questions as What is the F.B.I.? Does the F.B.I. actually protect one from crime? Is it even supposed to protect one from crime? If not, what is it supposed to do? Why *do* we have an F.B.I.? Do we really need one?

Even today, after Hoover's death, the Bureau's involvement in crime remains very suspiciously selective—the result of a handful of laws literally drafted for (if not by) Hoover so that he might maintain the highest batting average in the big leagues.

At the same time, an awful lot of what the F.B.I. does bears little relation to crime control and crime prevention. Much of its time, for instance, is spent running routine security checks on applicants for federal jobs.

As far as local police are concerned, the contribution of the Bureau to crime control has been limited to the provision of some technical services: the F.B.I. laboratory, which aids small, otherwise helpless police forces; the central fingerprint file; and the central criminal record index. Basically, these are library services, and might just as well be handled by the Library of Congress.

Question: If, then, the vast forces of the F.B.I.—more than eight thousand sworn agents, not to mention thousands of civilian employees—have not been involved in any of the gut crime problems, what *have* they been involved in ?

The most convincing answer is a very troubling one.

J. Edgar Hoover took over the Justice Department's little Bureau of Investigation in 1924, and proceeded to run it, through the terms of eight Presidents and sixteen Attorneys General. Not until his death in 1972 did some of the ugly truths begin to leak out. For fifty years prior to that, the Bureau operated as a law unto itself, with no supervision by Congress, which could have used the power of the purse strings, or by the Attorney General, nominally Hoover's boss. In any reading of American political history, it now appears axiomatic that power corrupts to the extent that it is unsupervised and not held strictly accountable. J. Edgar Hoover's fifty-year reign, remarkable and frightening in its longevity alone, was a study in the growth of unchecked power—a sort of permanent Watergate.

Not until recently has the existence of this skeleton in our national closet even been hinted at . Even today, for all the shocking revelations, the truth about the Bureau and Hoover is only partly known. Only those of us who have chosen to devote our lives to law enforcement, and who have had to suffer the suffocating presence of the Bureau, possess the dubious distinction of having had to live silently with the truth about this monstrosity.

Our silence was advisable (if not wholly commendable) because of Hoover, who operated behind the scenes as the unquestioned Rasputin of American law enforcement. Until the mid-1960s, when the gap between image and reality started to show like a fissure in the earth from a long pent-up earthquake, Hoover's power in the domestic territory of the United States was absolute; but it was not always, perhaps not even often, exercised in the proper performance of duty. Hoover became the classic case of the victim of one's own success, who if he did not actually believe in the myth of the Bureau's invincibility certainly was propelled by a vision of omnipotence. Though the appointment of Hoover to head the Bureau originated from an act of virtue (one of the reform measures in the wake of the Teapot Dome scandal), his half century on the Mount Olympus of American law enforcement turned into an American nightmare.

The violations of civil rights, the unsanctioned burglaries, the infiltration of suspected or disliked groups with the intent to make them appear to the public more violence-prone or lawbreaking than in fact they were—all have now become familiar to the careful reader of newspaper accounts.

But what was perhaps equally depressing to those of us in law enforcement was the ugly way in which Hoover worked to promote the Bureau at the expense of some desperately needed improvements in local policing—of *your* police department. To those of us concerned about the right of the American citizen to the best possible police service at every level, Hoover's transparent program to divide and conquer made him and his Bureau the biggest single bureaucratic obstacle in the country to better law enforcement.

Hoover's main concern was the image of the Bureau. Nothing else mattered, not even the reality of the growing crime problem in the country. Hoover, for instance, made no contribution at all to the effort to control narcotics traffic in the United States, no contribution to speak of to organized-crime control until dragged into the battle by then Attorney General Robert Kennedy in the early 1960s. In fact, organized crime could not have reached the proportions it has without the neglect of the Federal Bureau of Investigation. More than any other single law enforcement agency, the F.B.I. absented itself from all those areas of crime, like organized crime, that were important and also difficult to handle. In recent years the F.B.I. has begun to make some contributions, most notably through the mechanism of the federal strike forces against organized crime; but if the war against syndicate crime is still to be won, it will be a tremendous come-from-behind victory, to say the least. I would say that nothing in my professional work as head of police in four American cities was more frustrating than the historic failure of the F.B.I. to have had a meaningful role in organized-crime control.

Until Bobby Kennedy pushed Hoover into the swim, Hoover kept publicly denying the existence of a national organized crime syndicate —sometimes called the Mafia or the Cosa Nostra—when of course everyone knew (including Hoover) that denying it could not make it disappear. But the secret truth was that Hoover was deathly afraid to involve the Bureau in such areas as gambling control, narcotics enforcement, and other syndicated rackets because he feared that these were battles he could not win. Even with all the advantages of high-salaried, college-educated agents, complete independence from political control and civil service restrictions in recruitment (advantages practically no chief or commissioner of a municipal department ever had), Hoover lived in fear of the corruption of the Bureau by organized crime.

So—again showing the perversity of his genius for public relations —the Director succeeded in selecting organized crime targets with an eye not to the total contribution of the arrests to the overall organized crime picture but rather to the publicity angle. The emphasis was on visibility rather than on effectiveness and professionalism. Thus the image was preserved. Indeed, the image was related to a bit of reality in that the Bureau was, by comparison to most police departments, a cleaner, more bureaucratically efficient organization. But Hoover helped keep the standard of competition down; this was the Rasputin touch. He was assisted by the statutes; because of its nationwide jurisdiction, the Bureau is not held accountable for organized crime in any single jurisdiction. Of course, the local chief is.

Hoover personally manipulated American law enforcement from the inner sanctum of his office in a wing of the U.S. Justice Department building. With the unflagging assent of Congress, Hoover employed all his leverage as the federal government's most powerful law enforcement official and indeed the nation's most successful political figure.

Hoover's overall strategy was to try to control the selection of local chiefs. To this end, the F.B.I. ran a sort of short-term boarding school for ambitious police executives known as the National Academy; it offered local police so-called advanced training. On the face of it, the National Academy, which began in 1935, was an innocent contribution to the professed desirability of improving American police work. Indeed, the Academy, in view of the fact that it was the only institution of its kind, did help. But for those of us from big cities with our own police academies, little was learned in Washington.* The deputy sheriff from Mississippi sitting next to me hadn't had a single hour of prior training, so his educational needs differed somewhat from mine; nevertheless, we were all thrown into the same category.

Between classes and in the evenings many of those in attendance exploited the golden opportunity to exchange ideas, knowledge, and experience. In our grossly insular, fragmented police world, it might, we knew, prove to be the only such opportunity to do so in our careers.

But in the police world, many understood that Hoover had succeeded in making the National Academy a certification pit stop before advancement up the American police career ladder. No one who wished to get anywhere in policing was likely to be successful without an F.B.I. Academy ticket.† The reputation of the Academy

* The new National Academy building is located in Quantico, Virginia.

† Incidentally, that deputy from Mississippi wasn't wasting his time, even though during the three-month course he never once cracked a book. He ran for sheriff two years later on the platform that he was the only F.B.I.-trained deputy in the county, and he won in a walk.

was such that often the first question an appointing politician might put forth about the prospective new chief was whether or not he had graduated from the "FBI School."

But the catch was that certification by the N.A. was the same thing as certification by the Director, since Hoover was not only the Academy's Dean but also its Director of Admissions. Each year two hundred police careerists from all over the country were invited to Washington. They were hardly randomly selected. In fact, perhaps no group of Americans had ever been so thoroughly screened. What Hoover and his screeners were looking for were future local police chiefs who could be counted on to render blind obeisance to the Director, and who would pledge future service to the local branch of the F.B.I. as needed.*

In the selection process, the Director was assisted by the local S.A.C.'s. These are the special agents in charge who head the many regional F.B.I. offices throughout the country. These were Hoover's talent scouts, and hatchet men. Who had cooperated with the Bureau in the past? Who had handed us the spectacular cases on a silver platter? (Which we then later claimed as our own.) Who was tipping us off about what was going on inside the police department, so we could stay ahead of the headlines? Who could we count on once he was made (by us) chief of police to stay out of our way and do what he was told?

These were the sorts of criteria that Hoover and his S.A.C.'s looked for in their evaluation of applicants to the National Academy.

The special agent in charge was therefore a key figure in the Director's empire—the Strategic Air Command bases in touch with the Pentagon. The S.A.C. was a curious law enforcement figure. His main responsibility seemed to be to move among his territory's businessmen and leaders of commerce—to plug himself, and therefore the Bureau, into the power structure, to keep tabs on the politicians, to keep eyes and ears open for incriminating gossip about local Congressmen and Senators. This dirt could then be conveyed to the Director for whatever purposes he might find useful.

---

* I often wonder how I got by the selection process. Indeed, in view of the many run-ins I had with Hoover in the course of my career, it must have been by mistake, suggesting perhaps that the Bureau was fallible after all.

Aside from the Academy selection process, the S.A.C. participated in the selection of a municipal police chief in yet another way. It was not a formal thing, of course; it would just be that the mayor might want to be friendly with the great F.B.I. (he too might worry about Hoover's secret dossiers). In most instances, the S.A.C. would only have to make a suggestion one way or the other, and with the Hoover legend hanging over his shoulder (like the Sword of Damocles), would find his suggestion taken very seriously indeed. He might just mention to the mayor something along the lines of "Gee, all the agents think very highly of him." (Translation: As deputy chief, he always tips us off to the good cases so we can move in and claim credit for them.)

Hoover's domination of local police departments in this manner helped immensely to achieve whatever actual success in enforcing the law the Bureau enjoyed. With the better cases being gift-wrapped by the cooperative local police, how could the Bureau miss? The Bureau, luxuriating in the flexibility of the federal code, could then pick and choose from the tray of choice entrees offered up by the local gendarmes.

In a similar manner, Hoover and the Bureau dominated for a long, long time the only national police association worth mentioning. This was the International Association of Chiefs of Police.

Until 1962, when a former assistant F.B.I. director broke with Hoover and defected to the I.A.C.P., this organization was a weak, pathetic body* dominated by the small-town chiefs, who in turn were subservient to the Director through the process just described.

Hoover thus controlled the I.A.C.P. before 1962 from behind the scenes like a power broker in a smoke-filled room at a convention, his goal being to keep all possible rival power brokers divided among themselves. In pursuit of this goal, his tactic was to favor the small fry and work against the chiefs from the big police departments. In this way, the I.A.C.P., which represented police management as if it were a kind of American Medical Association, could not rise to a stature that might have posed an alternative to the Bureau's monopoly of wisdom and authority in the field of policing.

---

* "International" stands for Mexico and Canada; it is predominantly a United States organization.

But, ironically, the assistant F.B.I. director who ultimately rescued the I.A.C.P. from the Director's footlocker was originally one of Hoover's most trusted operatives. His name is Quinn Tamm. In 1958, before his defection, Tamm, a very bright man, engineered at Hoover's request one of the most astonishing and, in retrospect, hilarious power plays in my experience.

The story started in 1958 when Chief William Parker, the impressive and great head of the Los Angeles Police Department, sought the position of sixth vice president of the I.A.C.P. at the organization's annual convention, held that year in New York.

Chief Parker was a man of independent mind, with a progressive, professional approach to police management—and therefore a distinct threat to Hoover's pre-eminence as the Marshal Dillon of America. Hoover, naturally, could not abide him.

The Director's first countermeasure was to put out the word to his admissions officers not to admit any more L.A.P.D. officers to the F.B.I. Academy, and in short order L.A. cops were frozen out.

Then the Director moved against Parker's candidacy, which if successful would have put the reform chief in line for the actual presidency of the I.A.C.P.—and perhaps in a position to make something of the organization. He thereupon dispatched Quinn Tamm, then one of his assistant directors and shrewdest operators. Tamm lobbied furiously in New York among all the F.B.I. National Academy graduates at the convention, reminding them which side their bread was buttered on, passing word of the Director's displeasure with the naughty L.A. Chief.

How quickly the word was passed!

In short order, a new sixth vice president was elected, but it wasn't Parker, who in ordinary circumstances would have been elected by acclamation: he was, after all, *the* outstanding police chief of his time. The new sixth V.P. was an otherwise forgettable police chief of an otherwise forgettable force somewhere in Massachusetts. The I.A.C.P. delegates, manipulated from Washington, had chosen for their board of officers yet another small-town chief. And with small-town chiefs totally in control, the I.A.C.P. was not likely to amount to anything.

But the story ends with an ironic twist. Some years later Tamm broke with Hoover and looked for work at, of all places, the I.A.C.P. The job of executive director was open, and Tamm took it. He conscientiously and successfully began to make something of the association. The I.A.C.P. for the first time was making a major contribution to police improvement—and in the process slightly lessening the Bureau's influence. Hoover's underlings tried to unseat Tamm, but Tamm held on to the job despite the effort. In a surprise move, one of the members of the organization's executive board broke from the party line and came out for Tamm, against Hoover's express wishes. He was that Massachusetts small-town Chief who years ago Tamm had installed in the stop-Parker drive. Naturally this development outraged the Director, who with characteristic pique proceeded to make the Massachusetts Chief a non-person, in the manner of the communists. On the next annual roster of National Academy alumni the name of the Massachusetts Chief was nowhere to be found!

This was vintage Hoover. Whenever a bright light would come on in a local police department—Parker in L.A., the scholarly August Vollmer in Berkeley, the innovative O. W. Wilson in Chicago, and the articulate Stephen Kennedy in New York—Hoover would try to extinguish it. He was evidently so insecure that he could not relate in a serious, intelligent, professional way to anyone who might have been his equal. The style here was not collegial but despotic. There could be room for only one bright light in American law enforcement.

In this fashion Hoover put down every effort to raise the educational requirements for police.

It was small-minded stuff at best, but as a tactic, incredibly, it worked. Almost single-handedly, Hoover slowed down the painful march out of the Stone Age and kept exploiting local police unmercifully. This was another aspect of his power not generally known. It was axiomatic with Hoover and his S.A.C.'s that the F.B.I. was to have unfettered access to local police files; but reciprocity was a different matter. It was also axiomatic with Hoover that investigations begun, nurtured, and successfully wound up by local police could at the last moment, with only marginal eleventh-hour federal help, be snatched away by the Bureau for publicity purposes. At the same time, it would also be understood by all concerned that local police departments would not complain if the F.B.I. failed to include them in on operations in which local violations were involved.*

It was also part of the game that local P.D.'s would raise no embarrassing questions if F.B.I. agents should bend a Constitutional safeguard or two on a case—perhaps by conducting an unauthorized burglary, perhaps even with an honor guard of local gendarmes. Over the years, many such illegal operations were conducted by the F.B.I., in New York and elsewhere. The atmosphere in the relationship between local agents and local police was such that the police officers on the operational level simply assumed that the high brass could not and would not put a halt to such operations. Headquarters might not be notified, because even if it knew, there wasn't anything it could do about them, the officers at the operational level reasoned, such was the traditional influence of the Bureau over local police.

Hoover's frightening reign over American law enforcement was not, however, a 1000 percent disaster. As troubling as the Bureau was under his leadership, it has made some important contributions to American policing. Hoover, in his time, in some ways stayed well ahead of his time. He upgraded eligibility requirements for admission into the Bureau in an era when most law enforcement agencies were barely requiring literacy. He established strict controls and strict training requirements for the use of weapons by the F.B.I. in an era when restraint meant shooting first and asking questions later. He put together the Uniform Crime Reports, which though technically a dubious proposition, as we shall see in Chapter Five, at least established the desirability and the principle of crime reportage and collation. He also established the famous fingerprint file, which does no harm; the nation-wide criminal index; and the forensic laboratory, which makes some people feel more scientific about crime. And after 1924, in perhaps his most important contribution, Hoover removed F.B.I. hiring from the corrupt patronage system; even today, poli-

---

* To be perfectly fair, the F.B.I. privately believed that most municipal police departments could not be trusted in sensitive investigations, that they had been compromised by local underworld figures or politicians. There is some truth to this. However, since the F.B.I. rarely involved itself in organized crime investigations, this was not a main cause of the Bureau's reluctance to share the wealth with the locals.

ticians have no leverage over who gets into the Bureau and who gets the promotions. Even the National Academy, despite the perverse uses to which it was put, was useful, though not so much as an educational institution as a focal point for a chaotic law enforcement world.

But despite all these accomplishments, Hoover became a victim of his own success; he became a national monument. And like a monument he could weather storms but he could not bend with the wind. Instead of having a law enforcement leader, the nation was stuck with a statue of law-and-order.

All along, Director Hoover could have been addressing himself to the real crime problems of the nation. The law-and-order pose was actually a cover for irresponsibility. It took Attorney General Kennedy to shove the F.B.I. into organized crime enforcement; who knows what personality or what event will be required to get the Bureau involved in some way in violent street crime. Between organized crime and street crime you have most of the serious crime problem in the United States, and the Bureau has been doing very little about either of them.

The unique position Hoover held in the respect of the American people provided him the opportunity to speak honestly and directly about the complex question of crime. Instead, like the demagogic politician he was, Hoover wrapped himself in the American flag and walked the standard law-and-order line, feigning (or perhaps deeply feeling) bitterness about liberals.*

Worst of all, his stance included a strong dose of racism. It may be, of course, that Hoover's racist beliefs derived from the notion that continued repression of blacks by the law enforcement and the criminal justice systems was a better, cheaper solution to crime than ending the social and economic injustice they continued to suffer. But this is not a position I personally am sympathetic with, of course. Except for the historical circumstances of his exceptional power, Hoover's racism, though ugly, was hardly unique; racism in American law enforcement circles is a terribly common attitude.

The consequences of racism in American policing have been

* Hoover was ideologically so far to the right that a moderate in law enforcement became in his view a liberal, and a liberal a radical. Unfortunately, the police world is cut from the same cloth.

terribly serious. The image and prestige of our police have suffered as many Americans have perceived the police as unjust oppressors of blacks, enforcers of the status quo. At the same time, many Americans look at the police as incompetent in dealing with the crime problem. Although both views are exaggerated and unfair, they occur, to a large extent as a result of the inability of the police to articulate their own side of the story and to overcome the distorted impressions that grow into conventional wisdom precisely because they are unchallenged.

The issue of racial separatism in American society has manifested itself in a serious problem for police. Where the police were friendly toward white residents, they became distant to blacks moving into urban and even suburban communities. That distancing diminished the effectiveness of the police in controlling crime, because the police depend so much on citizens to help them accomplish their task. And, of course, the distancing alienated primarily the law-abiding blacks, who constitute the vast majority of residents in even the highest-crime neighborhood. Add to this the hostility felt by blacks about racial discrimination in hiring, discrimination that is either deliberately conceived or the inevitable consequence of civil service standards that are both discriminatory *and* lacking in job-relatedness. As a consequence of a number of factors, blacks feel that the police are unjust in enforcing the law at least in part because black thinking has been virtually excluded from high policymaking, and from the exercise of street-level discretion.

Hoover's racism was also politically expedient, helping to cement powerful alliances on Capitol Hill with committee chairmen whose own avowed racism was perhaps the most interesting thing about them. Thus, Hoover allied the Bureau with the most repressive racist forces in national politics. What made this volatile mixture of racism and law-and-order policing especially troubling was the Bureau's own special powers.

In the years immediately preceding World War Two, President Roosevelt assigned the Bureau the job of investigating fascist and communist groups. During the war this responsibility was expanded to include counterespionage activity in North and South America, and the problem of federal employees with questionable loyalties. With these new horizons came new powers. Chief among them was the power to wiretap and bug. Hoover, to his credit, was at first quite wary about wiretapping. But under wartime conditions he treated the practice as a necessary evil. After the war the Bureau retained the capability and the power, even though the special conditions were presumably gone. Only recently has the truth come out, that the Bureau has been wiretapping and bugging prominent citizens unconnected to either facism or communism.

The abuse of such power was the inevitable concomitant not only of Hoover's racism but also of the failure of our national government to hold the Bureau accountable to Constitutional principles and procedures. In this context, it is ironic that Hoover contributed to the increasing fragmentation of the nation's police structure by invoking the loathsome specter of a national police force. Much hard work by dedicated people in and out of government to improve policing by consolidation of small inefficient agencies was rendered useless when the opposition trotted out its best available argument (since it was J. Edgar's): Be on guard against the creation of a national police force. (Interpretation: no consolidation.)

Everyone, of course, opposes a Gestapo police. But there was through all this maneuvering a fairly subtle irony beneath the surface. The irony was that the consolidation of small departments, or even the creation of more powerful state police agencies, could not possibly have developed into a danger on the order of the often-stated menace of a national police; while, at the same time, the F.B.I. itself had the potential of developing the freedom-threatening characteristics of a political secret police.

The best approach to a reform of the F.B.I. is to bring the Bureau closer to the real crime problems of the country. All else should follow from that effort.

For starters, the Bureau's much-vaunted kidnapping exploits should be taken over by a special nationwide F.B.I. kidnapping unit, since the structure of virtually all kidnappings is the same. This consolidation would free the various regional and local offices to take on the more difficult crime problems. There are now about one hundred bona fide kidnappings in the U.S. per year, just the right size caseload for a special nationwide unit. The local and regional offices would also have more time on their hands to cooperate more fully with local police departments.

Clarence M. Kelley helped change the Bureau for the better upon becoming Director in 1973. It has been a painfully slow process frequently resisted by unreconstructed Hoover fanatics. Change in the top command has been gradual but is finally complete. With twenty years of prior F.B.I. service and twelve as police chief of Kansas City, Missouri, Kelley has won the abiding respect of chiefs by treating them more as equals and involving the Bureau more directly in assisting their departments with street crime problems. The effort has been modest but it is in precisely the right direction. In a variety of ways the F.B.I. should support the police in becoming more effective not only against street crime, especially the violent kind, but also every type of organized crime, the illicit drug and gun traffic, even white collar crime. The larger police training budget can be better utilized to improve police management and the exchange of knowledge concerning the best methods developed in any department. Training should be a vehicle for the dissemination and the discussion of practical application of current research findings.

The F.B.I. Uniform Crime Reporting system could be much more helpful to the police and criminal justice agencies if the statistics were more accurate and analyzed in ways that would permit comparisons of crime and arrest experience among jurisdictions. The inability to do so at present deprives administrations of potentially valuable crime analysis opportunities.

The Bureau's responsibilities in internal security and counter-intelligence should not be so demanding as to render inadequate its support of the nation's police network. The support role of the federal government is of crucial importance. It has not yet been sufficiently developed. The highest priority should be assigned to it. If future experience indicates a conflict between internal security or police support functions, a reorganization should occur to assure a strong support capacity whether in the Bureau or elsewhere.

In discussions with colleagues and students around the country, I've often referred to the F.B.I. as the *only* completely professional law enforcement agency in the country. For all my criticisms of the Bureau, this statement remains substantially correct. Though federal criminal law accounts for only a small fraction of our total crime picture (most crime is against individual states, and therefore is outside Bureau jurisdiction), the Bureau's record in investigating crimes against the United States has been genuinely splendid. And the level of personal integrity among agents has been astonishingly high. We could scarcely do without a Bureau. But one can only hope that the reforms initiated by Kelley will be expanded and improved upon. Although a continuing reform effort will be tricky and difficult, too much is at stake to allow the Bureau to become nothing more than a sophisticated public relations operation, or, less harmlessly, a law enforcement agency operating on the edge of the law. The F.B.I. is too important to be allowed to be either trivialized or perverted. The nation needs a very good F.B.I.— perhaps more than ever before.

Chapter Five

Transformations

By the late 1960s the American police service—in all honesty it could not yet be termed a formal *profession*—suffered a series of ugly setbacks. Their names were Watts, Detroit, and Newark, blistering urban riots that not only belied the ideological myth of racial harmony in the United States but also gave police chiefs all over the country a terrible case of nerves. In three major American cities, police had demonstrated an unexpected depth of incompetence, insensitivity, and lack of preparedness in dealing with these civil disorders; and, despite all this, there was unfortunately no indication that the bottom of the barrel had been plumbed. There were plenty of other American cities, all with substantial black populations, all too ready to give further test in the summer of 1968—the summer after the historic '67 explosions—to the proposition of whether American police, in a humane, sensible manner, could maintain domestic order. Which was, after all, the original and minimum justification for a domestic military. All that was required to touch off further difficulty, some of us felt, was (a) for the police to respond as amateurishly in 1968 as they had in 1967 to routine Friday or Saturday night ghetto arrests, which can explode into disorder and quickly escalate to a riot; and (b) for the country's ghetto residents to continue to be agitated by the rhetoric of the militants and the exaggerated TV news coverage (some of it demonstrably inflammatory). There were more than enough real issues to feed a great deal of emotion and frustration in those ghettos already on the brink of collective despair.

In the United States Department of Justice at this time, Ramsey Clark—a most caring, most far-seeing Attorney General—set into motion a series of high-level meetings toward the end of 1967 with an agenda on the anticipated "long hot" summer of 1968. Among the concerns uppermost in his mind was the urgent necessity of improving the performance of city police, whose sometimes provocative behavior in the early stages of these riots had in reality (we all knew) compounded what was without their unwanted contribution an already difficult situation.

At the time of Clark's concern—reinforced by a deeply agonized Lyndon Baines Johnson—I was a middle-level Justice Department official. I had by then taken leave from the N.Y.P.D., a formal retiree, at the rank of deputy chief inspector. More than a year before retirement I had left Syracuse (to the capable hands of William H. T. Smith, my deputy chief, whom Mayor Walsh had promoted without delay to chief at my unreserved recommendation) to return to my home department as commanding officer of the New York Police Academy. After a year a new commissioner interviewed me for two different top positions, but I was not selected for either. The disappointment was real. (The only other comparable setback in my career was the occasion of my first captain's examination. I passed the multiple-choice section of the exam but missed passing the essay section by one percentage point. Afterward, the civil service system was sued by a group of officers who failed the multiple-choice section of the test, and in response the passing grade was lowered, thus enabling many who had failed to receive a passing grade. However, the passing grade for the essay section was not lowered, leaving one Patrick Murphy out in the cold—with a four-year wait until the next examination for captain. I suppose my reluctance to embrace without stipulation the civil service examination basis of promotion within the department might at least in part be traced to this bitter personal experience.)

So when the opportunity to go to Washington came—to get in on the ground floor of the federal government's new involvement in the "war on crime" (the Law Enforcement Assistance program)—I found Washington much more exciting than treading water at the N.Y.P.D.

In Washington, some serious attention—perhaps for the first time since F.D.R.—was being given to unaddressed domestic problems (despite the preoccupying disaster in Vietnam). Under Attorney

General Clark the federal strike force approach against organized crime (initiated under R.F.K.) was refined and expanded, and new pilot projects to improve local policing were being raised off the drawing boards, under a program of federal assistance to local policing under a new agency—at first called the Office of Law Enforcement Assistance, but soon to evolve into the Law Enforcement Assistance Administration (L.E.A.A.). The urban riots prior to 1968 not only reinforced Clark's belief in the urgent need for new programs for the inner cities but also in the absolute necessity for programs for our local police departments—institutional ghettos in their own way. It was in this regard that as an otherwise inconsequential federal bureaucrat I came to the attention of the Attorney General. Clark felt that, like most federal officials, he did not know nearly enough about cops, and that, if only by comparison I did.* And so he asked me to conduct what he sometimes referred to as "tutorial" lessons.

It was out of such tutorial lessons that a series of conferences of the nation's police chiefs was proposed and arranged. Clark had caught a glimpse, almost from the start of our discussions, of the profound chaos in American policing, and the attendant isolation and confusion felt by many police chiefs. Even under the best of conditions, such chaos was not conducive to intelligent law enforcement and humane order maintenance. But in the circumstance of all the worries about the summer of '68, such confusion and isolation made everyone in the Justice Department, especially Clark, exceedingly nervous. It was as if hundreds of different fingers were on guns pointed directly at the nation's cranium—with every single one of those fingers inclining toward panic.

As an emergency move, Clark approved what I had suggested— a series of secret meetings at Airlie House, a conference center in Virginia. Invited to attend—at Justice Department expense—were about 125 police chiefs, the logical ones, from the largest cities and some of the bigger suburban counties. The subject matter of the meetings was unapologetically "relevant": the problem of urban disorder, police-minority relations, and police preparedness for riot situations.

* In reality Clark knew more than he ever realized; but since he was charmingly devoid of that characteristic federal arrogance about cops, he felt that there was a great deal more to be learned.

And the "curriculum," as Clark and a strong staff devised it, was uncompromisingly conciliatory in conception. We were less interested, for instance, in maximizing the fatality-effectiveness of a department's arsenal of submachine guns that in minimizing a department's potential contribution to heightened racial tension, and its occasional proclivity toward pointless exercises in brutality and other forms of macho-policing. The main point of the Airlie House exercise, in fact, was to calm the frazzled nerves of the police officials, who by the summer of 1968 may very well have held in their hands the fate of the nation's domestic tranquillity.

Revealingly, not a single chief, as best I can remember, turned down the confidential invitation from the Attorney General. In the police world the opportunity to meet expressly on such a sensitive subject had never presented itself. And rather than shrink from the controversial fare at the Airlie House conference, most of the chiefs seemed to be drawn to the novel idea of attempting to meet squarely the problems of reality. By the unanimous acceptance of the invitation, the Attorney General and I sensed that we had a winner on our hands.

The crash course for the chiefs—invited in waves of small groups at a time—lasted one week, but the effect was evidently longer-lasting. Each group was joined for the last two days by the mayors of the attending chiefs. Their understanding of and support for needed change were essential. Even the few enlightened chiefs benefited from having their "hard-headed" mayors understand that the traditional "show of force" approach was no longer an adequate police strategy for civil disorder.

The Airlie House conferences had, all knew, been a serious effort. (Pointedly, the press had not been invited, to avoid giving the impression that the conferences were no more than a publicity stunt.) It was exactly the sort of thing that should have been put together over at the great F.B.I. Academy had that institution not been compromised on the altar of Hoover's grand designs for the total conquest of the American law enforcement world. Perhaps most important to the overall program, however, was Attorney General Clark's regular weekly appearances: impressive, extemporaneous, fact-filled, highly astute, and often amusing disquisitions on the law and on law enforcement as these matters related to minority rights and preventing violence.

On the face of it, these sessions in Virginia with the nation's troubled police chiefs can hardly by themselves be credited with the full weight of the astonishing turnaround in police performance during the summer of 1968, when major cities on the brink of riots pulled back. The causes, both of the trouble and of the de-escalation, transcend any solitary factor. Yet the Airlie consciousness-raising sessions, in my opinion, did have a profound effect on the police world, or at least that portion of it significant enough to be invited to Airlie. To communicate with the nation's chiefs on an issue of this importance in such a manner and in such an atmosphere—where police were not being lectured down to by condescending, cop-disliking academics, but taking part in a free give and take among peers, with the Attorney General of the United States lending his office and his presence to the communication—did more than anything else to prevent a rerun in 1968 of the horrors of 1967 and summers past. To assert this is, of course, to concede regretfully that in 1967 police misconduct was a force not for law and order, as it were, but for very troubling domestic disorder.

It was painfully obvious at this time, to both the White House and the Attorney General's office, that the Washington Police Department, like the Detroit P.D. and many other police forces in the country, had poor relations with minority communities. But to permit the local police force, operating in the shadow of the White House, to remain in such a circumstance was, of course, risk taking at its worst.

It was also known that the leadership of the Washington Metropolitan Police Department was reporting not to the District citizens or official representatives (the majority of whom were black) but to a clique of Southern Congressmen who in fact were making the most important decisions regarding the District of Columbia. By this powerful clique of racist Southern Congressmen, the incumbent Washington Police Chief, John B. Layton, was considered properly competent. But Attorney General Clark and President Johnson believed that with a high police command in the capital more sensitive to the whims and prejudices of Southern outsiders than to the citizens of the District, it would be difficult to ensure the next summer without city-wide ugliness.

The initial political calculation, in the White House, was to try to remove Layton directly and replace him with someone who could work better with the black leaders and neighborhoods. Presidential muscle, the figuring went, could do the job. But with control of the District more or less divided between the House on the Hill and the White House, the frontal approach looked at second glance a bit costly; it could be done, but it would kick up a lot of dust. On top of the politics there was another serious problem: the white downtown businessmen of Washington supported the Chief and could create a tidal wave of protest against any attempt at replacing him.

In this endeavor, however, time was not on the White House's side; thus a clever back-door approach had to be concocted. The scheme involved the creation of a civil service–exempt position: the Director of Public Safety. In this scheme, the Director of Public Safety would be put over not only the Police Department but also the fire and civil defense departments as well. Accordingly, the creation of the new position could be justified to the public and to any of the Congressional powers concerned as a coordination move, and not seem like a direct power play against the Police Chief. Indeed, in many other parts of the country—particularly in New Jersey—where an incumbent police chief for one reason or another has been difficult to remove, this back-door technique has been employed, usually to good effect.

When Attorney General Clark asked me to take the new job if Mayor Walter Washington decided to offer it—and indicated that my nomination had been considered and approved at the highest level of the White House—I was flattered but not overjoyed. I knew, if only from reading the Washington *Post* and the Washington *Star*, that Chief Layton, on the basis of his political alliances, was practically an immovable object—and a chief who, like so many around the country, looked the part, if in fact he was not actually right for it. The assignment from the White House, of course, was to outmaneuver Layton and his group, thereby to gain control over the lower ranks, and thereafter to prepare as rapidly as possible for the risk-filled summer that we all knew lay ahead.

I met with Layton soon after moving into an office at the District Building near the White House. Layton, as he would be for almost all of our encounters in the coming months, was properly correct and superficially helpful. We chatted, mostly about nothing and the weather, but when I raised the crucial question of whether in his opinion the department had received sufficient instruction and motivation for the trying summer months ahead, Layton's eyes glazed over defiantly and he said, "I'm satisfied we're ready."

I was not completely reassured and felt even more uneasy as I recalled the Chief's attitude during a recent public discussion about police officers addressing black youths: "Boys!" Concerned groups and individuals sought a clear policy prohibiting officers from addressing black men or young men as "Boy" or "Boys." But the Chief had difficulty understanding how he could possibly prohibit officers from addressing a group of young black boys as "Boys." His attitude suggested to me a rigidity or lack of sensitivity that, if reflected in the attitudes of the Department's 3,000 officers, spelled serious trouble.

Like most American chiefs whom the times had passed by, however, Layton was not an evil or even an unpleasant man; but he understood power. It would be power, not equity or even social conscience, that would move him off the dime.

I thus needed additional leverage in order to make major changes quickly. Privately arranged reports from the field were reinforcing all my fears. As far as training and preparation were concerned, the department was ready for a bloodbath perhaps, but not for skillful crisis management.

One of the confidential sources of this information was a bright young commander named Jerry Wilson; and everything I was to find out about him in the coming weeks told me that, against Layton's opposition, he had to be our new assistant chief in charge of field operations. Ironically, however, it was Layton himself who handed me the incident which provided the leverage I needed.

The incident began late one night in early 1968. A handful of Washington's finest were doing serious drinking in the back of the Sixth Precinct House. Running out of booze, they piled into one of the officers' cars and headed for a Maryland suburb—home. On the way, amid a great deal of hell raising, their car passed the well-known residence of the president of Howard University, the largely black institution of higher learning in Washington. The car slowed down, then one or more of the inebriated officers proceeded to aim his Police Special in the general direction of the president's residence and fire off several shots. Then the car quickly raced away.

Private security guards posted at the president's residence, however, jumped into their car and gave chase. At a traffic light, these black guards pulled up alongside the fleeing car for a quick look. Although the white police officers inside were wearing civilian coats, the distinctive black police pants gave them away. They were obviously cops. But rather than confront the white officers, the black security guards wisely retreated, taking with them only the license plate number. By early morning, the white officers had weaved their way out of the District.

I knew nothing of the incident until very late the next day. I took a call from an aide to Mayor Walter Washington at my office. He asked what I'd come up with on the Howard University shooting incident. I told him, truthfully, that I had heard nothing at all, so obviously there could be nothing to it—because, after all, I was the Director of Public Safety. About an hour later a second call came in. I laughed. After all, I was the Director of Public Safety; surely I would have been among the very first to have heard about a police shooting incident.

Later that night, however, at my home in Northwest Washington, I took a call from a black radio station that really shook me up. The reporter had chapter and verse of the shooting incident; evidently he had talked to one of the black guards. Now I felt like a complete fool.

Worse yet, the situation itself had another quite frightening side. Would there be a second chapter to the shooting tonight? And why was the Director of Public Safety, like the rest of Washington, being kept in the dark?

I told the reporter contritely that I'd get back to him, and I dialed Communications at Police Headquarters. I had to practically browbeat several officers before I could get one who would talk. Finally, one cracked, confirming essentially the version of events given me by the black radio reporter.

What a coverup! Even the Public Safety Director was being locked out. I dialed Chief Layton at Headquarters but was told he was out to dinner. By now my Irish temper was on fire. As I left the house, I told Betty, "Tell Layton when he calls that I've gone to the Sixth Precinct." Betty was to tell me later that when Chief Layton called and heard where I'd gone, he made a sound like someone swallowing false teeth.

Aside from anger, I also felt something quite contradictory: relief. Chief Layton, in failing to report the incident, was handing us the key to the Police Department—and to the installation of young Jerry Wilson where I wanted him, in the top operational position in the department.

I arrived at the Sixth Precinct. The television stations had evidently picked up the shooting report from the black radio station. The building was crawling with cameras, klieg lights, and reporters.

And so I held an impromptu news conference.

"Director Murphy," one television reporter asked with cameras rolling and the lights scorching hot, "is there any truth to the report that white off-duty police officers fired upon the residence of the president of Howard University?"

"Yes," I said, simply; but my face was, I knew, turning red.

The room erupted into an uproar as I explained the dimensions of the incident. I had not, I revealed finally, been informed through channels. What you have here, I explained, is a typical police department coverup. I then attacked Chief Layton for failing to inform the Director of Public Safety.

"You weren't told?" asked a reporter incredulously.

"No," I said.

I proceeded, but in an uncharacteristic emotional manner. I was emotional because (a) that's how I felt and (b) I wanted to provide the cameras with as much television footage as they could use. I had caught Layton in a big inexcusable error, and I felt he should pay dearly for it. To reporters, I said, "The officers involved in this incident will be criminally prosecuted as well as departmentally disciplined if law was violated."

The reporters and cameramen ran out of the stationhouse like a posse. They had, they knew, a front-page story. By the time Chief Layton arrived at the precinct, the cameras, lights, and media paraphernalia were gone.

But I stayed behind, waiting for Layton to arrive. When he did, I commandeered a private office, pulled Layton inside and locked the door. My essential message was this: "Chief, don't you understand? I'm your *boss*. I'm *your* boss."

The next day Mayor Washington telephoned. He was quite upset, implying that I had gone too far. By then my performance had made all the television news shows, at considerable length: there was the new Public Safety Director, carrying on about a police coverup.

In retrospect, the concerns of Mayor Washington and Deputy Mayor Tom Fletcher were enormously legitimate. Naturally, I had been quite upset—and quite opportunistic in the attempt to make points against the Layton faction, which I believed to be on the wrong side of most of the major issues involving the Police Department. But in my desire to capitalize on the situation, I had violated a cardinal rule of the Police Chief: failing to alert the Mayor or the Deputy Mayor to what I was up to. They had been taken as completely by surprise as everyone else in Washington, and this treatment they manifestly did not deserve. After all, I might have come out temporarily ahead—and, indeed, I did—but they could have lost heavily in the long run, which, blessedly, they did not. The police chief sometimes forgets that public safety is only one of the politician's many concerns. More to the point, by alienating powerful people in Congress, I could have damaged the Mayor and his deputy irreparably. I had been incautious; in all fairness to them, I should have remembered that it was the Mayor and his deputy who time and again mobilized the necessary support for me and my reform program with the ever-dangerous House District Committee.

About a week later, Layton's allies regrouped on the Hill and, sensing trouble, scheduled an executive session of the House D.C. Committee. But several friends and supporters obtained the cooperation of a couple of committee members, who, at my prompting, forced Chairman John McMillan of South Carolina to conduct an open session. McMillan evidently believed that he could deal as summarily with me in the glare of a public session as in the privacy of an executive session.

But soon he knew he had miscalculated. With the public looking over our shoulders, Chairman McMillan and I had it out—and the TV cameras again had a good day.

Chairman McMillan clearly was not accustomed to being talked back to by a mere official of the District of Columbia government. When I left the hearing room, a few spectators rushed up to me to say I had held my own.

Frankly, I felt terrific. More importantly, the message had been conveyed: The Public Safety Director is in charge, the Chief is under him.

But, in truth, I had really just lucked out, and matters could have come out much worse. In a freewheeling, highly sophisticated political environment like Washington, the Mayor and his aides more than once taught me things I did not know, and protected me from dangers I had not seen coming. I did not once, as far as I can recall, ignore their advice, or fail to be impressed by it. Indeed, it is the foolish police chief who believes that the expertise he possesses on the subject of police work and police administration can necessarily be translated into all-around political savvy.

I believed I knew my subject mattter, but I also knew better— most of the time—than to show contempt for Congressional power. All the textbook knowledge in the world is useless if the police chief is bullheaded and isolated from that part of the political establishment which supports his program.

But the wild card in this poker game was held by the media. How would they play their hand? How would they cover it? I had met previously with several newspaper editors and felt that I had gotten my ideas across rather well. I thought: If only the two big papers and the television stations would cooperate, the Metropolitan P.D. could be turned around—at least for a summer. And they did.

I felt this about the skirmish for control of the department: Machiavelli, whom one might say receives a bit of a bad press these days, must, on a more careful reading of *The Prince*, be understood for his advocacy of politics for the accomplishment of desirable ends. The police administrator, to accomplish change and reform that count, must comprehend the power inherent in his office, and must know how to use it. In the case at hand, the Public Safety Director was an official position created out of urgency, even desperation; it was necessarily an office with no traditional leverage behind it (since it was so new) but also an official creation containing an enormous degree of visibility (also, because it was new). And it was this visibility which was to permit me the leverage to exert power over the traditional, since in the circumstance of 1968 it was literally the traditional way of policing that stood in the way of a summer we could live with.

The elevation of a young, little-known police officer to a top operational position, along with the promotion of a selected group of other junior officers over those far more senior, had a symbolic as well as a practical consequence. This symbol of genuine change attracted the attention of the District Committee, which once again thought enough of my presence to require it at a special hearing on the Hill, held entirely in my honor.

"Wilson is too young, lacks seniority," said one critic of Assistant Chief Jerry Wilson, echoing the reflexive criticism of all progress and change. "The promotion will demoralize senior officers."* But such touching devotion to seniority, developed virtually to a mystic ritual in Congress, had the corollary and perhaps intended effect of making blacks wait forever before reaching top management circles. Time, again, was not on our side. Washington was 75 percent black, the highest ratio of any city in the country; there accordingly could be no excuse for further delay in integrating the higher levels of the Washington Police Department. What I hoped, then, was to suggest in the unexpected promotions of a few junior officers new and hopefully immediate opportunities for other frustrated officers below, especially blacks.

The promotions were calculated to have a second effect. In virtually any sizable police department, the complexion of the top leadership will be inordinately crucial. Because of its paramilitary nature, a police department, more than any other civilian-government bureaucracy one can think of, houses souls who by conditioning and per-

---

* Some members of the House committee were perhaps not as concerned with morale at the senior level as with their own morale. We would receive letters of recommendation about the desirability of promoting so-and-so to inspector. The suggestion of a "contract" (i.e., a deal) was implicit. I always wrote back politely, but noncommitally. I tried my best to devalue this sort of recommendation. If I had gone along with their "recommendation," word soon would have gotten out that the way to get ahead in the Washington Metropolitan Police Department was to follow the lead of the District Committee not the Director of Public Safety.

haps by prior inclination look to those ahead of them to determine how to get by. The lower 90 percent of a department will take its cues from the top 10 percent. But this top 10 percent—the cream of the officers corps—will not present a united front to the officers below. Typically, in departments of some size, the top officers corps will be divided in half, into two contending factions, perceived by those below as, literally and figuratively, the "good" guys and the "bad" guys. When a new police administrator comes into power, it is his immediate task to identify that faction which to the younger, more idealistic, more potentially productive officers in the ranks below appears to include the "good" guys frozen out of the very top positions by the old guard clique. Once this potentially inspirational set of officers is identified, then the administrator must selectively but rapidly begin to move its members up at the expense of the bad clique currently in power. Once it is perceived that the new top police administrator has tilted in the direction of the "good" top 5 percent, then the entire bureaucracy below—the 90 percent—will lean in that direction, so susceptible are those below to the nuances of management change at the top.

Therefore, that handful of promotions in the Washington P.D., which included some blacks, had a calculated effect on street policies and attitudes in the lower ranks. In a matter of weeks there was a discernible change in the mood of the force. At bottom was an appeal —urgent in the circumstances we all knew we would be up against— to the pride of the average police officer in the sheer fact that he or she *was a law enforcement representative.*

The overall appeal—supplemented of course by a host of training programs aimed at tightening of command and control and increasing sensitivity—would have otherwise fallen on deaf ears had there not been real and symbolic changes at the top. But it had an emotional foundation: the idea that if we could motivate our officers to understand that, in essence, the whole world was watching, that the proper behavior of the law enforcement officer was central to the order of society, then we could proceed to the next logical premise— that proper, intelligent law enforcement might as reasonably involve the non-use of police guns as their use, that the enforcement of the law with dignity could as its essential feature require restraint as much as (if not more than) muscle, that we were a police service, not just a police *force*.

The appeal to pride can in certain circumstances be more powerful than one might imagine. The Washington P.D. was widely known as a sort of redneck police force; and as a generalization that gibe was not without some point. Many officers were, after all, more native to the small towns of white rural Georgia than to the ghettos of Northeast Washington. But still, despite the bad national reputation, all our officers had in common a consensual experience, and a training, as officers of the law; *this was the entire point.* "I am a lawman, I am a law enforcement officer, and my job is to enforce the law and the court order." This was something that had been stressed to them throughout their careers over and over again.

The appeal's strength hardly diminishes when the public spotlight is turned on. In the incidents in Boston in the mid-1970s over court-ordered school integration, Boston police officers (mostly Irish and Italo-Americans) were placed in a most difficult position. The court had decided the issue of integrating mostly white schools in certain densely ethnic Boston neighborhoods literally in favor of the Fourteenth Amendment. The legal decision conflicted with local sentiment, however. To enforce the court order, Boston police, then under Police Commissioner Robert di Grazia—a very bright man—had to swim against the tide of local sentiment—not infrequently the sentiment of neighbors and relatives—and of cops.

Nevertheless, the Boston police performed this unpleasant task with commendable and, to some, surprising efficiency. The cops were there where the front lines of the legal and political battle had been drawn; and when a white prepared to launch a rock at some black schoolchildren, the Boston police were there to do what they were supposed to do.

In this situation, the massive presence of the news media probably helped. In the spotlight the police officer is more certain perhaps to play his or her role according to the book than when out of it. I suppose it's the old back-alley story. Police officers who have become irritated with, say, an obnoxious drunk or fresh kid have been known to take care of the problem, if they know no one is looking, in the back alley. But with television cameras recording history, the spirit, as well as the letter, of the law has a better than average chance of close observance.*

Thus in Washington in 1968, as in Boston in the mid-1970s, it was clear to all whose heads were not in the sand that the Washington Metropolitan Police Department might well be at center stage. With just the right signals from above—utilizing the 90 percent formula— it was my belief that the Washington street officer could be made to see that roughneck (or red-neck) policing would just not do. My own personal view, in fact, was that the red-neck charge was unfair and inaccurate; the problem of racism in American police depart- ments was far too pervasive and serious to be explained in terms of the geographical origin of the officers. There was nothing essentially more racist or red-neck about the Washington P.D. than any number of other police departments, including some prominent northern ones.

By the time of the assassination of the Reverend Martin Luther King, Jr., in April of 1968, when Washington's minority neighbor- hoods, like others in the country, reacted with serious violence and destruction, the Washington P.D. had been mellowed, trained, and was psychologically ready. Jerry Wilson, in a very short period of time, had performed a minor miracle. When the tragic and moving spectacle of the Poor People's Campaign—complete with mule team and instant Resurrection City—camped on the Mall and lodged for weeks in the nation's conscience, our police, with few exceptions, extended themselves like fellow passengers in the same trapped train. What might have been a genuine first-class racial holocaust, generated in part by police overreaction, was contained reasonably within the bounds of the possible by levelheaded police work.

In point of fact, the inclination toward restraint in dealing with the looters and the window smashers and the amateur arsonists unleashed

* The role of police as enforcement officers of patently unpopular laws or court orders is troubling. As a police administrator, I often wished that there had been a better way. But the involvement is not altogether a new one. For example, seemingly the entire early history of the Pennsylvania State Police was as a "scab" force. The real reason for its existence was to break labor strikes in that highly industrialized state. For decades the Pennsylvania State Police made virtually no contribution to public order other than to keep the plants open, to permit strike- breakers to make it past picket lines, exercises which also involved the specter of the officers' brothers and sisters on the other side of the picket line.

in the wake of the assassination of Dr. King surfaced more rapidly than perhaps anyone had expected.

Because of their excruciatingly close contact with the poverty and desperation of the ghetto and the street, police officers, especially younger ones, can show enormous sympathy and compassion under certain conditions—especially when encouraged by the new attitudes of top management. Notwithstanding the ugly Howard University incident, the Washington P.D., in its essential form, was capable of great restraint, as its performance during the King riot demonstrated.

Indeed, the most intense resistance to our policy of restraint came not from within the department, once the old outmoded policy had been superseded, but from without. Depressingly, in the aftermath of the disorder I personally received a number of pieces of mail, some of them more literate and less threatening than others, from our "consumers." Leaving aside the matter of personal abuse and criticisms of my manhood, the net impression of this wave of mail was almost that some citizens were actually rather disappointed that there hadn't been a bloodbath, that Washington police hadn't taunted and goaded the poor black people of Washington into some form of self-immolation, that the official policy of the department was a respect for the value of life rather than for genocide. Some letter writers, of course, were no doubt sincere in their consternation over police policies which were on their face a shocking departure from what the citizens of the Washington area had been used to.

The basic intellectual content of these letters, taken together, rested on the premise that had the police employed more force during the several days of the King disorder in the District, less violence would have ensued. This premise, of course, was as wrong as it could be.

In the belief that police officials should play an educative as well as an enforcement role (this is something I believe strongly in), I composed a rather lengthy response to my critics, spelling out in it the essential philosophy of riot control, and sent it out in the form of individual replies. The letter began by briefly summarizing the circumstances of the April 1968 evening in question. "Following the assassination of Martin Luther King, Jr., trouble flared spontaneously in several parts of the city. Despite speedy mobilization, our police officers were outnumbered in certain areas, and were unable to stop the large-scale looting which quickly developed."

But outnumbered, I suggested, was not necessarily outsmarted. "Rather than apply the degree of force that would have been effective against a single thief or a small band of lawbreakers, our police, in view of the extremely inflammatory situation they faced, were instructed to contain the area of the disorder. To discharge their firearms into large numbers of people could well have caused the disturbance to overflow."

The payoff, in fact, was gratifying; the policy of police restraint seemed actually to have evoked a response of restraint, rather than increased lawlessness, from neighborhoods that were in understandable anguish and turmoil over the assassination. "Injuries to outnumbered lawmen were averted." There were only two police-related deaths during the large-scale rioting, both of which were clearly defensible. "When firearms are discharged and lives lost, the experience of other cities has shown that the amount of property damage increases." This was the paradox.

"I want you to understand that the decision to minimize the use of force in this manner was a conscious one, reached after a determination that such a course of action would not only save lives, both of police officers and citizens, but would also save property."

Some years later an incident occurred which illustrated a pathetic problem in American policing: the distrust of the press. A head of police in a large city during one high-level meeting went into an incoherent rage about reporters and politicians. All at once, all the accumulated paranoia, resentment, naiveté, and juvenile bitterness erupted. Eyewitnesses told me the performance was an embarrassment to all present.

Although pathetic, the scene was hardly unusual. It is one which in the police world is replayed constantly in cities and counties throughout the country. In part, what is open for inspection here is the civil service mentality. The police chief's job is the gold ring; it is his because he has earned it. In this view of things, the civil service system, in which one enters and rises through the ranks, is the Total Merit System of the World. The press and the politicians, as nonmembers of this Platonic merit world, are deemed to be nothing more than irritants, interlopers, carpetbaggers, troublemakers, perhaps even communists (or, worse yet, "eggheads"). That the politician and the reporter might actually be integral, legitimate, and possibly even valuable cogs in our system seems a subtlety lost on many chiefs, who act out a kind of blue-collar arrogance and military-collar smugness.

And it is the viselike grip of the civil service system on American policing that works directly against a logical distillation of a better police leadership. Originally created in understandable revulsion to the spoils system, the civil service system, now a permanently encrusted element in American political life, has become a classic case of the cure that may be as bad as the disease. Because of its suffocating hold on the process by which police chiefs are crowned, this system, perhaps more than any other single factor, must be held responsible for the routine mediocrity of police management in America.

This mediocrity is terribly costly, in several respects. In addition to the questions of arrest or freedom, even life and death, that often arise as a result of police work, there is the bread-and-butter matter of money. Even in a medium-sized American city, without the incredibly omnipresent crime problems of a city like New York or Chicago, the police get a tremendous share of the city budget. Take a nice American city like Cincinnati, which considers itself light-years removed from crime centers like New York. Fully 24 percent of Cincinnati's entire city government budget goes to the police. And in a medium-sized city like Cincinnati this is not an extremely high share for police. Policing is a very expensive function of government; in many respects it is the Tiffany's of public service. In one year, again in Cincinnati, the citizens spent $23.8 million on their police alone. The variety of ways in which this huge hunk of the budget was disbursed to serve the citizens illustrates the tremendous complexity of the police business, and, in my view, strengthens the argument for professional, modern management at the highest levels of a police department. For instance, in one year Cincinnati spent some of its money for policing as follows:

• $2.7 million responding to 250,000 citizen calls for service; this came to $10.74 per call;

• $10.58 every time a drunk had to be picked up off the streets, processed, and presented to the Alcohol Detoxification Center;

• $80.81 for each police presentation to a community meeting;

• $8.00 per man-hour for 125,280 man-hours per year to conduct walking patrol and to interact with the community;

• $13.91 per case for each of 20,000 criminal cases sent to court each year;

• $72.13 per place per check, after discovering 1700 business establishments or other commercial buildings left unlocked during the year;

• $8.25 an hour, 36 hours per month, in training 10 canine units;

• 37 cents a call, to review and screen roughly one million incoming phone calls per year;

• 10 cents a transmission, to dispatch police units on 400,000 radio runs;

• $849.13 per investigation, to probe each of 220 criminal or suspicious deaths;

• $277.38 per investigation, for each of 575 business or financial-institution robberies;

• $4.19 to process each piece of physical evidence that, for whatever reason, must temporarily be retained in police custody;

• $206.64 per investigation of possible misconduct or criminality by a police officer.

This list, though abbreviated, gives one a sense of the dimensions of the police management problem. A police force is not a little toy dollhouse, and the deployment of its resources and manpower is not a quaint game of pushing tiny tin soldiers around. And yet few police careerists, either through professional training or as amateur buffs in management, are actually qualified to manage significantly sized police departments—that is, the ones that count.

The contribution of the news media in Washington in helping relieve the 1968 difficulties, as I have mentioned, was a crucial factor. Without their help, we could not have made that 5 percent change at the top that tilted those 90 percent below in the right direction. The decency and good will—not to mention honest professionalism—of the news media in the tense circumstances of that moment in history may, for all I know, have been *the* crucial factor in the relatively acceptable outcome.

In any case, the news media and the police could routinely be natural allies rather than suspicious neighbors. The fact that with all too many departments antagonism rather than mutual understanding prevails may, however, say more about the police than the press. In my own experience, cops—not just the chief—tend to be unnaturally suspicious of and paranoid about news organizations. The suspicion most often expresses itself not in wiretaps on reporters' phones or round-the-clock tails on the city editor but—far more seriously in a sense—in what might be described as an endemic case of police lockjaw. This is the proclivity of police, in the face of the temptation to respond to a question from the press with the whole truth, to issue instead the time-honored two-word statement "No comment."

The sources of police reluctance to level with the press may vary from place to place, but one common thread is the old paramilitary philosophy in which a police department is regarded as virtually a clandestine institution. Necessarily, then, its relationship with the press, an institution which thrives on easy access, would have to be adversarial. This mentality accounts for the reliance on reticence, or on the "No comment," when a full and honest disclosure of fact would not harm (and would perhaps even help) the department's essential interests. But the old tradition, which put such store in the dogma of secrecy, meant that in essence the "public relations" philosophy was practically a code of silence. The problem is that any institution which reflexively treats the press as the enemy obviously runs the risk of alienating itself from the society and constituencies it serves.

The paranoia about the press is also bad politics. In reality, the most meaningful measure of the performance of a police department and its top management often comes from the news media. A bad press can quickly bring down even a good chief. A good press can keep a bad chief in power. A capable chief, even if he has the respect and support of the mayor or city manager, can become a political liability if constantly under fire from the news media. A chief who is intensely disliked by the mayor or the city manager may nevertheless be invulnerable to removal if the department continues to receive rave reviews in the press.

The power of the press in police politics is awesome, perhaps more than it should be; but the press has a monopoly on the field. For outside of press accounts of police performance, no good critical measures exist. As inexact and often impressionistic as they may be, the press ratings are all we have. How ironic, then, that some police departments have failed to develop or even consider sensible strategies of handling public information, aside from infinite calculations of different ways to say "No comment." It is unfortunate in another respect. Few police departments are all bad, for in most of them as a daily matter a great deal of good does get done. But police departments, by staking out in many instances an adversarial relationship with the press, simply fail to tell their own good story.

The question of trying to level with the press arose acutely in Detroit in the very early days of 1970. I had just become Detroit's Police Commissioner.

Roman S. Gribbs, a lawyer, had just been elected Mayor of Detroit, and had gone about looking for his own police commissioner. Gribbs, a former sheriff, had sent one of his staff members to Washington to visit me. I was then a senior staff member at the Urban Institute and a refugee from the Justice Department, which was then being restaffed with Nixon's men. My biggest project at the Urban Institute, which I will discuss at length later, involved a design for reorganizing patrol —a design which was to figure in Detroit.

But it seemed as if I had not been in Detroit for more than a few minutes when the first hint of the department's endemic difficulty in relating to the press appeared. The incident began late on a Friday. A team of white officers had arrested four black teenagers following a traffic violation. I was out of town, back in Washington, helping Betty and the children prepare for the last leg of the family move to Detroit. During the entire weekend, though I had left my Washington phone number with the department's communications center, no one called from Detroit; and so on Monday morning, when I picked up a paper on my return to Detroit International Airport, before ducking into the Chrysler Imperial* for the ride to Headquarters, I was not prepared for what I was to read.

* All the top brass in Detroit, from the rank of inspector and above, were provided departmental cars—all American-made, of course. In Detroit, Motor City, if a police officer drove to work in a foreign car, he was practically asking for a demotion! The Chrysler Imperial plant was located within city limits, and it provided the Police Commissioner's official vehicle. Mine was a lush, almost obscenely luxurious automobile, far more excessively appointed than the official car I was to use later as New York Police Commissioner. But, after all, Detroit *was* Motor City.

The first thing that caught my eye in the paper was the lead story—and that it was a three-day-old story. It had built up over the weekend like bad weather, so that by now the Detroit P.D. had been made to look as if it had been trying to hide from the truth. White Detroit police officers, it was implied, had unjustifiably and brutally arrested four black teenagers for no discernible reason. With the backdrop of the 1967 Detroit riot still on everyone's mind, even now, two and a half years later, the story left a powerful impression reminiscent of the infamous Algiers Motel shooting incident of 1967.

In vain, and with growing anger, I searched the papers for our side of the story. Some official version of the events. Even a flat denial. Even some promise of future comment and clarification. The allegation was clearly of great consequence. But the stories, though quoting just about every black spokesperson in the city about what a terrible thing our racist police department had done, had nothing from the Detroit P.D.—only silence.

As my driver worked his way to Headquarters, I read further. I was assuming, unpleasantly, that our side was in the wrong, that Detroit's finest had blundered, that there was no justifiable reason for the arrests. Otherwise—right?—we would be saying something.

Still, I was infuriated by the "No comment" stance. Even if we had blundered, the mistake was only being compounded by the policy of lockjaw. Better to admit it, get it out and over with, and move on to the next day.

When I arrived at Headquarters, the brass packed themselves hurriedly into the conference room, and I began immediately the interrogation of senior officers. Who did what to whom first? Were standard procedures followed? . . .

Finally one top official offered a coherent version of the weekend's events, and as the story began to unfold, I almost had to cry. Incredibly, the officers involved had done exactly what they should have done—and I verified this version of events through independent means later.

The story was this: White police officers had stopped a car for a serious traffic violation. Inside were teenagers, all black, all without either license or registration for the vehicle. The youths, however, protested that all necessary documents were available at home, so the police officers extended them the courtesy of driving them home to get them.

The courtesy, however, was not reciprocated. The youths disappeared into a ghetto building and did not come out. Finally, the officers went in after them; but when finally located, the youths intensely resisted arrest. Alerted by the presence of the parked patrol car, a small crowd soon congregated outside the building, and by the time the officers got the teenagers into the car and hustled them off to the precinct for interrogation and booking, an incident had developed.

I heard the story, but I could hardly believe I was hearing it. I sat down in the Commissioner's chair, gazed intently at the clock on my desk, and began shaking my head to silence the ringing in my ears.

"Why, then, did we spend three days trying to cover this up? What exactly did we do wrong?"

The questions had no answer. The brass in the conference room looked dumbfounded, stumped. Someone at the far end of the table began weakly with an explanation, but then trailed off into silence. The questions could only be answered with: *Why hadn't we told the public exactly what had happened?*

Few in the conference room understood it, but the answer to this question lies in the innate reluctance of a police department to level not only with itself but with the press and public. It was as if, having been caught in the wrong so many times in the past, a police department did not believe that it might have a story that would actually reflect well on the department. And so here's what we had: a perfectly defensible, even routine, police action, hardly a racist incident, with the department going through the weekend as if it were sitting on the hottest scandal of the year.

I got up from my desk, dismissed the brass, and walked down the hall wondering if police departments would ever change.

A few hours later the department issued its first official statement to the press and public. This was Monday afternoon. The incident had begun on Friday. It took the department three days to explain itself. And, all along, the Detroit P.D. hadn't had the slightest thing to hide. The officers were right. The kids were wrong. That was all there was to it. And yet we had behaved all through the weekend as though our fingers had been caught in the cookie jar. Just incredible.

The Detroit P.D., five thousand officers strong, was a better police force than it appeared to be.

For one thing, it enjoyed its *own* civil service system, by which the department retained considerable leverage over examinations, entrance requirements, and promotion procedures. The Detroit system was a potentially happy blend of two worlds. The ideal of integrity and non-political fairness in letting in and moving up was preserved; however, since the system was not under the aegis of some abstract commission that was unaware of department's special needs, but under the direct influence of the Police Commissioner, the mind-numbing and demoralizing inflexibility of a typical civil service system was avoided. One practical and immediate payoff, for instance, was the ability to tinker with the admissions standards to increase the hiring of blacks, so often shut out by the inherent bias of civil service entrance exams that were discriminatory in their net effect.

Another plus in Detroit was Roman S. Gribbs, the Mayor (he's now a jurist). A good chief executive can make all the difference in the world, and no one I ever worked for was better than Ray Gribbs. Intelligent and honest, he skillfully maneuvered himself and his office to insulate me from the hardball politics of Detroit. In the relative calm which he created—as in the center of a hurricane—police administration could be practiced. Without a mayor of Gribbs's character, a police commissioner's energies can be entirely consumed in the effort of not being blown away by political winds inimical to good, independent policing. But right from the outset Mayor Gribbs gave away the key: independence. I inquired about this at our first meeting in Detroit, and Gribbs sensed instantly what I was driving at.

In this atmosphere progress was possible, but not inevitable. For one thing, the new Police Commissioner, for all his experience, moved perhaps more slowly than desirable because, quite simply, he just did not know the lay of the land. When one becomes the head of a police department, there is no bluebook—no set of detailed instructions covering the location of bureaucratic landmines, corrupt practices, entrenched hacks, and skeletons in the closet. One has to feel one's way around, as if in a dark attic fumbling for that light switch. One moved tentatively, fearing to stub one's toe or to fall through the attic studs over an unseen object in one's path.

There was an additional problem as well. In Detroit there was no provision for hiring civilian professionals for attachment to the Commissioner's office. In Syracuse, under such an arrangement, I was able to hire a lawyer as legal adviser, and in Washington, Jerry Caplan, as Executive Assistant to the Public Safety Director. Both were essential to whatever was done for the better; so by this time I was persuaded that one could not accomplish much solely with civil service police officers in staff positions.

In a sense, the business of policing had become entirely too difficult to be managed only by cops. The Detroit experience, for me, clinched the argument. The first thing a new commissioner should do on taking office is to bring in a handful of top-notch non-cops to help him manage the policing business. In Detroit, because of a budget crisis, funds for such amenities were sadly unavailable. Gribbs could protect me from the political vipers, but he couldn't, alas, print money.

This shortcoming might have proven more serious than it did except for the absence of a crisis atmosphere in Detroit. Unlike Syracuse, where I entered in the wake of a corruption "scandal," or Washington, where a summer of hell was possible, the Detroit appointment was almost a position contemplated in tranquillity; a considerable tenure in which a long-range, sustained program of reform could occur seemed entirely possible. But had the circumstances been otherwise, had the Detroit P.D. required immediate radical surgery, the unavailability of civilian expertise might have been devastating. Cops, no matter how bright, are no substitute for a few very well educated professionals in several disciplines to grapple with the wide variety of complex problems encountered in police administration.

Several pieces of relatively minor surgery were immediately desirable, despite the absence of a crisis atmosphere. The city was still, for instance, living in the shadow of the 1967 ugliness, so that in a sense a certain crisis of confidence existed, especially with regard to the Police Department. No wonder that a study of the riot revealed an incredible fact about the organization of the Detroit P.D.

The infamous Detroit riot occurred on a weekend. On any given weekend (prior to one of my first administrative changes, an obvious one, really, as you will see), the highest-ranking officer on duty department-wide and city-wide was a sergeant or lieutenant. This would be the rough equivalent of leaving a General Motors factory in the hands of a single foreman. By five P.M. on any Friday, every higher-ranking officer had utterly, totally vanished (and don't try to call them). Their concept of success in the police world was most endearing: to get up there so you won't have to work late or on weekends. Thus, when the rioting began, the Detroit P.D. had ingeniously staffed itself so that the individual in charge was not the Police Commissioner, or a chief, or even an inspector—but at most a lieutenant.

As one of my first moves, therefore, I required the presence of a duty officer on the weekends—on call, out in a car—at a rank no lower than a full inspector.*

Another curious quirk in the Detroit P.D. concerned employee relations. On the face of it, this may not seem like such an important concern, except that in recent years police strikes around the country have done little to enhance the public's confidence in the police, much less to improve law enforcement. The trouble was that the Detroit P.D. had no permanent staff to deal with employee grievances and other labor problems. Surprising in a way, since Detroit was such a thoroughly union town; but to make matters worse, the head of the Detroit Police Officers Association was practically the stereotype of the bombastic, garrulous police-union spokesman who seemed unaware that his act was more hilarious than effective.† I began to

---

* Ironically, there was a tremendous incongruity of rank and assignment in the Detroit P.D., along with a tremendous lack of correlation between rank and authority. In addition to the ludicrous spectacle of a sergeant trying to run the Police Department during a full-scale riot, one also saw the assignment of a full inspector to be in charge of the motor pool!

† Privately, he was a much more reasonable person. Regrettably, like many other leaders of police-employee organizations, he felt it necessary to employ the militant rhetoric for the purpose of pacifying the dues payers. This says a great deal about the kind of people who are our police officers—about their morale and attitudes. The military model of organization and management in most large city police departments was put in place decades ago. As the military has improved over the years, police departments, isolated from the positive changes in the military establishment, have continued to perpetuate some long-outdated, and often overbearing, attitudes of top management, attitudes that weaken morale in the rank and file. Better policing in the future will depend upon improved personnel administration, which, with the recruitment of better-educated personnel, should develop more professional attitudes among those who exercise such important power in keeping the peace.

suspect that perhaps even some of the officers were less than tickled to be so represented. We therefore put in a new employee relations process; we wanted the troops to know that there was another way to deal with their grievances besides going through union channels.

One evening, on invitation, I made an appearance at a monthly meeting of the D.P.O.A. Fortunately, I had been briefed in advance about what to expect; the monthly "meeting" was in reality an excuse for a drinking session. Thus the presence of the Commissioner would somewhat hamper their style, requiring for the moment the staging of a bit of a show. I admired the orchestration. There were just enough sober officers present so the Commissioner would not be embarrassed during his short little speech; but my guest appearance had not been scheduled so late in the evening that I would arrive to find everyone bombed. It was a fine calculation indeed, and I was in and out of there in a half hour with no untoward incident occurring!

A serious problem with the Detroit P.D. concerned narcotics enforcement. This was the *one* area of police work that had become, since the mid-1960s, the most troubling and the least satisfying. During my stay in Detroit five police officers were to lose their lives, several of them in the course of raiding narcotics "shooting pads."

The deaths of the officers were partly attributable not only to bravery but also to a reckless departmental practice. Raids of pads (apartments) used by shooters (heroin users employing intravenous or subcutaneous injection) were set up on the basis of "intelligence" information, i.e., tips from police informants. On the basis of these tips, the pads would be raided in blitzkrieg fashion. It was an ineffective and dangerous practice, not the way to make the greatest impact on drug traffic and traffickers. It did not allow for sufficient time to plan and organize a risk-filled undertaking. Neither New York, Washington, nor Syracuse used such a method, but Detroit did not know this—another example of the insularity and primitive state of knowledge in American policing. In Detroit the tendency was to charge in gangbuster-style, submachine guns (which were still carried in unmarked "cruiser" cars) at the ready. In the rush to make the scene, Detroit officers were getting shot at—and for what? The arrest of a few miserable narcotics addicts? With what effect on the overall narcotics traffic in the city?* Finally, after several meetings in our conference room, we rationalized procedures, making the decision to raid a prerogative of higher management. But before the review, we had the classic case before us of a police department whose own procedures had created unnecessary risks for its officers.

The relationship between police work and crime control was often coincidental. The traditions of policing tended to remain fossilized, whereas crime patterns and trends seemed, if only by comparison, far more dynamic. The average precinct commander in the average precinct in a city in the U.S. could feel, given his relative lack of success, a bit like the designer of the Edsel. Police work could be very rewarding—especially in acts of, or even the appreciation of, heroism by police officers with a frequency that bordered on the routine—but it could also be terribly frustrating. Precinct commanders, moreover, could find themselves removed from thinking about crime, in the constant daily worries about actually running the precinct, even though the precinct commander is far closer to the problems of crime than, for instance, the police commissioner and his high command. But was the head of a precinct doing his or her job if he or she wasn't worrying about crime—and its increases? Could the management of a police department become so abstract that a concern with crime could somehow be lost by the wayside?

The involvement of precinct personnel in thinking about crime— getting the precinct heads to think *as* the commissioner, and *for* the commissioner—was a worthwhile effort, because this was where

---

* As law enforcement strategy, in my view, an attack at the point of use is hopeless. Once the narcotics have been introduced into a city, police operating under democratic rules and procedures face an impossible situation. Where the problem is most vulnerable to law enforcement pressure is not at the point of consumption but at the point of supply. The best place to deal with the heroin problem is not in the streets or shooting pads of Detroit (which perhaps possessed more heroin addicts per capita than any other city in the U.S.) but in Mexico, Southeast Asia, and Turkey—at the points of supply. In this respect, then, the heroin sickness in America is perhaps less a local law enforcement problem than a foreign policy problem. One of the main reasons for the growth of narcotics trafficking is that American foreign policy places such high priorities on military pacts with regimes of dubious worth when it should be protecting citizens from the ill effects of the heroin-exporting nations.

fluctuations in the degree of public safety were most directly affected. It is interesting that whenever there is a crime "wave" of the proportion that attracts the attention of the news media, the response of the police commissioner or the high command is typically to set up a special "unit," with special responsibility (i.e., a city-wide "rape" squad, a special "crime against the elderly" squad). This response, more often than not a public relations effort, in my view works against the precinct organization of the department. With a special city-wide unit to take care of that problem, why, then, the precinct doesn't have to worry about it. In this way, for instance, does the crime of rape become removed from the attention of *every* police officer in the department, to the detriment of comprehensive law enforcement.

In contrast, the precinct must be the place of origin for good police management; it is the answer to the conflicting ideals of modern centralized management (which tries to derive the maximum benefit from available resources and manpower, as well as to establish uniform policies and procedures) and intelligent, neighborhood law enforcement (which seeks to avoid overcentralization, insensitivity to local variations in crime problems, headquarters abstractions, and bureaucratic immobility). The properly run precinct, with just the right amount (but no more) of direction from headquarters, can prove to be the best of both worlds; but precinct commanders (the local police chiefs, as it were) must be encouraged to think and act as if they were, at their level, the police commissioner, who is all too far removed from the front lines of the local situation.

During those first months in Detroit I put together a lengthy memorandum addressed to each one of the department's thirteen precinct commanders, in an effort to get them to think more about crime. (Sometimes the reader of the average newspaper might get the impression that all cops think about is pension benefits, job actions, grafting, and duty schedules; and sometimes the reader is right.) The memorandum, somewhat lengthier than was my usual style, tried to draw out the precinct commanders into a little colloquium with the new Commissioner, to get them to develop a little introspection about their work, to help them to understand the tremendous complexity of their job, as both a reassurance that what they were doing was both important and susceptible to analytic comprehension. The memorandum, in part, read:

I am asking each Precinct Inspector to analyze and evaluate the [F.B.I.'s] Uniform Crime Reporting Index experience in each precinct during 1969 as compared to 1968 by category, patrol area, monthly variation, and tour of duty variation. . . . I want you then to explain, to the best of your ability, the reasons for increases or decreases in crime in your precinct, considering such factors as the following:

- *Population* increases, decreases, other changes
- *Income* levels of residents
- *unemployment* and underemployment
- *number on welfare* and aid-to-dependent-children recipients
- *police personnel* and man-hours available to you
- *number of parolees,* probationers, released convicts, and so forth in your precinct
- *school drop-out rates*
- *gangs*
- *narcotics traffic*
- *organized crime*
- *addiction* and alcoholism
- *working mothers,* fatherless families.

The memorandum, with the call for replies, seemed perhaps something like a test, but it was intended really as a sympathetic attempt to relate to the precinct commanders. In this respect it seemed to have failed, just as, as a test, practically every precinct commander failed it spectacularly. Indeed, the replies were uniformly embarrassing, with a level of analysis that never quite rose above stock law-and-order thinking. Few sensed that we could have more of an impact on crime if we could figure out new strategies for employing such personnel as we had more efficiently. Most argued that crime could be reduced by the simple expedient of more manpower. At best this analysis was arguable; at worst academic. More cops were simply too expensive a governmental commodity; already they consumed all too great a proportion of the city budget as it stood, possibly to the detriment of the effectiveness of the courts and prosecutors' offices. Police officers

As a young rookie in the New York Police Department: the silver shield was handed down from his father. (BUREAU OF PUBLIC INFORMATION, NYCPD)

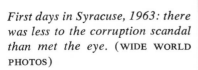

First days in Syracuse, 1963: there was less to the corruption scandal than met the eye. (WIDE WORLD PHOTOS)

With William H. T. Smith, the new first deputy chief, in Syracuse: it was supposed to be a far more troubled place than New York. (UNITED PRESS INTERNATIONAL)

The Murphy family in 1969: from left, Paul, Jerry, Betty, Mark, the recently named Detroit Police Commissioner, and Kevin. (WIDE WORLD PHOTOS)

The swearing-in ceremony in New York, 1971: Mayor John Lindsay had a problem with his police department. (WIDE WORLD PHOTOS)

Press conference, 1973, after the hostage crisis at a Williamsburg (Brooklyn) sporting-goods store: often the best game is the waiting game. (WIDE WORLD PHOTOS)

Meeting the press, 1975: with (first row, left to right) Robert de Grazia, the Boston police commissioner; Edward Davis, the controversial police chief of Los Angeles; (second row, left to right), Hubert Williams, Newark police director; Joseph McNamara, the Kansas City chief; and James Parsons, police chief of Birmingham, Alabama. (WIDE WORLD PHOTOS)

On John Lindsay's television show: the Mayor sometimes made more media commitments than he could keep. (WIDE WORLD PHOTOS)

Work in progress, 1971: Mayor Lindsay, with his new Police Commissioner (second from left), at the site of the new Police Headquarters building. (SPRING 3100)

St. Patrick's Day, 1972: The parade made the point, with St. Patrick's Cathedral as a backdrop, that there were more than a few Irishmen in New York. (SPRING 3100)

St. Patrick's Day, 1972: off the left shoulder of the new Police Commissioner, the new Chief Inspector, Michael Codd, later to become Police Commissioner. (SPRING 3100)

Shakeup, 1971: in the wake of the failure to take action against an illegal "bottle club" in upper Manhattan, William T. Bonacum was named commander of the difficult division in question. (UNITED PRESS INTERNATIONAL)

Up-and-down, 1971: with Chief of Detectives Al Seedman looking on (right), two announcements are made. One is the promotion of undercover detective narcotics officer Kathleen Conlon (partially veiled) to detective third grade. The other is the transfer from their commands (i.e., demotion) of six captains. (WIDE WORLD PHOTOS)

With Robert Daley, the Deputy Commissioner for Public Information (right), in 1972: announcing the arrest of four suspects in connection with the robbery of the swank Hotel Pierre. (WIDE WORLD PHOTOS)

Pressure from without, 1971: Whitman Knapp, with pencil, holding a hearing on police corruption in New York. (WIDE WORLD PHOTOS)

Frank Serpico, with his lawyer Ramsey Clark, the former U.S. Attorney General, 1971: at the Knapp hearings, Serpico testified a captain had told him that if he kept talking, he "might end up floating in the river." (UNITED PRESS INTERNATIONAL)

Frank Hogan, the Manhattan D.A., in 1971, at the age of 69: had he actually been running the New York Police Department? (WIDE WORLD PHOTOS)

Leaving a state hearing on narcotics trafficking in New York, 1971: it was as much a question of foreign policy as domestic police work. (WIDE WORLD PHOTOS)

The luck of the Irish: with Cardinal Cooke of New York. (SPRING 3100)

Target practice: under new rules and regulations, every member of the department had to undergo periodic firearms training. (SPRING 3100)

A public burning, 1972: $2 million worth of heroin being returned, in a pouring rain, to ashes. (SPRING 3100)

An unpleasant business, 1972: an injured plainclothes police officer is dragged to safety by a fellow officer during the disorder at a Muslim mosque in Harlem. (WIDE WORLD PHOTOS)

Escape from terror: New York's finest aiding hostages fleeing from their captors through a hidden staircase in a Williamsburg sporting-goods store; they had been held hostage for more than forty hours. (UNITED PRESS IN-TERNATIONAL)

Hostage situation in progress, 1973: a police officer peers cautiously at a sporting-goods store in Brooklyn where nine hostages are being held by gunmen. (UNITED PRESS INTERNATIONAL)

A bad day in New York: with Deputy Commissioner William McCarthy announcing the disappearance of a large amount of heroin from the Police Department's Property Clerk's office. (WIDE WORLD PHOTOS)

High-level huddle: with (from left), Michael Codd, the Chief Inspector; William H. T. Smith, the First Deputy Commissioner; Elmer Cone, Assistant Chief Inspector; and Sydney Cooper, Chief of Personnel. (WIDE WORLD PHOTOS)

Conference in Washington, 1970: with Attorney General John Mitchell (back to camera) and other leading police executives around the country, discussing the wave of terrorist bombings and attacks on law enforcement officers. (UNITED PRESS INTERNATIONAL)

Swearing-out, 1973: with John Lindsay and Donald Cawley, the young Chief of Patrol who was now being made the new P.C. (UNITED PRESS INTERNATIONAL)

As president of the national Police Foundation: at an international workshop on police–community relations at Syracuse University. (WIDE WORLD PHOTOS)

tend not to understand that the ultimate answer to crime will not be found in the transformation of half the society into cops.

Additionally, there were ramifications to hiring more officers (even if this step were feasible) which our commanders out in the precincts had not perhaps fully considered. One ramification was the effect that even larger police departments might have on the *perceived* performance of the precinct, if its effectiveness were to be measured in terms of reported crime; for it was on the basis of reported crime data that police departments unconsciously contrived to hang themselves on their own petard. "Several precinct commanders," I wrote back, considerably understating the number, "have told me that they could reduce *crime* with more officers. They may be correct, but would they reduce *reported* crime?"

The question should have been, for them, a most troubling one. In other words, if one deployed more personnel out on the street, would one not receive in return more reports of crime? Then, with evidence of crime "on the rise," how could a police department claim to have been using its new personnel effectively? Perversely, questions of an entirely different nature might well be raised by the curious sequence of (a) more cops and (b) more reported crime: "How do we then answer the charge that more crime would be reported by us to justify the budget, or even to obtain a larger budget?" For this, and for other reasons, simply putting out more cops might not prove the unalloyed joy that many of us sometimes assume.

There was another question scarcely considered by the advocates of more police. What do we do with them when we get them? The question was, unfortunately, more difficult than it might appear at first glance. There tended to be more bravado in policing than clarity. You could be charmed by what we did, but not necessarily enlightened. The presence of more cops on the streets was perhaps reassuring to the citizenry, but it was also perhaps reassuring to the criminals, who in the circumstances of such intense visibility might be credited with intelligence sufficient to avoid staging their crimes under uniformed gaze. More than this, mere routine patrolling, however comforting in the abstract, seemed intuitively like a dumb way to use police.

At the Urban Institute, before I went to Detroit, I had developed a design for reorganizing patrol at a basic level, relying little on mere patrolling but heavily on citizen participation in the act of policing. In this model, the officers would be required to do more than simply parade up and down the streets, in and out of the car. On the contrary, it would be considered part of the job to regard citizens as extensions of police rather than solely as targets of police work—to confer, for instance, with citizens as often as with fellow officers, to talk rather than walk. The hoped-for payoff was this: the valuable intelligence information which, in my view, most citizens possess. In this conception, time now spent on patrolling unproductively would be spent productively in obtaining valuable citizen assistance in preventing and perhaps therefore even controlling crime.

In Detroit the design was implemented on a trial basis in one small area as the "Beat Commander" project. For the first time, one supervising officer would have charge of a beat. A sergeant would direct the work of officers in obtaining citizen cooperation and involvement in crime intelligence work, which would at the same time drastically reduce the amount of time wasted in traditional, undirected patrol.

Beat Commander thereby combined two new elements. One was the emphasis on putting one identifiable sergeant in charge of one beat—one piece of turf. The second was the administrative insistence on multiplying citizen-police contacts (aside from arrests or interrogations). In Detroit the experiment was restricted to a single beat, with a single pioneering sergeant in charge. (In a traditional system a dozen sergeants in the course of a week might be rotated over three different pieces of turf.)

Even so, as small as it was, one had a sense we were onto something. The experiment seemed to generate some real enthusiasm; and in policing, enthusiasm, from either officer or citizen, was not in most places a common emotion. For the future, the taste of success in this Detroit project was crucial, and the original flavor of the enthusiasm generated by Beat Commander was captured engagingly by the pioneer sergeant in command of the original demonstration beat. In one of the earliest internal reports—addressed to his charges, not to higher-ups—the sergeant summed up one month of activity in this way:

> So far this month, you have spent one hundred twenty-two hours on what we are calling public relations time. I have received numerous

telephone calls, written comments, and most important, vocal statements from residents and businessmen who are pleased and impressed with your work on the street. . . . I found witnesses who volunteered information on your behalf and in support of your actions. They have spoken out because you have taken the time in your daily routine to stop and talk to them, explaining the purpose of the Beat Commander program, and making friends. In these trying times, it is difficult to find many people who are willing to come to a police officer's defense.

We are criticized on all sides for our actions with no one coming up with solutions for our problems. You, however, in a short time, have become known in this community as individuals and not faceless men in a cop's uniform. Surely, there are many people who don't like us but the more time we spend talking to people, the more friends we will win over to our side. They may not remember your name but they will remember the pleasant conversation and your concern for their welfare.

When the chips are down and you need help, they will be willing to speak out because they "know" you. We cannot eliminate crime. At least we can hope to cut the crime rate down. We *can* make friends.

In the Beat Commander project, as in every attempted innovation, the police union—the D.P.O.A.—was on the opposite side of the fence. Police unions, in the process of trying to represent the broad rank and file, inevitably reflect the lowest common denominator— which in the police world, with extremely right-wing political and sociological views very well represented, was *painfully* low.

The struggle to make changes in the department would have to proceed tooth and nail against the D.P.O.A. Sadly, the power of the Police Commissioner was such that the police union virtually possessed veto power over change in the face of a weak commissioner. But the matter of a commissioner's power was thus relative to the expertness of its use, and from the beginning, once I took the measure of the full extent to which the D.P.O.A. would stupidly oppose virtually any suggestion for improvement, I began plotting, searching the inventory for an issue with which to expose the D.P.O.A. for what it was. With such a demonstration one might hope to discredit the union as a serious critic.

The issue on which the D.P.O.A. decided to do battle concerned, incredibly, higher education for police officers. They were opposed. I had made a little speech proposing that in the future all promotees ideally be required to have completed some minimum of college education.

To most people the proposal seemed reasonable enough, and in some circles urgently in need of adoption. Only in the police world, with its occasional propensity for staking out positions that prompt public ridicule, would an argument for the improvement in the caliber of its members require explanation and defense.

But the D.P.O.A.'s opposition to the proposal was so shrill, indeed almost hysterical, that it attracted a great deal of unexpected attention. The Detroit newspapers jumped into the quarrel, delightedly endorsing in editorials the higher-education concept, wondering out loud why anyone would be so strongly opposed. By the time the dust had settled, the public was left with the impression that the new Police Commissioner had made a serious, honest suggestion that was worth considering—and that the D.P.O.A., in its flat, crude rejection of any further discussion of the matter, must not be a serious organization.

The idea of higher education for police was hardly new, of course. The President's Commission on Law Enforcement and Administration of Justice in 1967 spelled out all the arguments, dealt with all the possible objections. For decades the British, with possibly the most thoroughly thought out policing system in the world, have recognized the undesirability of allowing their police forces to attract only the least-educated members of society. As the Royal Commission on the Police observed back in 1962, "The police play a vital role in our national life and well-being, and it is deplorable that they, to a far greater extent than any of the other public services, law, commerce, industry, or indeed any major branch of our national life, should for years have been failing to recruit anything like their proper share of able and well-educated young men. We do not suggest that graduates are necessarily more likely than others to make effective chief constables; our concern is simply that the police today are not securing a sufficient share of the better educated section of the community."

This is the essential rationale for the higher education of the police officer: Did we as a society really desire to be policed by the less-educated, less-acculturated, less-sophisticated of our number? Did we truly wish to arm with deadly weapons and the force of law those of us less qualified by educational and cultural experience? And yet the argument against higher education for police officers, made re-flexively, instantly, by the Detroit Police Officers Association, took just this position—and a terrifying one it was.

But it was hardly more than a routine head-in-the-sand demurrer from the police union. Rank-and-file organizations apparently feel so threatened by the idea of elevating their service that an astonishing variety of arguments against higher education, some of them posi-tively ingenious, have accumulated over the years, like barnacles on the bottom of a boat.

Taking them in some sort of logical order, which is not how they tended to be presented, one begins with an incredibly self-deprecating assertion about police work: "There are certainly numerous functions in the police service," writes former Washington Police Chief Jerry Wilson, ". . . which not only do not require a college education but would be deadly boring to an imaginative college graduate."* The answer here, of course, is not to shut policing off to college graduates by keeping police work boring, but to make major changes in the police business to render it more attractive to the college-educated and the non-college-educated alike. Too many police leaders, like my old friend Wilson, fail to understand how stupidly policing is orga-nized at present, and how urgently it needs to be reformed.

Neither is it understood that the redesign of American policing is not at all impractical. Take as one example the Fremont, California, Police Department. At this writing, the Fremont P.D. is 47 percent civilian and 53 percent sworn officers. Less expensive civilians perform a great many of the less demanding functions like traffic control, radio dispatching, and record keeping. But in seeing the basic patrol officer's job as a miserable one,† Jerry Wilson and many others in policing sell short the possibilities of their life's work. The truth is that by breaking away from the stultifying, antiquated, and unproduc-tive military model of rank and organization, and the tin-soldier concept of patrolling—in short, by *liberating*, as it were, policing—

---

* *Police Report,* Little, Brown: Boston, 1975. This is the same police careerist I promoted in 1968 to Assistant Chief for Operations in Washington, D.C.

† Interestingly, teachers and other professionals tend not to feel a vast difference between the basic job and supervision-management. Neither will police as the work becomes more professional. It will gradually, I hope, cease being a job of con-suming interest only to superior officers—i.e., "a bosses' job."

we can make our work more meaningful not only to our consumers but also to our fellow officers.

The unproductive time now spent on "preventive patrol" should be used in citizen interactions involving an active two-way flow of information between the community and the police (recognizing how ineffective the police are until they mobilize the community to assist them in controlling crime); crime analysis; information collection, evaluation, and dissemination; coordinating with detective, juvenile, and other branches; planning strategies to make the most effective use of resources and time. Each officer should have twenty-four-hour-a-day responsibility for a small area and population. His basic task should not be patrol but managing the crime control program of his department in an area small enough to be manageable. Such an arrangement will minimize boredom. The added authority and responsibility will upgrade the police officer to a more appropriate level for one with his power and discretion. The menial tasks to be found in an accurate description of his current job should be reassigned, to the fullest possible extent, to support personnel functioning under his supervision.

Wilson and others further insist that the sort of discretionary decision making that logically requires a sophisticated, educated decision maker can be minimized by administrative control. "The fact is," Wilson writes, "that in most departments, the actions of beat patrolmen and of working detectives are quite closely constrained by either law or by departmental policies and regulations."

In truth, there is an enormous disparity *within* a single police department like Washington's, which Wilson headed soon after my departure, not to mention *among* departments, as to who is subjected to arrest and why. It is sheer nonsense to believe or assert that administrative guidelines can ever substitute for the judgment and maturity of individual officers.* Higher education necessarily will help equip officers to meet the challenge of making a variety of decisions far more diverse and unanticipated than could possibly be predicted by bureaucratic decision makers at headquarters with their "guidelines."

---

* Better guidelines are urgently needed in every department in the country. But they have their limitations. For example, the critical decision to shoot or not to shoot is influenced more by an officer's values and life experience than by even the best guidelines.

A further objection to higher education—one that the D.P.O.A. shared—is somewhat disingenuously hypocritical, coming as it does from quarters that have not demonstrated notable concern in the past for the recruitment of minorities. This objection argues that the requirement of college education will tend to screen out a higher proportion of minority recruits.

But this is an unproven assumption at best. On the contrary, the recruitment of college graduates will mean attracting a very different cut of individual—black or white. Indeed, the experience, for instance, of New York City was that when entrance standards were lowered, ostensibly in an effort to attract minority candidates, the composition of the new recruits tended to include not a sufficiently higher percentage of minorities but a higher percentage of white high school dropouts—not necessarily ideal police candidates.

Corollary to this assumption, and equally immaterial and unproven, is the idea that "the proposed . . . standard will close to lower socioeconomic groups the stepping-stone into the middle-class which historically has been provided by employment as a police officer," as Jerry Wilson writes. With this criticism, however, we are putting the cart far in front of the horse. The purpose of the police service is not to provide employment for the otherwise unemployed or unemployable, I should think, but to make the nation safer and more civilized for those who have to live in it. Thus the great need is not to preserve things the way they are for the demeaning purpose of serving as a "stepping-stone," but to improve and upgrade the service.

Boring patrol, for starters, could be eliminated. Neighborhood policing—i.e., some extension of and variations on the Beat Commander concept—should be tried. College graduates should be regarded by the police establishment not as threats but as desirable "catches." In a country with such a high level of education, the police should not be drawn from among those with a lower than average education. At the very least, the idea is quite terrifying.

For the future, moreover, the problem becomes even more acute. Sadly, the relative level of education of the police compared to that of the general population has probably *decreased* since World War Two. Before then, many cities required a high school diploma; now, following the ultimate logic of such as the D.P.O.A., it would seem that even literacy might be viewed as a drawback.

Despite the opposition of police unions, the idea of having better-educated police officers is catching on. Pressure is growing for some reform. In response, however, overanxious police administrators are endorsing the community college concept as a convenient way of seeming to accept change while actually circumventing the problem. But acceptance has only gone so far as to include post-entry studies for the already recruited; indeed, the current federal program of financial assistance places a high priority on educating officers already employed in departments.

This policy misses the point of attracting a greater variety of people to policing. As Professor Herman Goldstein has observed, "Throughout the country . . . support for education without change is demonstrated most clearly by the preference of police establishments for educating the recruited rather than recruiting the educated."

For the decades when I had been a police officer in the N.Y.P.D.—rising to the rank of deputy chief inspector—there had remained one man in New York whom I respected greatly but had not had the slightest hope of ever meeting privately. To serious-minded police officers this gentleman was a constant reminder of the possibilities of professional law enforcement. Yet not even a deputy chief inspector (one of the top fifty officers in the N.Y.P.D.) would ordinarily have a ghost of a chance of a private audience with him—perhaps less of a chance than an acting student spending an afternoon with, say, Alfred Hitchcock.

Appropriately enough, then, my first private session with the late Frank Hogan, the Manhattan District Attorney, was in 1970—when I was Police Commissioner of Detroit.

The idea for such a meeting grew out of discussions involving the Wayne County Prosecutor, the County Sheriff, and myself. For decades, prosecutors had been impressed with the effectiveness of the New York County (Manhattan) Rackets Squad, formed back in the 1930s by the famous Thomas Dewey for dealing with organized crime. His work catapulted him into the New York governorship, national fame, and two unsuccessful races for the Presidency. Ever since, Frank Hogan, Dewey's successor, had utilized the Rackets Squad to nail the big and little fish of organized crime.

Bill Cohalan, the Prosecutor, wanted to strengthen his office for organized crime investigations and prosecutions. Bill Lucas, the Sheriff, and I were delighted to support such initiative. Over the years, the cooperative efforts of the Rackets Squad and the N.Y.P.D. had proved to be the most successful approach to high-level organized crime. A visit to New York to learn from the master made a great deal of sense. Why shouldn't a rackets squad be organized in Detroit? After all, Detroit had more than its share of organized crime.

And so one day in September 1970 I found myself enjoying the company of the great Frank Hogan, along with the Sheriff and the Prosecutor of Wayne County.

I have two recollections of that meeting. One was my genuine awe of Hogan—incorruptible, a model of probity, intelligent. The other was the extent of Hogan's courtliness and attentiveness. As we discussed setting up a Detroit version of the Manhattan Rackets Squad, I began to wonder whether his attentiveness might not be attributable to something beyond manners.

Did he know about my secret meeting with Mayor John Lindsay just a few hours before?

Indeed, did the selection of a new police commissioner for New York require prior consultation with, or perhaps even the explicit approval of, Frank Hogan—"Mr. D.A."?

Chapter Six

Going Home

The New York Police Department was such a huge, consequential, closely watched police department that, like the Mayo Clinic in the field of medicine and the Harvard Law School in the legal world, nothing that happened within its territory could evolve in total obscurity. By the fall of 1970, in fact, the troubles of the N.Y.P.D. had become, as they so often had in the past, national news. Even the Detroit papers had been covering the story of the scandal in the N.Y.P.D. with more attention than they ordinarily afforded Big Apple developments. In part, the nature of the story itself compelled attention. Patrolman Frank Serpico, an otherwise obscure cop, had come forward to the New York *Times* with allegations of corruption in the department and with the additional allegation that the department was covering up despite his best efforts to persuade it to take action. In a sense, the story was a pre-Watergate Watergate-style story. Another reason why the story was national news was that New York's mayor had become national news. He was John Lindsay, and he was not only running the biggest city in the nation, he was running for the Presidency. This ambition entitled him to special attention, which he might in this case have been more than willing to do without.

And so it was in a context of urgency, if not panic, that a meeting with John Lindsay had taken place. The arranger, working long-distance phones between Detroit and New York, had been Henry Ruth, a former Justice Department aide who was now director of the New York City Criminal Justice Coordinating Council. Ruth had decided that the long-planned meeting with Hogan to establish a

139

Detroit counterpart to the Manhattan Rackets Squad would provide excellent cover for a secret meeting with Lindsay to discuss the suddenly vacant position of Police Commissioner of New York. The position was suddenly vacant because of the unexplained resignation of Howard Leary, who had been John Lindsay's police commissioner since the beginning of his first term in 1966.

The meeting at Gracie Mansion with the tall, handsome Lindsay had been kept confidential for several good reasons. One, I suspect, was that to Lindsay I was an unknown quantity. I had retired from the N.Y.P.D. in 1965, just before John Lindsay had come in, so that in a sense, although the N.Y.P.D. had been my home, John Lindsay did not know me any more intimately than any other police commissioner from Detroit. But another reason for the hush-hush was that I was not sure I wanted the job. Or perhaps, even if at bottom I really did, I wished not to think of myself as one who under these circumstances should wish to take it.

More than risking the possibility of failure—for, having been born and raised in the New York Police Department, I possessed more than a vague idea of the problems currently being opened for inspection— I knew that acceptance of any offer from the Mayor, assuming one would be forthcoming, might draw upon me Ray Gribbs's eternal condemnation. The picture was this: Pat Murphy had been in Detroit less than a year, under more or less ideal conditions thanks to Gribbs's integrity, and suddenly at the first knock of a better opportunity he was off and running to New York, leaving Gribbs behind to explain to his constituency why talent was leaving the fold. It was a position in which I did not relish placing this man, whom I had come to recognize as perhaps the most outstanding person for whom I had ever worked. And so I had supported the idea of a secret meeting as much as Lindsay.

Unfortunately, the papers had caught on to my presence in New York, and with the one-and-one-equals-three sort of thinking which is the essence, as I understood it, of certain forms of journalism, were touting me as the next Police Commissioner of the city. As it happened, the secret meeting with John Lindsay had, in fact, gone better than either of us had expected; and the job was offered and accepted.

This left me in the position of not only breaking the news as rapidly as possible to Ray Gribbs but of explaining my decision to abandon Gribbs to myself. Ironically, the first task proved not quite as difficult as the second.

Back in Detroit the day after the meeting with Lindsay, I met with Gribbs. The hurt that he may have felt, in view of the fact that I still had promises to keep, he did not let show. Instead of coming down on me hard for abandoning a ship that we had just begun to renovate, he extended further friendship and indicated, as only a person of his degree of sensitivity could, that he understood the emotional basis of my decision. I was, after all, being offered a triumphal return to the department of my father and my brothers, to a position that in the police world was regarded as the best job there was.

Perhaps Gribbs, in a sense, understood me and my motives better than I did myself. For I had to balance in my mind my belief in the desirability of not remaining within one department all one's life (and thus the decision always to *move on* rather than to remain provincially wedded to the familiar) against the desirability of a sort of mutual contract of, say, at least four years, within which a genuine reform of a department could be planned and executed. Gribbs was offering the four years' time; Lindsay was offering the "move on." I would thus have to conclude charitably of myself that if the move to New York had not been a return to my home department I would indeed have been immovable from Detroit.

For against the glamour of the New York job there had to be weighed the instinctive thought that what Howard Leary's successor would be asked to accomplish might well be impossible to achieve. The lesson of New York would be not a local lesson but a national one. The whole police world would be watching as if it were the late 1950s and the Navy rocket Vanguard were poised on the launching pad. Would the unproven thing go into orbit or keel over of its own weight? This was what a reform program and a reform commissioner faced: the threat of the unknown. For a *real* program of reform had in fact never been tried in New York, indeed had barely been tried anywhere else in the entire United States, because (a) few knew how even to begin the effort and (b) few knew beforehand how it might in the end work out.

The problem of reforming the N.Y.P.D.—or any department of significant size—was in my view (and it was widely shared) endless and enormous. In a way, it was a no-win situation. Anyone who tried might very well be consumed in the effort. At the very least, the effort would not be entirely pleasurable, and the person who was placed in the position of being hired to effect a real reform would surely find himself divided emotionally. It was not unlike the parent of a wayward child being placed in the position of having to inflict pain on one he loved. And, as a political matter, a reform commissioner without tremendous support from the Mayor could find himself at the mercy of the very people to whom he would be applying the rod. If Ray Gribbs had been Mayor of New York rather than the Mayor of Detroit, I could have more comfortably, for more reasons than one, accepted the offer. But I did not know anything more about John Lindsay than what I had read in the papers and observed on national television and gleaned from that one meeting. In the circumstances, then, the decision to go to New York was not one of calculation but of emotion. I was to return home, to the department of my father and my brothers, in the capacity of one who might attempt to improve that which he had five years before abandoned.

It is important to review the first meeting with John Lindsay, at which the offer had been extended and accepted, as background for subsequent developments.

Gracie Mansion is the official residence of the Mayor of New York, a little White House for New York in which some of its occupants were able to dream about occupancy of the big White House in Washington. It is an impressive old place, and the study in which we first met was as fitting a location for a confidential tête-à-tête as could be imagined.

Lindsay himself was taller and handsomer in person than he appeared to be on national television, and the charm which he displayed in public was no media creation; it was as real a part of him as his height and his ambition, both of which were larger than average.

I was seated at a sort of coffee table in a large overstuffed chair. Betty and Mary Lindsay, the Mayor's intelligent wife, who in the years to come would befriend Betty beyond the call of duty, had joined us for dinner, but now they left us alone to our business. In a way I wished they had stayed.

The truth was that I was wary. I was not entirely sure that John Lindsay was as serious as he might be about reforming the department, or that he understood fully the political risks that were involved, and the political capital that might be consumed.

It was, for instance, no secret that the relationship between City Hall and the New York Police Department under John Lindsay had taken a sharp turn for the worse from the very inception of the Lindsay administration in 1966. During his first year in office, Lindsay, with the backing of such political heavies as the late Senator Robert Kennedy, had gone to the people with a referendum on the creation of a civilian review board. The purpose of the board was to handle citizens' complaints of alleged brutality and other misconduct by the N.Y.P.D. The battle over the referendum was as pitched as any in the history of the city. And when the dust cleared, the referendum had been roundly defeated by a margin of two to one, in no small measure because of the organized opposition of the New York cops. In essence, then, the N.Y.P.D. had handed Lindsay, heretofore relatively untarnished by defeat, a perceptible political disaster.

For his part, Lindsay proceeded to handle the N.Y.P.D. roughly and peremptorily. While he resented cops, he also imposed his ideas on them. He had either encouraged or condoned blatant interference in the operations of the department by a select group of mayoral aides who became known as the "Kiddie Corps." Their interference in bona fide police operations during protest demonstrations was deeply resented by the rank and file. Whatever punishment the department deserved for entering into political action against the Mayor on the review board issue, the demeaning and contemptuous treatment it received seemed excessive.

I also had attained, almost by accident, personal knowledge of the relationship between City Hall and the Police Department. Early in 1966 I received a call from Howard Leary, who had been summoned from the police commissionership of Philadelphia to become Lindsay's police commissioner. Leary had called me at my office in the Justice Department to sound me out about a man named Sanford Garelik. I told Leary over the phone all I knew—which was not much, though none of it was very favorable—and hung up puzzled. There was an urgency about the call that seemed difficult to understand, since Leary had been Commissioner for but a few days. The mystery cleared up, however, in a matter of forty-eight hours. The New York papers carried the story that Sandy Garelik had been "chosen" by the new Police Commissioner Howard Leary as Chief Inspector. This was then (and still is, though the position now has a different title) the top *uniformed* position in the department (all the deputy commissioners as well as the Commissioner of the N.Y.P.D. are, in law, civilian positions) and was the most important operational position. The Chief Inspector was the rough military equivalent of chief of staff. The timing seemed to me to be such that Howard Leary, who had just arrived from Philadelphia, had barely had time to un-pack his bags when the naming of the Chief Inspector had been an accomplished fact—a result not of the logic of the available candi-dates, or of his own knowledge of the contenders, but of a fiat from City Hall. In essence, the Police Commissioner had not been per-mitted by the political circle to choose his own number two.

This, in my view, was not a healthy situation. Several things were wrong with it. One was that the selection by City Hall of Leary's chief inspector would necessarily have sent a signal through the city (and, more importantly, throughout the department) that the new Police Commissioner was not entirely in charge of his own show. Therefore, one might infer from this example that the way to get ahead in the N.Y.P.D. was not to please the Police Commissioner but to answer to the calls of City Hall. Nothing similar to such an act of overt inter-ference had ever happened to me in Syracuse or Washington, nor had anything even remotely comparable occurred under Ray Gribbs in Detroit.

The Mayor's principal motives were correct, and perhaps even noble. The late 1960s were a time of palpable tension in the cities between blacks and police. Violent confrontations were commonplace. The Kiddie Corps specialists were intended to provide extra dimen-sions of sensitivity in avoiding violence should the police handling of a complex problem fall short in any significant respect. But concern for avoiding a riot was not matched by a concern for reducing corruption.

Now, more than half a decade later, with the benefit of hindsight, it is possible to take stock. The riots had been prevented but other problems had grown: an intensification of corruption within the department, a major-league newspaper scandal, a special investiga-tory commission (called the Knapp Commission, after Whitman Knapp, the Wall Street attorney whom the Mayor appointed chairman), and, finally, the biggest political toothache of Lindsay's until-then charmed political career.

To be sure, there are two sides to the question of police inde-pendence and City Hall interference. But the history of modern American policing overwhelmingly supports an independent police department. Interference, experience has shown, has usually been negative, rarely positive. As far as I was concerned, I was convinced that the principle of independence was utterly axiomatic.

Thus when I walked into the study of Gracie Mansion to meet with the Camelot Mayor, I brought into the room considerable misgivings, and a determination not to be charmed out of a statement of my reservations about taking the job.

After the preliminary pleasantries, we got down to business. The position that I took was deliberately couched in the sort of terms likely to appeal to the political side of the Mayor.

My little dissertation opened accordingly. The power of the office of the Police Commissioner was not inconsiderable, but was it real? There were a certain number of levers to be pulled, but not a limitless number. Every single piece of leverage removed from the Police Commissioner would serve to undermine the reform. Specifically—promotions above the rank of captain, roughly 180 senior positions. Would they be within the domain of the Commissioner to make—or within that of City Hall? If the latter, the reform would not go forward, because the Police Commissioner would be stripped of his power by the Hall.

Lindsay seemed to be listening carefully, seemed to be nodding in agreement. I had placed the issue not in terms of ego but in terms of the future of the reform. The department could not be cleaned up, i.e., corruption minimized, by the Police Commissioner if it was being run by the Hall.

The issue of interference in the operational concerns of the depart-ment was raised delicately. But it did not have to be spelled out. Lindsay, perhaps, had anticipated that it would come, and he dealt with it swiftly with an unequivocal assurance of independence.

Finally, the issue of most immediate concern was raised. "Mr. Mayor, in the first few months, it is entirely likely that I would have to fire, demote, or transfer much if not all of the Leary team." I thought this one would be a difficult one for the Mayor. In essence, the action of replacing Leary's appointed commanders would be a summary repudiation of an entire subcabinet—and a team of police commanders with whom Lindsay's aides (who were not, after all, being fired) had closely worked.

But the Mayor, either not comprehending the import of the concept or not caring, responded to the effect that he understood the point of my having my own team.

It was going so smoothly, with no unpleasant undercurrents that I could discern, that the difficult question of the Knapp Commission, which the Mayor had created by executive order, raised itself. Lindsay spoke to it first: "Its mandate expires on December thirty-first of this year," he said, "Also, so does its money. By the New Year, you won't have it looking over your shoulder."

Although I had not had time to figure out what my posture would be vis-à-vis the investigatory commission, I was reassurred by the sense of certainty that the Mayor conveyed.

"Finally, Mr. Mayor," I said, folding up my presentation, "I've been a very fortunate police commissioner, perhaps the most fortunate I know of. Under a succession of three fine mayors, I've enjoyed virtual independence in Syracuse, Washington, and Detroit. If I don't have it here, I'll resign and publicly state my reason. And that would be an unfortunate situation for both of us."

This was, I felt, as far as I could push it.

"Pat, let me assure you," said the Mayor, "you have nothing to worry about."

And so I took the job.

But I had plenty to worry about, for nothing is gift-wrapped for free. To remain independent of City Hall, my reform effort would have to produce. And production, I knew, would not be a cinch.

The minimization of corruption and the maximization of police service in a department whose performance levels would be circumscribed by the rigidities of civil service, tradition, and surely politics would require a tremendous effort of management. To buy a hands-off policy from City Hall would require the new Commissioner to sell his program not only to the high command and the rank and file but also to the public. A reform administration was necessarily a high-risk proposition and would ultimately depend for its energy not only on the excellence of the new reform administration but also on the perceived political power of the Mayor. We were presented then with a bit of a paradox. One needed both the Mayor's muscle and his non-interference to fuel the reform. Either a decline in the perception of his political power or a rise in the level of City Hall interference could embolden those forces in the city and in the department with a vested interest in the reform's failure.

The nature of the reform, abstractly, centered on a single concept, from which everything would flow. The concept was one long known and appreciated by professional managers, experts on administration, and students of the management of large institutions. The concept was accountability. The concept meant that the administration of an institution would be designed in such a way that throughout that institution identifiable individuals with clear-cut responsibilities and authority could be and would be held accountable for the success or failure of the programs under their command. And the principle would be applied to the whole department, from the lowest patrol officer to the highest-ranking chiefs. In the past, in the N.Y.P.D. as in most other large police departments, responsibility and authority had been so dispersed through the institution that whenever something went wrong it was often difficult to determine who was to blame. Without a clearly identifiable pattern of authority and responsibility, it was therefore impossible to correct mistakes; in essence, the institution was beyond improvement, and the service it provided beyond enhancement—except in various haphazard ways.

The effort to bring the managerial principle of accountability to the N.Y.P.D. would necessarily prove the most difficult administrative innovation of my career. It would be fraught with both personal and political peril, but without this innovation nothing could really be changed. Every single one of the problems that had caused the department trouble—the Detective Bureau, the non-management of corruption prevention, the alienation of police work from the neighborhoods of the city—could be traced to the failure of top management to hold all segments of the department accountable.

Changes could not be made overnight. The arrival of a new police commissioner was hardly a cause for celebration within the department. There were officers in the N.Y.P.D. with decades of service under their belts who had observed new commissioners come and go like television cop series. Many had survived the infamous police corruption scandal of the 1950s, the Gross scandal, in which even some high-ranking commanders were tied to a major gambling syndicate.

Younger members of the force would be no more impressed. In addition to picking up on the cynical posture of the world-weary veterans, they would inevitably feel only a distant identification at best with the new P.C. To them, Headquarters might as well be as far away as Peking, China. In addition, on a personal basis, I would be judged at best an unknown factor. Although I had been "one of them" until 1965, on the minus side I had been since 1965 outside the department—on the run in Detroit and Washington, an obvious head-quarters type jumping from one perch to the next. Could I be trusted to make the proper public noises about corruption but in private permit business as usual? Even to the many cops who secretly wished for dramatic and real change, Murphy's arrival would seem like some-thing less than the second coming. Corruption and inefficiency in the N.Y.P.D. were regarded not as diseases but as symptoms of a larger malaise. Ever since my days as a rookie walking a beat in Brooklyn, the muffled cry in the locker rooms of the department was "You can't change the job." This meant that corruption was like death and taxes.

The Police Commissioner's office was located on the second floor of an old steel and granite building on Centre Street a dozen blocks north of the financial district. Through the arch entrance the Police Commissioner had access to a private elevator (the tiny sort one sees in those old European films) which on the second floor opened into the P.C.'s office. Up one more floor and it opened on the First Deputy Commissioner's office. Only the P.C. and the "First Dep," by tradi-tion, had use of the little elevator.

The Commissioner's office was a delightfully old-fashioned room of dark oak paneling, dark red carpeting, an overhead chandelier, a wood-burning fireplace, and a larger than life portrait of former New York Police Commissioner Theodore Roosevelt. Almost in the center of the room was an antique walnut desk, exquisitely appointed. To the side were glass doors leading out to a terrace.

Outside the office, a long narrow hallway, bisecting a small con-ference room on one side and a large bullpen area for the Commission's private staff on the other, led to a delightful anachronism that you will not find in today's police offices: an elegant rotunda with wall seats on the circumference. The rotunda was used as a waiting area, and you could be sitting outside in the rotunda, with its stately white columns and plush red carpet, and almost feel like a papal aide waiting for an audience with the Pope.

In the bull-pen area, divided up with various wall sectors, was the Commissioner's staff—officially known as the Police Commissioner's Office, or the P.C.O. The P.C.O. consisted of thirty staffers, including ranking officers, detectives, police officers, and civilian employees, and it had its own commanding officer.

The P.C.O. staff dealt with highly sensitive material. A disloyal or corrupt person on the staff could have quite an ill effect on the Commissioner, the department, or an individual life or career. If one were thinking of planting just one person in the N.Y.P.D., one could do no better than a penetration of the P.C.O.

The commanding officer of the P.C.O. was a deputy inspector, Jim Agoglia.* The first day I walked into the office—October 1, 1970—I was glad to see him. He had been an instructor at the Police Academy when I was the training officer. Jim took charge and selected my two drivers.

The Commissioner's drivers were important, quite possibly more important than a great many officers with superior rank. They were aware of the places the Commissioner goes, the people with whom he meets and transacts business, the content of sensitive conversations either in the back seat of the car or over the radiotelephone. Outside the Commissioner's presence they would naturally be badgered for rumors and inside information, and, obviously, they would know a great deal. Deputy Inspector Agoglia had to find two officers who would be content in the role of drivers, not as gossip columnists of the N.Y.P.D.

On the Commissioner's desk were two sets of telephones. One was a console system with about a half dozen outside lines—including a hot line to the Mayor. Another was an office intercom with direct lines to the highest officers in the New York Police Department, including

---

* Later, on promotion to inspector, he left for a desirable detective assignment and was replaced by Bill Devine.

the First Deputy, the Chief Inspector, and the Chief of Detectives. Everyone in the top echelon of the N.Y.P.D. had, of course, served under my predecessor. I planned to ask all of them to retire.

Only one had offered a resignation. In view of the sudden departure of the commissioner who had appointed them, and all that had transpired in the creation of the Knapp Commission, courtesy alone, I thought, would have produced offers to step down. But only one offered.

In the early weeks, relations with John Lindsay were affable, but dealings with the aides around him were somewhat more difficult. I could not tell at first whether City Hall was re-enacting the old nice-cop, bad-cop routine on the Police Commissioner, with Lindsay providing the pleasantry and ego massage, and his aides providing the heat and the hassle. Whatever the explanation, there was a bifurcation of attitude from the Hall, and in some instances the differing attitudes caused problems.

The most troubling early problem of all was the seeming indifference of some aides to what I had understood to be the nature of the agreement I had reached with the Mayor that Sunday night in accepting the job. The agreement stipulated that to effect a reform program the Police Commissioner must have a blank check from the politicial establishment to run the department. Without that blank check, the inevitable obstacles to reform could not be overcome.

It seemed to me that the eyeball-to-eyeball understanding with Lindsay permitted no other interpretation. And yet not long after I took office something happened that was deeply troubling. It made me wonder whether the Lindsay administration was indifferent to the need for thoroughgoing reform; or, even if it wasn't, whether it was willing to pay the price for what had to be done.

A conversation was initiated at the request of a man named Sydney Cooper. Cooper, who had been the Bronx Borough Commander—he had made his mark as chief architect of the Bronx cleanup that was undertaken in the wake of allegations of corruption by Frank Serpico—had just been promoted by me to Chief of Personnel.

In the past, the personnel office had been a Death Valley position, lacking the glamour of the job of Chief of Patrol, the prestige of the job of Chief Inspector, or the mystery of the job of Chief of Detectives. But the very fact that Chief of Personnel was accorded the least attention by ambitious and upwardly directed commanders in itself said something about the N.Y.P.D. For under great reform police administrators like Chicago's O. W. Wilson, personnel management was the most important function of a police administration, especially of a reform administration. The personnel function was the puppet's string by which the various joints of the huge bureaucracy below could be made to move and act. At this time in the N.Y.P.D., there were 37,000 employees—32,000 of them sworn police officers—and all were insulated in the womb of the civil service system. Personnel, with the strings of promotion, demotion, assignment, performance evaluation, discipline, separation, and training, would have to provide the missing link by which the Police Commissioner could "communicate" with his department. By appointing Cooper, one of the most visible, popular, and talented commanders in the department, I was sending, I hoped, a signal to the rest of the department. In addition to the symbolic advantage, Cooper would, I knew, bring innovation as well as integrity to the job. He was the sort of person who could not be satisfied doing things the way they had always been done; and in the N.Y.P.D., where the way things had been done was usually the wrong way to do things, Cooper as the choice for Chief of Personnel was, I thought, exactly right.

"Boss," Cooper said, one fall morning in my office, "we may have a problem with the Hall. I got a call this morning from the Deputy Mayor's office concerning the usual list of requests from councilmen about department personnel."

My mind began to race. "Were any of these requests unusual?" I asked.

"Yes," said Cooper, eyebrows bouncing up and down like fireplace logs.

It was, of course, entirely proper for members of the political community to bring to the attention of the department bona fide hardship cases, e.g., the police officer stationed in Staten Island whose mother living in Queens was dying of cancer. What was far more worrisome were the non-hardship cases; in short, the political contracts, which if executed would make the police officer forever beholden not to the department or the P.C. but to the politician who put the contract through.

I tried to hide the hurt. Was that Sunday night talk with the Mayor just so much ego stroking? Or did we have independence?

I asked, "Who was it that called?"

Cooper answered that it was the Deputy Mayor, transmitting requests from councilmen for advancement to detective or transfer to a precinct closer to home.

I said, "An obvious contract?"

Cooper replied that it was not the first wave of requests since he'd taken over Personnel. "How often?" I asked.

Cooper replied that whenever a half dozen or so have accumulated over at City Council they're sent over.

I looked out past Chief Cooper, in the general direction of Detroit, wondering about the possibility of running back to Ray Gribbs.

"Well, don't take these calls any more. Just don't take them," I said.

Cooper's thick eyebrows lifted perceptibly. "But he'll call back, boss."

"Then," I said, "transfer his call to me. Or tell him to phone me directly." Cooper now coughed nervously. So I made the order more explicit: "Any more like this, refer them directly to the Police Commissioner. Tell whoever is calling, this is a matter of deep personal concern for the Commissioner."

Cooper got up to leave. "One more thing, Syd," I said. "In the future, any intervention by a politician is to be considered a very negative factor. Our people must be personally reviewed and moved along by *both* of us."

When Cooper left my office, I was worrying about City Hall's response.

I was deeply worried because under our handsome Mayor, a different political game between City Hall and the Police Department was being played. Lindsay's predecessor, Robert Wagner, had been Mayor for twelve years—three consecutive terms. During that time he gave his police commissioners a free hand, and had honestly selected the best he could identify. (However, he did not look beyond

N.Y.C. for talent.) Not totally by coincidence, there were no serious police corruption scandals under Wagner.* Indeed, it was accepted as a "reform" period under a mayor whose policy toward the P.D. was "hands off." Lindsay's policy, I was to learn, was "hands on."

Tragically, however, Wagner's twelve years added up to one big lost opportunity. Only a fraction was accomplished of what was possible in improved management, accountability, corruption control, discipline, and leadership at every level.

Wagner's commissioners, paradoxically—Adams, Kennedy, Michael Murphy, and Broderick—were all head and shoulders above almost all other large city police administrators. Perhaps only Chief Parker in Los Angeles and the great O.W. Wilson in Chicago were superior, as better managers, with a deeper understanding of the principles of organization and management through which the head of a police department can get a handle on problems. Almost no one else was worth mentioning across the entire country, which is some measure of how bad police management in America was.

But Wagner's P.C.'s, for all their personal integrity, were all lawyers—and lawyers who not only failed to address basic management problems but failed even to bring in aides as either consultants or staffers who might have helped. If Wagner's police commissioners had in fact accomplished more than they had by 1965, when Lindsay came in and brought Howard Leary from Philadelphia with him, the department would have been a lot closer to the L.A.P.D. in knowing how to deal with the ever-present danger of corruption. Put another way, the well-intentioned Wagner P.C.'s could not grasp the intricacies of managing a huge police bureaucracy and as a result only nibbled around the fringes rather than going to the heart of the problems. There were such profound weaknesses in organization and management that in essence Headquarters was not in control of the department. Their ignorance was personified in their reliance on a man named John Walsh. He was the first big hurdle in the attempt to reform the N.Y.P.D.

---

* This is not the same thing as saying that there was no serious corruption. The atmosphere may not have seemed conducive to corrupt behavior, but management control may not have been strong enough or clever enough to see that the atmosphere at Headquarters filtered down to the ranks below.

As a result of the failure of Wagner's four independent police commissioners to have had more of an impact on corruption control than they did, a terrible impression was left on the troops: to wit, "You can't change the job." Perhaps more than anything else, this pessimistic, cynical attitude stood in the way of generating any substantial or serious enthusiasm for beginning anew during those first few weeks. And perhaps more than anyone, First Deputy Police Commissioner John Walsh personified this pessimism.

I inherited John Walsh when I took the job the way I inherited Teddy Roosevelt's portrait. And, in a way, I felt both men were always looking over my shoulder.

John Walsh had become perhaps the most entrenched single police administrator in modern police history. Over the years, and surviving police commissioner after commissioner, Walsh became an institution, a sort of Sam Rayburn of the N.Y.P.D.

Ironically, John Walsh became known as the department's top-ranking corruption fighter. It was ironic because, as the book and film *Serpico* imply, Walsh was the police official to whom Frank Serpico's story of police corruption had been bucked, and in whose office said reports had allegedly remained.

Walsh—and probably most police departments in the country have a John Walsh—was a paragon of personal integrity (at least no one had ever had any reason to challenge it, despite the mishandling of the Serpico case) but he was an individual who could prove to be a severe impediment to any real reform program, since he would have little sympathy with the prospects of any such program, no matter how carefully conceived. Practically axiomatically, John Walsh believed in sin; by comparison, I believed in virtue.

Under other circumstances it might have been possible to work around Walsh. But these weren't ordinary circumstances. Even now the investigatory commission was hard at work, prowling on the dark underside of the department, and despite John Lindsay's assurance that by January first—in a few short months—the commission would be out of business, some instinct deep inside the political portion of my brain told me that somehow, some way, the corruption commission would survive. It was this assumption—shared, I should add, by almost no one in the high command, who believed Lindsay's assurances that the commission would die a natural death after its agreed-upon life had run its course—which fueled my determination to move as rapidly as possible in New York, as contrasted to the slower pace in Detroit.

During the first few weeks it was necessary to have occasional contact with Walsh; he was, unfortunately, the number two man in the department. But I made these unavoidable meetings as painfully uncomfortable and as brief as possible, pausing only once in a while to afford the First Deputy Police Commissioner a graceful opportunity to resign. But Walsh obviously wouldn't go gracefully.

John Walsh was a very powerful—and clever—man. One did not last as long as he had at such a height without having built up a tremendous political base in the city. And that base had been extended, shrewdly, to points of political power outside the department. It was not, then, such a simple matter as demanding a letter of resignation. To that request the First Deputy Commissioner might simply respond with a no, and the Police Commissioner would then have his work cut out for him. With Walsh, an outflanking maneuver would have to be tried. This meant that I had to pay a call on Walsh's most powerful political ally—the great Frank Hogan.

In New York City, as elsewhere, the most powerful law enforcement officials were the district attorneys. There were five of them, one for each borough, and taken together they were as an accumulated force more powerful than the Police Commissioner, despite the latter's great visibility and legion of 32,000 soldiers.

In New York the most powerful district attorney was the Manhattan D.A.—for the same reason that, in the worlds of finance, commerce, communications, and so on, Manhattan reigned supreme over the city's other four boroughs. In addition to the power of the office, Hogan's power was extended by virtue of his reputation for incorruptibility and his tenure in office—more than three decades. Thus, with the arguable exception of the Mayor, probably the most powerful public official in New York was Manhattan District Attorney Hogan.

Walsh—and we knew, did we not, that here was a man not to be underestimated?—therefore had early in his career allied himself with Frank Hogan. Mayors and police commissioners might come and go, but Hogan had become an institution—and to become which was also Walsh's ambition. In such circumstances was an elaborate arrangement crafted between the two shrewd gentlemen of law enforcement.

What Walsh provided the D.A. was this: a pair of eyes and ears inside the N.Y.P.D., a direct pipeline between his office and the department. Nothing of consequence would therefore be planned, much less executed, without advance word being relayed to the D.A. Walsh would be like the C.I.A. liaison's daily intelligence briefing for the President, except that Hogan would be able to trust Walsh more than any President could ever trust the C.I.A. For Hogan knew that in return for an inside hold on the department, he was providing something very valuable to John Walsh.

This item of value was something that no other New York district attorney's office seemed nearly as willing to provide. Only Hogan, evidently, could consistently give it. The item of value was the ability to prosecute with skill and integrity any police corruption case brought to it by John Walsh, the department's chief official in charge of corruption fighting.

Hogan's record of successful prosecution of police corruption cases over a long period of years so far exceeded those of the other D.A.'s that Headquarters believed it highly likely that any such case would be blown in another borough. This state of affairs reinforced the Walsh attitude of struggling against almost impossible odds in attempting to reduce corruption. It was also a way of passing the buck —shifting the blame outside the department, while failing to tighten controls within.

And so Walsh, whose power depended on being the avenging angel, relied on Hogan's office, without which Walsh's power would have crumpled for lack of credibility. For Walsh's power within the department would revolve around his potential for striking at a small, unpredictable fraction of the corruption cases coming to his attention while the core of the problem remained unaddressed. Of course, this was a terrible way to run an anti-corruption program. It started out by conceding the hopelessness of the situation. Then it proceeded to hypocrisy by ignoring the underlying causes, many of which were rooted in such traditional management follies as "the sheet"—the monthly gambling arrest quota (see Chapter Nine).

Furthermore, Walsh's policy of cynicism extended to the foundation of the Internal Affairs Unit. This was a Headquarters unit—sort of John's Angels. The principle of collection was to identify those honest officers, axiomatically few in number, according to Walsh's theory, and to bring them into Headquarters as a little band of honest men.

The cynicism of assuming that most police officers would be corrupt and that only a small fraction could be counted on to be honest explained a lot of things about Walsh—and the failure of four honest police commissioners under Wagner to have had more of an impact. It explained, for example, the mystery of why Deputy Commissioner Walsh did so little about Serpico's allegations of corruption—until they appeared in the New York *Times* exposés.

The mystery is explained by a paradox: Walsh believed in the pervasiveness of police corruption, therefore it was his contention that it was beyond administrative control. So far from not believing in the veracity of Frank Serpico's allegations of widespread grafting among plainclothes units in the Bronx, Walsh believed them wholeheartedly, but in a trembling fashion. It did not occur to him that the response to Serpico's portfolio of horrors was to attack them under a systematic program of reform, any more than it would occur to a Haitian peasant to treat an allegedly Voodoo-related sickness with the techniques of modern medicine.

My own position was that police officers were not fundamentally or irremediably corrupt. They were human beings who had been corrupted by a larger system only partly of the department's making. It wasn't the honest cop who was the freak; it was the failure of administration that had helped produce an atmosphere in which corruption could exist. Whatever the actual evidence for my contention, however, it seemed mandatory to *assume* a hypothesis of optimism regarding the essential nature of police behavior and to steer clear of defeatism and cynicism. Thus John Walsh's negative approach, as an administrative policy, had to be discredited.

Perhaps as importantly, the departure of John Walsh might signal to the rest of the department that we were going to try something new. By the same token, every day he remained in my administration would add to the belief, within and outside the department, that more of the same could be expected under Murphy, since the man who had had so many years to accomplish his assigned goal of assuring an honest police department and had failed would still be in charge as number two.

There was only one way to topple Walsh without an unseemly show of power—that was to pull the rug from underneath his power base. And so one morning I whispered to Peggy Triplett, my administrative secretary, that I had an unscheduled appointment to keep and slipped down the back elevator into the waiting black Mercury. The car threaded smoothly through the snarling morning traffic. At a traffic intersection a cop, seeing the Commissioner's car, drew up to attention and saluted. I wondered how he would feel about Murphy after he found out what was in store for the department. Would there come a time when cops wouldn't salute?

The car continued toward Leonard Street, toward the Manhattan District Attorney's office.

Hogan, from behind his desk, was affable but cautious. Had John Walsh called ahead to let him know what was coming?

The living legend congratulated me on the fine start I was making, how he'd heard so many great things about what I was planning to do.

(And I knew exactly from whom he had heard them.)

We fenced for a few rounds.

Then I came to the point. I said, "Mr. District Attorney, I need the cooperation of this office in all that I do, but I'm thinking seriously of building a whole new team at the top."

Hogan said, "I can appreciate that. It even seems like a good idea to me. However, it is difficult to understand how you could get along, at least for a year, without Deputy Commissioner Walsh."

Hogan was trying to buy his man time. Round one was even.

I said, "Everything one hears about the distinguished First Deputy deepens one's respect and esteem. This has made me pause and wonder many times whether the decision I have made is correct. But, nevertheless, I must have my own man in that sensitive position, a real alter ego."

A quiet descended over his long book-filled office. Hogan, wearing a three-piece suit, focused pale eyes on some far-off wall. Then he frowned. I suspect that he may not have anticipated the extent to which I seemed willing to push the matter.

Not sure, I pressed home the point. "I don't feel I can serve the Mayor properly without my own number two man."

Well, there it was. All of it. And John Lindsay could either support me or find a new commissioner. The Hogan-Walsh alliance could only hurt the reform.

Hogan stood up. "I understand," he said and extended his hand. We shook on it.

Or had we? Did he really understand? Would I get a call later in the day from the Mayor?

I got into the Mercury for the ride back to Headquarters wondering about two things. One, would Hogan work against me? Two, did Hogan really understand the immense danger of the Knapp Commission, or was he taking this whole thing much too lightly?

The 180 police commanders above the rank of captain were gathered in the assembly room of the Police Academy. The occasion was the Commissioner's little inaugural address, drafted by Lieutenant Herman Lederman of the Public Information Office. Every officer in the audience held rank at the pleasure of the P.C. I thought I would have their attention. "Strong winds of social change have propelled us into new areas of activity," the speech began. "Demands on the police service have never been greater, and the social significance of what we do or fail to do has attracted considerable public interest. It calls for quality performance. . . .

"The police officer needs and respects leadership. . . . The New York City policeman is capable and highly trained. He has the ability to take charge of a confused situation on the street, to bring order where there is disorder. He has the ability to exercise good judgment and restore peace where there was violence. These are talents gained by experience *and* training. They are developed by supervision and leadership, which are the continuing processes of instruction."

I then took the opportunity to announce that Assistant Chief Albert A. Seedman, then commander of Manhattan South detectives, was being put in charge of department-wide training. Cops generally tended not to take training seriously. But Seedman, a sort of Kojak figure in the department, cops would take seriously. I hoped to put one and one together and create a revitalized training program that all commanders would take note of.

"The great majority of police officers," I continued, getting to the point, "are honest men, proud of their profession. . . . It is this large majority that welcomes strong leadership—the kind that has the courage to denounce corruption.

"Except for your paycheck, there is no such thing as a clean buck. . . . I will hold each of you accountable for the misdeeds of your subordinates. . . . I expect borough and division commanders to make frequent visits to stationhouses. . . . Corruption in any form is odious and repugnant to this administration. State your position to your men eyeball to eyeball.

"I will hold each of you personally accountable for any misconduct within the ranks at any level of command. . . . It will be my policy to increase significantly your authority, with a view to achieving greater effectiveness and efficiency. In return, you can expect to be held to greater accountability for your exercise of direction and control.

"The law provides that each of you serves above the rank of captain at my pleasure. It is my responsibility to remove from high rank anyone among you who cannot, or will not, meet the high standards at the executive level."

A short time later we "flopped" back into uniform a large portion of all plainclothes officers—those responsible for gambling enforcement. Almost all of those transferred had been in plainclothes for five years or more. My next target for transfer were those in the four-year category.

The abrupt transfer had an unsettling effect at Headquarters. Taken in conjunction with my maiden speech, which stressed accountability at the level of the high command, it seemed to make some sort of impression. Yet on the surface everything seemed to be running all too smoothly. I was therefore concerned, on the alert. Meeting after meeting was held, and though nothing in the way of organized resistance had formed, something which rather resembled organized clay kept getting in the way.

Take the high command conferences. I suppose there is nothing quite so breathtaking in servility as a roomful of police brass prepared to say yes to the Police Commissioner on his every whim. I believe I might have proposed that all officers start wearing blue evening gowns, and half the brass in the room would have nodded their heads in agreement. Everything I said was brilliant, witty; everything I touched turned to gold. One was reminded, as an indication of the atmosphere, of the title of the biography of Hollywood mogul Darryl Zanuck: *Don't Say Yes Until I Finish Talking.*

The accountability concept was a huge new element, but as yet it was an abstraction. And the massive transfers had not yet touched the brass. I suspect that for most of them accountability was nothing more than some little pet project of the new Commissioner's, which in due course would be whittled down to a toothpick by the bureaucracy.

Because of this general impression, among other reasons, my conviction grew stronger than the final responsibility for corruption and ineffectiveness was not so much out in the precincts as it was in Headquarters.

After one high-level meeting, I waved Chief Cooper into my office for a word.

"Any interesting phone calls lately from City Hall," I asked several weeks after our discussion.

He smiled broadly, a winner's smile. "Not a one, boss."

I smiled back. Really, I was quite pleased.

A few days later First Deputy Commissioner John Walsh cleaned out his desk.

The body was gone, but sometimes I wondered whether like Christmas past the ghost of John Walsh wasn't still making the rounds at Headquarters. There were 180 executive positions above the rank of captain (the 380 captains, who had achieved rank through the civil service system, were not subject to the P.C., except as to the nature of their assignments). It was this executive group of 180 that had to be manipulated and inspired first—so that the 99 percent below would get the message. So I began to make changes, some of them as dramatically as possible. Perhaps the most dramatic was the sudden elevation of a lowly deputy inspector—Donald Cawley—to Chief of Patrol, over dozens of candidates more obviously senior. Cawley would be in New York what Jerry Wilson was in Washington: the symbol that a new era had arrived.

Still there was more dead wood at the top levels of the world's most famous police department than in a petrified forest. From what I could observe, it was remarkable that those below were not more dispirited than they seemed to be. No matter how good a department's rank and file—and in the N.Y.P.D. one was pleased to observe some of the savviest and best-intentioned police officers to be found anywhere—without the right sort of leadership from the top, very little good could be accomplished.

At one high-level meeting I pounded the conference table, as if a man possessed, in an effort to communicate a sense of urgency: "We've got a real problem here in narcotics and with the division plainclothes squads, and you know it. This guy Mike Armstrong [Knapp Commission Chief Counsel] is smart. He is not going to have much trouble finding what he's looking for, and he's going to expose it all over the papers. Now we can look like we couldn't care less, or like we know what's wrong and are trying to do something about it."

The existence of the outside investigatory commission had by now become an essential element of the attempt to motivate commanders reared under the Walsh system. My dependency on it had been formed because of the clear absence of any sense of shame or purpose at high levels, despite the New York *Times* series on corruption. Without the Knapp Commission hovering about, the case for moving quickly to institute reforms would have been, in this crowd, more difficult to make. Thus I felt secretly that I needed the Knapp Commission, that without it real reform might not be possible, that if it expired on December 31, as John Lindsay predicted, I would face even more resistance.

The existence of an outside body investigating police corruption has become almost an inevitable problem for heads of police of major departments around the country. Within a span of a few years a number of cities (and chiefs) were to be put through a similar sort of ordeal, complete with newspaper exposé and investigatory commission. In 1973 and 1974, allegations of corruption hit police departments in Philadelphia, Cleveland, Houston, Denver, Indianapolis, and Chicago. For police chiefs in those cities the primary question would become whether to cooperate with (a) the outside commission, or (b) the grand jury. Thus, in a sense, the New York melodrama of 1970–1973—the years of the reform—was to become a sort of prototype for police departments around the country.

From the beginning, the key question had been how to relate to the Knapp Commission, and before long I had concluded that the reform would depend on pressure from without as well as from within.

This was something I could not, of course, admit publicly at the time, for it would have enraged virtually everyone in the N.Y.P.D.—people who were angered already by my obvious policy of tacit cooperation. But in truth, to move an institution as large and as entrenched as a police bureaucracy, especially on an issue of decades-old patterns of corruption, requires all the effort a community can bring to bear; quite possibly, a serious-minded, competent police administration may not be enough.

Constantly the Knapp Commission threat was invoked in private one-on-one sessions held in my office with commanders whom I felt should be moving more briskly on the corruption issue than they were. I usually tried to time these sessions so that they would occur in the wake of some dramatic "shakeup" announcement. With one borough commander I announced the demotion of two ranking officers, the removal of six from command, and the forced retirement of two others.

The atmosphere was thus one of suspense. This borough commander, trying to get on key, went into elaborate detail in my office about the anti-corruption work of his staff.

I had personally chosen to conduct this session because I had known this very successful police department climber from way back and I knew that he was a phony. Although he was well connected with city politicians, he was a terrible commander; whether or not he was corrupt I did not know. But under the reform, personal integrity was not enough; competence was also necessary—competence as a manager and as a leader of police officers.

I pulled my chair from behind my desk and placed it directly next to the commander. I looked him directly in the eyes and spoke softly. "The Knapp Commissioner is going to take a bite out of us by dragging police corruption into the papers," I said, as ever invoking Knapp as the Sword of Damocles. "Tell me, Chief, and tell me man-to-man. What are your *real* corruption problems?"

The borough commander squirmed in his chair, flapping his weight like a fish in the bottom of a boat. He looked around the office as if searching the walls for some answer, but the walls held no cue card, so he turned back to me and blurted out, "Commissioner, I tell you in all honesty, we still got a lot of guys taking cups of coffee."

I rose slowly to my feet in exasperation at being so transparently underestimated and trifled with. Cups of coffee! Perhaps in thirty years we could begin dealing with cups of coffee. The commander's response was like the Captain of the *Titanic* worrying about leaky faucets.

I buzzed the intercom, asked for a certain lieutenant in the Internal Affairs office. "Would you promptly bring in," I said, "the commander's files."

Fear crossed the chief's face like a remembered embarrassment, and the thought occurred to him that he should try to say something in advance as a defense; but nothing would come out of his throat, and I silenced him, to put him out of his misery, with a show of the palm of my hand in front of his eyes.

The lieutenant came into my office smartly with a thick bulging file. It looked as thick as the Manhattan phone book.

With the young lieutenant looking at the two of us aghast, I started on the chief again: "I'm not talking about damn cups of coffee, Chief, and you know it. You want me to spell it out?"

The lieutenant, perhaps startled at hearing me in the unusual circumstance of raising my voice, handed me the heavy file with a rapid shove and scurried out the door.

I spread out the folder on my desk, as if a poker player showing my opponent my hand. "Here," I said. "What about this? [Pulling out an urgently red-flagged Internal Affairs report on the commander's borough.] What about this bottle club? And this gay bar? And this coop? And this whore house? And this dope-shooting pad?" I flipped through the reports as if conducting a guided tour of corruption in the commander's borough.

"What you fail to comprehend, Chief," I said, "is my unwillingness to take the fall for *your* mistakes, *your* errors of command. It's you who's going to go down the tubes on this corruption business, not me. It's a new ball game. I'm not responsible for every darn piece of ugliness in this department. You commanders are. I'm responsible for you; you're responsible for the corruption, the inefficiency, and the blunders. If I have to, I'll remove you from command, force your retirement or demote you.

"You are gong to be held accountable by me for the mistakes in your command. So clean your place up. And do it now. I'll help you in any way I can, back you up to the hilt. But if the axe falls, it'll be your neck, not mine."

The Chief mumbled something incomprehensible, averting his eyes from mine, and somehow managed to extricate himself from the office.

I went back behind my desk, dragging the chair behind me. I reached into the top desk drawer, pulled out a roll of Life Savers, and bit into a handful of them; if I were a drug user or an alcoholic, I certainly would have popped a Valium or a shot of whiskey. Instead, being raised in a business where heavy drinking had ruined more lives than gunshot wounds, I concentrated on the clean whiteness of the Life Savers. This accountability stuff was a rough business.

A few days later one of my top-ranking chiefs came in with a report on a bottle-club operation in Manhattan. At my suggestion, the chief had gone into a certain busy precinct looking for trouble; that is, for an obvious, or at least potentially obvious, corruption situation. Messages were being sent from Headquarters now as quickly as we could invent appropriate symbolic action. In this instance, the message under transmission was a scarcely veiled warning to the borough commander that we knew that in this division's precincts some of the worst corruption in the department flourished. We wanted this commander to start worrying—day and night.

The operation was a classic N.Y.P.D. Internal Affairs operation. Operatives were planted in surveillance on a notorious bottle club— an after-hours nightclub at which liquor was sold; these clubs might not close until eight or nine in the morning, if that soon.

Our plants sat in surveillance one night, then a second, then a third. They observed noise, drunks, women of glitter, and men of style coming in and out of this club well into daybreak. What they did not observe, strangely, was even a single patrol car in the area—not once in those three nights, not even by mistake!

By the fifth night, our operatives were pretty sure that they had located the sort of place they had been looking for. Now they went about contacting the precinct.

One of the operatives went to a pay phone booth in the vicinity and dialed the precinct switchboard. He put the microphone of a tape recorder on the receiver. Then, acting like a sleepy, irritated local resident driven into phoning a complaint, our operative gave the address of the "noise" and a plea that something be done by the police to correct the situation. "After all, man," said the operative, "it's five in the morning. A working man can't get no sleep." The precinct switchboard operator, naturally, promised immediate action.

The operative went back to the unmarked car where his buddies were planted. They all waited. They waited that night, the next night, the next. Even after a second call, no precinct car reported to the scene of the alleged after-hours club.

This was step one of the operation. It was established that the precinct had been notified of a suspicious situation by a citizen, and the precinct had not taken any action. (At this point, the precinct's only crime was failure to respond.)

The next step, in N.Y.P.D. lingo, involved "giving the precinct a piece of it." Headquarters composed an official memorandum to the commanding officer of the precinct. The memorandum said that a citizen has phoned us here with a complaint, to the effect that he had called the precinct about a noisy after-hours club in your territory, but that despite promises of action, nothing from your end was forthcoming. Probably nothing here, but give it a look, will you?

Now the trap was baited. Remember, we still had the tape recording of the complaint from the "citizen" being received. Under N.Y.P.D. rules and regulations, every complaint to a precinct switchboard must be logged on a daily chart as having been officially received.

A few days later the precinct's official response comes into Headquarters. It reads like a short table speech out of *Alice in Wonderland*. The bottom line: Said alleged complaint about said alleged bottle club was never received at the precinct switchboard. And the memorandum was signed not only by the precinct's commanding officer but endorsed also by both the division and borough patrol commanders. End of round two.

Round three. Headquarters, now spelling out to the borough commander exactly what was involved, sends a strongly worded memorandum, in response to which any honest, alert chief would have to come back with a serious, embarrassed reply; but instead what we got was "We will give continued attention to this problem." The

Going Home • 167

translation: Come back in ten years and we'll still be giving it "continued attention."

Disheartened and not nearly amused, I met with First Deputy William H. T. Smith—my replacement for John Walsh—who had worked with me so well in Syracuse. We left it with Bill Smith to slip the borough commander a bit of advice, to the effect "Maybe you'd like to add a few *touches* to your report on that incident." The translation: "Hey, we know what's going on. Maybe you don't, but you're the commanding officer. The ball's in your court. Do something, or else. Headquarters will back you up all the way, but *you* do it." This was the essence of accountability: not passing the buck. And the essence of good police management: knowing what was going on under your command. It was either corruption or incompetence, one or the other.

Under the old system, the commanding officer could have feigned insulation. Under the reform, we were insisting on greater accountability, knowledgeability, professionalism.

Soon after, Bill Smith got an anguished call from the chief: "Please don't make me do it. We've never done it this way before. It will undercut my hold over the troops. You do it, save me."

Bill Smith came in to convey the plea for mercy.

I thought about a stay of execution for about a second, then ordered the First Deputy to send back the unequivocal, heartless, ruthless message: Stop ducking this, get moving.

A few days later, after the dust settled, a local newspaper carried an account of a shake-up in this division. The paper noted correctly that twenty police officers were charged with failing to act against a bottle club in their territory, and added that the case was notable not only for its massive impact on the division but also because the charges against the officers were brought by the commanding officer of the borough, not by some special hit-and-run Headquarters unit. The newspaper story then quoted the commanding officer to the effect that he was very much in favor of this new system of accountability.

Of course, First Deputy Smith and I were highly entertained by the commander's public position. For this was the chief who had to be repeatedly pushed before he would take the necessary disciplinary action.

Lindsay was lying back, as if amused (and possibly pleased?) that Bill Smith, Syd Cooper, Mike Codd (who had been made Chief Inspector), Don Cawley, Bill McCarthy, and the rest of the new reform administration seemed to be moving in the right direction.

Except for the irritant of nagging, sometimes niggling calls from various City Hall aides, the Hall had apparently decided on a cease-fire in its relations with the N.Y.P.D., which had now almost attained a state of semi-independence approaching what it had enjoyed for twelve years under Mayor Wagner. You could, and you would, the message from the Hall appeared to be, fight your own battles.

Lindsay—as a personality, as opposed to a political operator and manipulator—was a charmer. He was direct and often, to put it in a carefree way, fun. He would never be a Ray Gribbs as far as non-interference was concerned—it was not in the nature of the sense of self he projected, not only to others but to himself—but he was a pleasant man to be around. The fact that I was getting to like him personally would, I hoped, not be obvious to the troops, who had little tolerance for J.V.L. and his "liberal" ideas.

For his part, Lindsay was actually infatuated with the *idea* of a police department, even while he was scared to death of cops as realities—especially as political realities—having been burned on the review-board referendum and wary ever since of a repeat conflagration.

But there were aspects of the department's intricacy and complexity that held his interest repeatedly, for if nothing else, the Police Department was (to him) the most interesting department in his cabinet. At the meetings of cabinet held often at Gracie Mansion, it was the Police Commissioner, perhaps more than anyone else, who got called on by the Mayor to illuminate aspects of his programs and as yet unseen corners of his department. Despite the presence of individuals at these meetings whom I considered manifestly more high powered— Edward Hamilton, the brilliant Budget Director, for instance— Lindsay seemed most fascinated by various elements of the reform program, especially the emphasis on accountability as a way of decreasing corruption and increasing the level of productivity.

For all this, however, Lindsay's most passionate concern about the

N.Y.P.D. involved one of our least important—and in my view, most cuttable and forgettable—services. This was the picturesque Mounted Division. The trouble was that Lindsay was an amateur equestrian, and he regarded any threat to the Mounteds the way any animal lover would regard a budget crisis at the A.S.P.C.A. animal shelter. One afternoon, after whole days of non-interference from the Hall, I actually took a call from John on this.

"Yes, Mr. Mayor," I said in my very official commissioner voice, not knowing what to expect. One never knew quite what to expect from City Hall these days. They were worrying more than we were, and often over matters that only we should have been worrying about. Was a new rumor coming out of the Knapp Commission? New feedback from the City Council over the Detective Bureau reorganization? (See Chapter Eight.) Or was somebody wondering when the next stationhouse dedication ceremony was? (The Mayor was now availing himself of opportunities to appear with the reform Commissioner at virtually any newsworthy or photoworthy police function.) Or was this possibly yet another request to fill in on some impossibly unfulfillable mayoral television commitment?

"*Commissioner*," he began, having established the serious tone of voice, meaning this was business, "I'm very concerned about something, and I want to discuss it with you openly."

It sounded like the beginning of a full-dress riot act. "Do you want me to come over, Mr. Mayor?" I said, believing as always in the accountability of our police to civilian control—*remote* control.

"No, no. It's about the Mounted Patrol Unit, Commissioner. I hear the rumor that you're going to have it abolished."

I thought: All one has to do in this situation is to concentrate on not cracking up over the phone and one could maybe do it. The horses were about to be immunized by the Mayor against Ed Hamilton's fancy-pants "productivity" medicine.

I answered, "No truth to that rumor whatever, Mr. Mayor," knowing that Mr. Mayor knew better, knew that in truth what the Commissioner really wanted to do with those darn horses was to retire all but one and encase that last one in bronze for display at Times Square. The annual cost of this equestrian's fantasy of a police unit could have budgeted a small precinct.

I added, "Of course, everything here at the department is under constant review and cost-benefit analysis under our continuing productivity drive [blah, blah, blah]."

I could hear Lindsay chuckling now. "Okay, Pat," he said, having shifted down into the friendly-intimate tone, meaning this was just between friends, "but I don't want anything happening to my horses."

And that, I knew, was an *order*.

I hung up the phone and wondered, How would I look standing before a battery of microphones and the glare of the klieg lights, resigning as commissioner on—the horse issue?

Not all mayoral interventions were, unfortunately, so innocent or amusing. One that caused me enormous personal anguish concerned the Deputy Commissioner for Public Information. The story illustrates the tenuous nature of total independence, and the extent to which a police department is often its own worst enemy when it comes to public relations.

The Public Information Commissioner's name was Robert Daley; and I had hired him not long after becoming Police Commissioner, at least partially out of urgency. The press commissioner I had inherited from Leary was a well-meaning advocate of the Detroit school of public information, where one could refuse for an entire weekend to comment on a story that was in reality worth telling. With the Knapp Commission working us over, and the public wondering in the face of a rising wave of crime about our effectiveness, not to mention our integrity, the "No comment" or grudging-comment style was stupid. More than any type of police administration, in fact, a reform administration needed a good promotion effort to sell its rather unorthodox ideas about policing and police management to a public whose expectations about police work have been at least partially shaped by such fictions as television crime shows and police novels—and the previous non-reform administration.

So, soon I had a new press commissioner, and a good one he turned out to be. Virtually overnight Daley—a novelist and journalist who had been a foreign correspondent for the *Times*—converted a lumbering, reclusive, defensive, and sometimes even amateurish public information operation into an aggressive, creative, upbeat shop. I knew we were in for our share of knocks on the corruption issue as the investigatory commission went public with its findings. All I asked from Public Information was a share of stories that showed a police department at work. For even in a troubled police force, a great deal of what went on—in the form of the routine good, and often even brave, work—was clearly in the public's interest, and in our interest to publicize.

But a few months after Daley had been in place, I began receiving very negative and concerned signals from the Hall about my press commissioner. At first I ignored them. But then several events occurred which made my cool approach difficult to maintain.

Early spring of 1972. The Mayor called in the morning with the urgent request to join him at Gracie Mansion for a special get-together the following day.

Worry, wrinkled brow. Perhaps on the average of once a week I might be at the Hall for some meeting or other (never being there simply for a social chat, or the good company). Meetings at Gracie Mansion occurred about as frequently.

This, noticeably, was a personal request from the Mayor to *be there*. Most unusual.

Yet I was a civilian commissioner, subject under the law (and moral obligation) to civilian control.

So off I would go to the Mansion, worried.

It wasn't, ultimately, all paranoia, for when I arrived the next morning all of Lindsay's staff heavyweights were lying in wait: Ed Hamilton, Deputy Mayor Aurelio, Tom Morgan, Jay Kriegel—and Lindsay.

Was it the budget?

What would be the issue? Not hiring any more cops? My position was already clear—the answer to the crime problem was not more money for the police but for the courts and the prosecutors. The P.D. had to do a better job with the resources already allocated. As I wrote to the high command in a memorandum, "It is likely that the crime control dollar in New York, and other cities, is not very well spent. Stated another way, if all the money available for controlling crime in New York City could be allocated among the various functions (police, prosecution, courts, corrections) in the best possible, optimal manner, some share of police funding might be shifted to other functions. It is obvious that the police are producing more work than the remainder of the system can handle effectively."

So it couldn't be the budget. Even the Mayor had been mildly amused, even caught unawares, by my philosophy about the totality of the criminal justice system budget. (He had anticipated, naturally, the usual empire-builder resistance.)

With Jay Kriegel in the room, my mind raced back to all the recent machinations (see the next chapter) with the Detective Bureau. Had all the due bills with City Council finally been called in? And was it now the day of reckoning? Kriegel, after all, had been the first aide from the Hall to moan every time we made a move with the detectives.

My eyes came to rest on Thomas Morgan, the press secretary to the Mayor. Could it be the Bob Daley issue?

On one level I had not calculated my public information commissioner to be weighty enough in the overall scheme of things to merit such a turnout at this mansion of heavies. But perhaps I had been mistaken. Why else would Morgan be attending? It was Morgan, I remembered, who recommended Daley for the job a while ago when I was absolutely desperate for a new press man. Was Morgan now prepared to admit a mistake?

I had sensed a growing concern with Daley from the Hall, but it was difficult to define clearly what might be bugging them. Oh, part of it, one suspected, was a clash of style. Daley was awfully flamboyant, even boyish; there had been an amusing little item about him in the *Times* recently taking droll note of our gun-toting public information hotshot.

So the issue had to be Daley.

But when the aides started to lunge at me, I realized I had underestimated the depth of feeling. Morgan, Kriegel, and Hamilton came at me in waves. Never before had I faced this sort of overt antagonism from the Hall.

I made the point, as strongly as one could under the circumstances of being surrounded, that it was the Mayor's aide Tom Morgan who had urged the Daley appointment on me.

They replied that Daley was uncontrollable. He was going berserk. He was issuing press releases without coordinating with City Hall, with the occasional result that a police story would bump a story important to the Mayor off page one.

On and on it went, for well over an hour. I defended Daley vigorously, and considering the length of the debate couldn't have been doing all that bad; but it became clear that the continuance of Daley as press commissioner would be regarded by Lindsay's inner circle as practically a war declaration by the Police Commissioner.

But *that* I knew I could handle. I was less confident of resisting the Mayor's opposition. After all, I had been successful so far in the risky detective reform, even against City Hall aides acting as cutouts for the detectives; but that success probably had hinged on the Mayor's backing, or at least non-interference, in the clutch.

As the rage subsided, the Mayor, who had popped in and out all morning to catch the drift of the debate, took me by the arm and escorted me to the door. When he was out of range of hearing by the others, he said, "You do what you think best, Pat, but frankly I think Daley's hurting you."

And so I left, troubled. In my role as a necessarily innovative reform commissioner, I had rarely been subjected to such direct pressure. Still, in the inner councils of the department, Daley invariably came down hard on the activist side of every issue, and his energy with the press was valuable. Thus, if nothing further occurred, if he did not pull something that caused serious embarrassment, he still retained the confidence of his leading admirer, the P.C. But something happened, sadly; it concerned a racial incident.

Quite possibly, what I now consider to be a low point of my administration occurred over the incident involving blacks and our poorly managed police officers in April of 1972.

A lot of emotions and thoughts came into focus in my mind one unpleasant morning that April. I was behind my desk in my office, looking over paperwork, fidgeting, popping Life Savers into my mouth, waiting for the appearance of a minister, Louis Farrakhan of Harlem, of Mohammed Temple Number Seven.

The source of my anguish was an incident of a few days before. As a result of an administrative failure, the minister in truth had the N.Y.P.D. on the edge of a cliff. Would he try to push us over? He wouldn't if he didn't want a riot. I assumed that nobody except a maniac was gunning for a replay of Watts 1965 in Harlem 1972. In my view, the unacceptability of a racial disorder in New York was clear to all concerned, whether conservative or liberal or even radical and politically ambitious, like the good reverend from Temple Seven.

This was the thinking behind my decision to meet with Farrakhan in a circumstance in which I did not really hold a very strong hand. A race riot would inevitably trigger more loathsome consequences than in any other city, if only because of our size, our total accumulated tension, and our propensity toward excess in both sin and virtue.

The incident at the mosque on April 14, 1972, was behind the unwanted visit of Louis Farrakhan to my office. I had asked Mike Codd to attend because of something he had told me after the incident. Codd and Al Seedman had the previous Friday taken command at the scene of the incident, with Deputy Commissioner Benjamin Ward, who visibly demonstrated the black presence at the top of the police hierarchy.

The incident began just before noon one April day. A 911 (the emergency police number) operator took an anonymous phone call. The caller reported an "officer in trouble" at Farrakhan's mosque.

This sort of call is known in the trade as a 10-13. The address, near 116th Street and Lenox Avenue, was one of the most famous, most frantic intersections in black America—the Times Square of Harlem. It was across 110th Street, and as close to the center of black America as any place in the country. And it had its own Muslim mosque— one of the dozen or so in the city of New York.

The mosque at 102 West 116th Street was quite a special building. It was a gleaming, modern monument to black consciousness; though, of course, it meant nothing to whites, any more than St. Patrick's Cathedral on Fifth Avenue and 50th Street meant a whole lot to black Muslims.

The tragedy was that the 10-13 call was a cruel hoax. And it resulted in the death of a police officer—and the near demise of a cease-fire spirit that had existed between blacks and whites in New York despite the continuing unjust economic gap between the races.

Two New York police officers responded to the 10-13. Evidently they rushed into the Muslim house of worship wearing their guns. Before long one of the officers lay bleeding on the floor, shot twice; and the other, wounded, escaped and fled to the street.

The details of the incident remain in contention. But, from all appearances, one of two things happened. Either the officers were shot with their own pistols, taken from them in the scuffle with Muslims inside. Or some of the faithful inside were living in sin—toting a forbidden rod while bowing to Allah. Just possibly.

Whatever the actual sequence of events, two officers were shot, and now there was a real 10-13 on our hands.

Within minutes dozens of radio cars surrounded the mosque. Officers leaped out of the cars, some with revolvers drawn. An ambulance screeched forward. The corner of 116th and Lenox, ordinarily not the quietest, least-populated place in the world, suddenly became a human anthill. It wasn't quite yet a riot situation—certainly nothing as widespread and out of control as Detroit or Newark in 1967—but it had every potential in the world for growth.

N.Y.P.D. personnel—there was only one notable exception, to be discussed later—behaved with commendable restraint. Although two officers had been shot, no officer sought revenge on the spot. (One, tragically, died later at the hospital.) The department's true colors were showing. Although the N.Y.P.D., like other forces, had perhaps benefited from the Airlie House conference, it also enjoyed a special tradition of restraint in the use of weapons. The environment of the city, as well as the character of the department, was involved. With its high-density population and high-rise construction, New York City was no place to come out shooting.* In addition, the N.Y.P.D. had compiled a considerable and astonishingly creditable history of handling crowds, demonstrations, strikes, protests, and so forth.

Even in this instance, the department could hardly be faulted for overreacting *after* the initial sequence of events. Where we were on trickier ground was over that initial sequence. It was here that the minister Louis Farrakhan had a point, unfortunately.

That morning the minister was ushered into my office accompanied by aides. The advance intelligence memo on the minister was that he was smart.

---

* Also, beginning in the late 1950s, when Bill McCarthy, now a deputy commissioner, upon promotion to captain took over firearms training, a heavy emphasis had been placed on the moral responsibility of officers in using firearms and the need for restraint. Since 1971, when the training was strengthened further, the results have been impressive and reassuring.

He didn't have to be brilliant to know that he had us over the barrel. That was what made me uncomfortable, what had made it impossible to deny the minister's request for an interview.

The previous Friday, at the mosque, Farrakhan had shown himself to be anything but a rabble-rouser, had in fact worked skillfully at the scene as a force of restraint, attempting to quiet the crowd, to remove the venom from the ugliness.

Farrakhan moved in my office as an obvious master of indirection, speaking in tones of deep resonance and clear conviction. He looked you straight in the eye, but then would quickly focus elsewhere in the room. There was a cold menace in his voice, but his larger style was not entirely confrontational.

My aides sat in chairs arrayed against one wall. The minister and his party took up positions near the opposite wall, on which hung the portrait of T.R. I remembered that the former New York Police Commisioner's solgan was "Speak softly and carry a big stick." That seemed like good advice now.

I rose from behind my desk, bringing my chair with me, and put it down next to Farrakhan. I was the gentleman, trying to reason.

Finally, Farrakhan spoke directly, powerfully, to the central point. This was his ace card. He played it casually, like a cool-tempered poker player with a large pot in front of him; but everyone in the room knew that it was coming.

Chief Inspector Michael Codd saw Farrakhan's gambit coming and now seemed perhaps even more depressed about the initial sequence of events than the rest of us. Codd, though not an innovator by temperament or a planner by conviction, was, to be sure, a professional police officer, and it irritated him enormously to be put in this position.

The secret of the mosque incident was this: prior to my returning to New York as Commissioner, a detailed agreement had been reached between Muslim ministers and police commanders with mosques in their precincts. This detailed agreement provided that mosques be accorded treatment as "sensitive locations," by police officers. Part of the agreed treatment was that police officers would not rush into a mosque with guns. Like scores of other "sensitive locations," as we called them, a mosque was a special situation.

Under the Muslim religion, guns were forbidden in the mosque.

The agreement between the N.Y.P.D. and the ministers had initially been hammered out several years before; indeed, when Mike Codd was then Brooklyn North borough commander. It was a clear, unequivocal, sensible agreement. And we had violated it.

Our violation, however, did not arise out of racism. Or being trigger-happy. Or corruption. Or even police brutality. It wasn't anything commissions investigate or newspapers much write about. But what was missing that Friday noon struck at the core of the problem with the N.Y.P.D. The core was very weak management; under better managerial control, every officer in the Twenty-sixth and Twenty-eighth precincts (Harlem) would have been reminded about that standing order on a regular basis.

In the N.Y.P.D. there were literally thousands of standing orders. These were special instructions to the troops, issued usually over the signature of the Chief Inspector or one of his commanders. They dealt with exceptions to rules, new rules, advice on "sensitive locations." A sensitive location was a place where the ordinary rules of procedure did not apply. A sensitive location was a Harlem mosque.

Under the ordinary rules, a 10-13 is a 10-13, no holds barred. But a 10-13 response at a sensitive location required a special procedure. Such special treatment was advisable even without a special standing order because of the vicious nature of the 10-13 call. The truth was that many such calls were phony.

As was this one. It had been made by a vicious, mean, deranged individual. And because our police officers had violated the agreement with the Muslim ministers in responding at the sensitive location as if no special standing order existed, a very tricky situation had developed. And, of course, it was precisely this sort of ugliness that the special standing order was designed to avoid. A department with better management (and here I am admitting that even after eighteen months of the reform the department was still far from up to snuff) would have hammered this standing order home to the officers in every precinct where there was a mosque.

There weren't many officers in the department, however, sympathetic to Farrakhan's point of view. They felt that whoever shot at the officers should have been strung up on the spot. Only Codd and Benjamin Ward, the Deputy Commissioner for Community Relations, notably, saw the other side of the story. They saw that from the

Muslim point of view, once an agreement had been worked out, even though years ago, in their minds it was as alive and valid as if it had been negotiated the day before.

This was Farrakhan's most valid point. It was this that he was now pressing on me with great force. I wish that there had been no standing order. I wish that Mike Codd had not told me *after* but *before* the incident about the special order. It seemed, at least in retrospect, something that we should have pounded away at in precinct briefing after briefing. But when Codd had come up to me later that Friday with the admission "Boss, I think there's something you should know," I realized that an officer had been killed and another wounded very possibly because of the weak management which would take so long to correct. I felt very helpless.

And so, in the privacy of the Office of the Police Commissioner, I looked Louis Farrakhan straight in the eye and admitted to the blunder: that there had been a secret agreement, known technically as a standing order, that the officers in forcing their way into his mosque with guns drawn had violated that pact.

Farrakhan pressed me on several other points—to remove all white officers from Harlem assignments, to admit publicly to the existence of the standing order—but he shortly saw that there was no give. I had gone as far as I could go, was going to go.

Then, to my astonishment, Farrakhan looked at me as though he understood, could feel what we had been going through, and man-to-man would not push us any further. He stood up, shook my hand, thanked me for the admission of the mistake, and took leave.

I had expected to be browbeaten. In the past there had been very few black leaders, even radical ones, with whom I could not establish some sort of rapport. But I had not expected Farrakhan to be one of them. I could not have been more wrong.

Perhaps the minister understood intuitively that it was just not possible to apologize in public. The officers, after all, had been responding to a 10-13. Although in public the minister had said that the 10-13 was merely a pretext for troublemaking by racist white cops, he probably knew better, knew in his heart that the officers responded instinctively, protectively. At the same time, he knew we had broken our promise, and that his people were entitled to just that admission and apology from the Police Commissioner.

Later, Chief Inspector Codd described the black Muslim leader as a charismatic man, urbane, intelligent. I would have added that he also struck me as a black leader who didn't want a riot in Harlem any more than we did.

After the shooting at the mosque, one of the responding officers was taken directly by ambulance to St. Luke's Hospital in serious condition.

Mayor Lindsay and I went to the hospital to observe the ritual of standing outside the hospital room showing our respect and concern. Lindsay looked terrible, and my own face probably looked as drawn. This was to be the thirteenth cop shot and killed in the last twelve months, the sixteenth in my administration. Each one became exponentially more difficult to take.

The Mayor was also concerned, naturally, about the situation back at the mosque. In a crowded place like Harlem, with all the different tensions at work, even with the police trying to do a good job of community relations, one of these things can blow up and get out of hand, and in a matter of minutes years of good and hard work go up in smoke. At a time like this, one way to defuse the situation was not to overreact: hysteria about what might happen could become a self-fulfilling prophecy.

Lindsay feared cops, did not trust them. Ever since the 1966 civilian review board defeat, his attitude toward the N.Y.P.D. had been highly ambivalent. On the one hand, he budgeted more money, approved more capital projects for the police than any previous mayor. But on the other hand, he was uneasy around cops, worried. Now, in the wake of the mosque incident, he felt that the chickens had come home to roost. He saw the Police Department undoing years of hard work in black relations with just one dumb move.

I was not as worried. Although I did not know at this time of the secret agreement (the Chief Inspector was to tell me only later), I had basic confidence in the officers of the N.Y.P.D. as regards street-smart restraint. They would make mistakes, but they were not idiotic, not by any means. And as far as the use of force went against blacks and radicals, the N.Y.P.D. was not a shoot-first, ask-questions-later police department.

But at the very moment that the Mayor's attitude about the

N.Y.P.D. and the mosque situation was tense and troubled, Deputy Commissioner Robert Daley arrived at the hospital.

Bob came running down the hall; to me he looked like an escapee from a psycho ward. His eyes were bulging, he was shouting in a high-pitched, almost soprano voice. "There's a riot out there, don't you know that?" he kept saying over and over again. He shouted that so many times that traffic seemed to stop in the hospital corridor and people began to stare at him.

As I mentioned, the Mayor had some time ago resigned his charter membership in the Robert Daley fan club, but now he really turned on the Public Information Commissioner.

Both men were taller than I, but as a patrolman in the tough Red Hook section of Brooklyn once, I had separated combatants bigger and rougher than these. Lindsay kept bearing down on the deputy commissioner like a prosecutor in utterly contemptuous cross-examination of a defense witness: How do you know it's a riot? How can it be a riot if it's under control?

Daley's answers were a gush of confused emotion: I was there on the street; you weren't. But he was weak, stunned, out of control. Nurses and orderlies began to give us hard looks. If it had been anyone other than the Mayor, the Police Commissioner, and some shouting aide in the corridor, we might have been asked to leave. I was embarrassed.

Suddenly Lindsay walked away enraged down the corridor, trying to cool off. He shot me a look from a doorway down the hall but I avoided his eyes. I was the only person who for these past few months had been defending the press commissioner.

Over the next few days Daley compounded the irritation. He kept pressing me to issue a full N.Y.P.D. statement on the mosque incident. For reasons which should now seem obvious, to issue such a statement would have been provocative to say the least. I did not wish to admit publicly the violation of the standing order; but I did not wish to throw gasoline on the flames by coming out with a version of events which if it did not reveal all would have been unfair to Harlem. We were caught, quite simply, on a tightrope; and at a time when a bit of soft-shoe tiptoeing would have been prudent, Bob wanted to stage a big production number.

And so it was for such reasons that the best press commissioner the N.Y.P.D. ever had was soon to leave our midst.

Shortly after the dust cleared, James Markham of the *Times* ran a story which began, "Police Commissioner Patrick V. Murphy yesterday defended the action of policemen at the Black Muslim Mosque Friday. The police went to the mosque, he said, after a caller, who falsely identified himself as 'Detective Thomas of the 28th Precinct,' reported an officer was in trouble on the building's second floor."

Shortly after that call, a deputy inspector in charge of the Twenty-eighth Precinct resigned. In a statement to the press, he criticized me for not defending the officers.

I wondered whether the deputy inspector had been reading the same newspapers as those carrying stories in which I was accused of excusing a racist attack.

The second moral to the story was of a phoenix rising from the ashes. The severe embarrassment of the mosque incident actually paved the way for the most sensational operational triumph of the reform administration. For without the ineptitude of the mosque operation, we probably would not have been as well prepared to handle the Williamsburg sporting-goods-store shootout as we were.

The incident took place in January of 1973, a few months before I resigned as N.Y.P.D. Commissioner and went to Washington as head of the Police Foundation. It began on a Friday night and ended on a Sunday afternoon. At stake were the lives of some dozen citizens being held hostage at gunpoint by robbers and/or revolutionaries inside a Brooklyn sporting goods store. Three policemen, by the time I had arrived on the scene, had already been shot, and as the store was surrounded by special police anti-sniper teams and special armored-car equipment, the scene began to look less like a depressed community in Brooklyn than a war zone.

Only exceptional police work by the N.Y.P.D. kept the situation from getting out of control. There was no L.A.P.D.–S.L.A. shootout scene here. We simply waited them out. Once we established that the lives of the hostages were not being endangered by the waiting game, hell could freeze over before we were going to charge the store à la a

John Wayne posse to bring the thing to some conclusion once and for all.

We waited through Friday night, all day Saturday, and most of Sunday. In the end all the hostages escaped without injury, and every one of the gunmen was captured, also without further injury to either the criminals or to police officers.

The key was police restraint. At any time we could have blown away the building, or done something to jeopardize the lives of the hostages. We had not done so, for in the back of all our minds, in addition to the special hostage training course we had all taken recently at the Police Academy, was the desire not to repeat a Harlem mosque performance.

Chapter Seven

The Detective
Mystique

In my era, Albert A. Seedman was the most famous detective in the New York Police Department, a virtual character out of a Raymond Chandler novel. An aura and a reputation surrounded him that would later be fictionalized, in a fashion, in the television series *Kojak*. Seedman and I went back a long way, to the days when we were both instructors at the Police Academy. I did not know him well, that is as a close friend, but I believed that I understood him better than most. Because despite the school-of-hard-knocks air which he carried proudly, like a war decoration, there was another dimension to Detective Commander Seedman of Manhattan South. He was, actually, a first-rate administrator of detectives who could crack the whip while still remaining one of the boys. With these qualities, then, Seedman was the best man for what would prove a difficult and sometimes ugly job: the reorganization of the N.Y.P.D.'s famous Detective Bureau, and the redefinition of the very concept of the police detective.

An important part of any sizable police department was the detective bureau. But it was often important for reasons which were not exactly well advertised. Two hushed-up propositions, known to many police administrators, were involved. One was that in almost any police department the worst corruption might very well be located in the detective bureau. A second was that for all their splash, panache, and uncanny ability to make headlines and friends, especially in the press corps, detectives tended to make an arguably insignificant contribution to the control of crime.

The second proposition even more than the first was caused by poor organization and poor management of detective work—rather than individual venality or incompetence. But poor management was a tradition at the N.Y.P.D., so that by the 1970s the Detective Bureau was a scary skeleton in the closet of the department. Everyone in the newly reorganized high command feared the consequences if ever that closet door were opened. Now a competent investigatory commission was knocking at the door.*

For decades the Detective Bureau had gone its own way, lived by its own rules. The Chief of Detectives had rarely had to answer to the Police Commissioner, the civilian head of the force. Only on a neat organizational chart was the Detective Bureau a province of the larger jungle that was the N.Y.P.D. In reality the bureau was an independent breakaway entity, with its own laws, customs, and marching orders. From the reform's point of view, accountability meant nothing to the detectives if they only had to answer to their consciences.

In essence, the textbook understanding of the modern big-city detective was in error. The actual number of cases solved, studies would show, was suspiciously low. The average working day of the average detective was spent either behind his desk with paperwork or at a bar, either shaking down the owner or planted on a bar stool listening for "information." This generalization wasn't, to be sure, true of every detective in every department in the country or in New York; but the image had so overshadowed the reality that the generalization was far more likely to be correct than most citizens realized.

Left to its own devices, the mighty Detective Bureau would continue to plague the reform by remaining outside of it. What was at stake was more than the outcome of a serious power struggle between the new reform administration, and the old bureau; at stake too was the entire principle of accountability, which logically was defective to the extent that any part of the institution escaped its ethic.

The ultimate logic of accountability rested with the people of the

---

* From the outset, we were faced with the question of whether to cooperate fully with the investigatory commission. We could open our files, make certain discreet transfers of personnel for the purposes of its investigations, cover their operatives as necessary, or, on the other hand, refuse to have anything to do with its staff. Interestingly, a few years later the Philadelphia P.D., confronted with a similar situation, flatly refused to cooperate. But we did the right thing. We helped, all the way.

city. Were the detectives a law unto themselves? Could they do what they wanted—à la Watergate—without the concern that their actions might be reviewed? Or were they a unit of government, and as such responsible to the people?

It was frustrating to have to deal with the reality of the big-city detective against the grain of the image created in the minds of the people. In no area of police work was there more difference between image and reality than in detective work. Thus, to attack this runaway institution, I felt some headway had to be made against the mystique of the institution as well as its organization.

The mystique was promoted by the popular entertainments of our time. The image of the detective working his leads, dusting for prints, pumping informants, hitting the case from every angle until it cracked, was a pretty picture, but it was also an unforgivably misleading one. For the citizen concerned about what the Police Department was doing about crime, probably this is a good place to set the record straight.

Our Crime Analysis people were asked to do some homework on the Detective Bureau's batting average. Specifically, what percentage of crimes referred to the bureau were actually being "cleared"? The study went back to the first six months of 1967 (you go that far back to give the bureau enough time). The results were devastating. The clearance rate* for robberies was 5.58 percent. The clearance rate for burglaries was 1.85 percent. The clearance rate for grand larcenies was 2.2 percent. Remember that these were *clearance* rates. Who knew how low the *conviction* rates would be. (Many cases were still tied up in court, so final figures were not available.)

To enlightened police chiefs and administrators around the country, such figures would not have been surprising. The ineffectiveness of big-city detectives has for a long time been one of the better-kept secrets in American policing.

Indeed, it was not until some years later, with the publication of a

---

* The "clearance" rate is a technical police term. Because of the vicissitudes of the court system, and problems peculiar to prosecution, not all crimes which the police believe they have solved are so regarded by the rest of the criminal justice system. The clearance rate, then, refers only to the percentage of crimes which, as far as the police are concerned, are "solved."

provocative Rand Corporation study, that the myth of the detective was to be fully documented. This 1976 study (which I wish I had had in 1971, as further ammunition for the points I was trying to make about detective effectiveness) was based on an extensive examination of twenty-five major police departments in the United States, and supplemented by information from 156 municipal and county law enforcement agencies.

The Rand study went to the heart of the nature of reported crime and the nature of the investigatory process. Both are poorly understood, even by otherwise informed observers. The Rand study demonstrated that on those rare occasions when detectives are credited with solving, i.e., clearing, a crime, the special detective process was practically irrelevant. Most serious crimes were solved through information obtained from the victim or the witness, not through leads developed independently by detectives. In more than half the solved cases studied nationally, the suspect's identity was known or readily determinable at the time the crime was reported to police.

These conclusions did not square with the underlying rationale for separate detective bureaus: that there is an important difference between *detective* work and all other police work, and hence the need for a separate bureau. On the contrary, the Rand study in digging further found that the detective bureaus tended to be so poorly organized that it was remarkable that as many crimes were solved by them as there were. One finding was that less than half of the felonies reported to these twenty-five detective bureaus around the country were actually worked on. Aside from banner-headline crimes like rape, kidnapping, and murder, most serious crimes reported to detectives were actually accorded "no more attention than the reading of the initial incident report." Indeed, the majority of investigated cases received less than one day's attention.

The Rand study in 1976 also questioned the detective's choice of cases to work on, suggesting that much of the detective's time seemed to be consumed with cases that from the outset were unlikely to be solved. Digging further, the Rand study suggested that some cases appeared to have been pursued only because of their notoriety, with fingerprint dusting, mug-shot showing, and witness questioning performed largely to satisfy victims' or reporters' expectations. There was, the study seemed to be suggesting, an element of public relations, if not of show-biz, in the performance of detectives.

All in all, the Rand study—on whose board sat such citizens as Cyrus Vance, Joseph Califano, and Brock Adams—would prove troubling. Hidden behind a mystique, detectives in big-city police departments throughout the country have become the victims of their own self-deception. For the management of police departments in America, the end recommendations were clear enough. "The effectiveness of criminal investigations," the Rand report concluded, "would not be unduly lessened if approximately half of the investigative effort were eliminated or shifted to more productive uses." In the report's covering statement, Gerald M. Caplan, the Director of the National Institute of Law Enforcement and Criminal Justice (which funded the Rand study), said, "We now know that the work of the detective need not be viewed as an art form that is not amenable to advanced management practices."

The truth about detectives is that, taken as a whole, they are not likely to be effective police officers. There is more featherbedding in the average detective bureau than in some construction gangs. There were, of course, always notable exceptions, but as a general rule crimes were solved not by detectives but by ordinary patrol officers.* Precinct police officers were usually the ones to identify the eyewitnesses and the victims. Most criminal cases never progressed beyond this state of knowledge. Cases that could not be cleared on the basis of the original set of facts were likely not to be cleared at all. In reality, the vast majority of a department's "detective" work was being performed by patrol officers in the normal course of their duty.

* Other conclusions of the Rand study:

1. In cases where the suspect was not immediately identifiable, routine police work, rather than the "imaginative exercise of investigative experience," led to the clearance.

2. Most departments collect more physical evidence than they can possibly process.

3. In cases where the suspect is identified, an investigator spends more time in post-clearance administrative processing than in identifying the offender.

4. Differences in investigative training, staffing, organization, workload, and procedures do not appear to affect crime, arrest, or clearance rates.

5. Most departments fall short of thoroughly documenting key evidence a prosecutor needs to obtain a conviction. This failure may contribute to a higher dismissal rate and a weakening of the prosecutor's plea bargaining position.

The mystique to the contrary is fueled by a constant glittering public relations job that takes up such a large part of the average day in the life of an ambitious detective. To the public generally, the detective is the brains of the outfit, and it is not until his arrival at the scene, and the shuffling off of the uniformed officers, that the real hard-core work of detection begins. In reality, of course, the real police workers had just walked out the door.

To the police officer, nothing is quite so much an inside joke as the dusting for prints. The number of cases cleared on the basis of "latents" is so minuscule that some cops at the sight of dusting have all they can do to keep from breaking into gales of laughter. But the dusting and the bar hopping for "information" are all part of the glittering ritual—or, at best, the longest of long shots.

In truth, a detective bureau of a big-city police department is a place where often little police work is done. Too many factors stand in the way. And many are beyond anyone's control, but not all.

The minds of our detectives often wander far from the reservation. The ambitious ones might be bar hopping with reporters, politicians, or judges; the shakedown artists, bar hopping too, might be "shopping"; the lazier ones could be glued to a bar stool ostensibly picking up "information." The real characters, known in the locker rooms as "sock peddlers," would be on the prowl for "discounts" for the boys. Some of the minor crimes besetting the city were sadly of the bureau's own making.

None of this was new stuff. The Leary administration did not invent it. No one can speak honestly of totally eliminating detective corruption. The perpetrators were, after all, conversant with the techniques of insulation and co-optation and even of the benefit of isolated scoring. Hypocrisy was the suggestion that any police commissioner could move in and clean it *all* up.

But with five years in office, the Leary administration might have made a more substantial effort to control it. Chief of Detectives Fred Lussen, like too many police managers in the United States, was a traditionalist accepting the same old unevaluated methods: "What's the problem? This is the way we've always done it." Commanders like Lussen had little trouble surviving, because neither police chiefs, mayors, nor city managers had the sense to hold their detective bureaus to some sensible standard of performance. One set of standards applied to patrol officers; no set of standards to detectives.*

Chief Lussen had an additional liability as far as I was concerned. He was aggressively powerful, so powerful that the previous administration had difficulty controlling his bureau. He allied himself firmly with Sanford Garelik when he was Chief Inspector. The alliance permitted Lussen the leverage virtually to ignore Commissioner Leary. It was leverage not infrequently used. Now that Garelik, retired from the department, was president of the City Council, reforming the Detective Bureau while Lussen headed it seemed an impossibility. I might get ulcers, and he would be happier than ever, having frustrated another P.C.

He was also one of the top commanders of a previous administration that had not covered itself with glory. If my hunch was right, that administration would come close to being destroyed by the Knapp Commission. I already had enough evidence to convince me that Lussen's Narcotics Division could be exposed in dramatic fashion as a viper's nest of corruption of the worst kind.

The almost invisible traditional corruption of the bureau would perhaps also be exposed. I recalled what a wise Internal Affairs commander had once told me: "Corrupt plainclothesmen have the money shoved in their pockets. Corrupt detectives squeeze it out of their victims."

Lussen—whose own honesty had never been questioned—was a terrible liability, but I needed time before picking a successor. During his honeymoon period a new P.C. can change the types of personnel that become less removable with each passing day. Each day you keep one is another day in which it is assumed that you consider him or her satisfactory.

It took several patient conversations to convince Lussen that, despite his sincerest beliefs, he was not indispensable.

---

* Performance standards for detectives were virtually nonexistent, since it was not entirely clear or resolved what exactly could justify a special bureau, if what the bureau was involved in differed in no essential respect from what the entire department was charged with, i.e., crime service. This criticism did not apply to the various *Headquarters* detective units, which specialized in, for example, such crimes as security frauds and theft, art theft, bank robberies, homicides, and so on. These were valuable units, but accounted for only a tiny fraction of the bureau's manpower.

A few days after the Chief put in for retirement, one of the papers ran an item on Al Seedman, detective commander of Manhattan South. (This is the area of Manhattan most tourists are familiar with: the big hotels, the Empire State Building, the nightclubs, the U.N., Times Square.) The story was that Seedman was the overwhelming favorite to head the bureau, and that would put him in charge of the department's three thousand or so detectives—including such exotic units as the various Headquarters detective squads like the Bureau of Special Services (subversion, dignitary protection, labor disputes, and sensitive investigations), the Safe, Loft, and Truck Squad, the Wall Street Unit, and many others—not to mention line authority over every detective in every corner of the city. In short, the newspaper gossip was that Seedman was about to become one of the most prominent and powerful government officials in New York.

At about this time among the business appointments on my calendar was a series of breakfasts with Whitman Knapp and Michael Armstrong, the Chairman and the Chief Counsel, respectively, of the Knapp Commission. The breakfasts were highly confidential, with no report given out to the press; only a handful of top aides at Headquarters were aware of the nature of the talks.

They were held at the Yale Club, of which both Knapp and Armstrong, I believe, were members, and they tended to last an hour or two at a time.

The purpose of these meetings, initiated at the suggestion of Knapp and Armstrong, was never entirely clear. My best guess was that they were to symbolize a certain clubbiness and an above-partisanship alliance against police corruption. They also symbolized, it seemed to me, confidence in the new police administration, i.e., that we were on the *same* side.

Armstrong and Knapp talking about police corruption were like young boys under a Christmas tree stealing a peek before Mommy and Daddy got up. This was understandable. They were newcomers. The world of cops and robbers was exciting to them. Courses in shakedowns and narcotics pads weren't listed as electives in the Yale college catalogue. One doubted that plainclothes officers were regular lecturers at the Yale Club library. It was so terribly exciting.

I put up with these breakfasts for several reasons. One was that I desperately needed the Knapp Commission. I needed them to put the fear of the Lord into the lower and middle ranks of the department that were protected by civil service from the Commissioner; I could handle, I hoped, those officers above the rank of captain. And I needed one other thing: that little line at the bottom of every one of their press releases which stated that the N.Y.P.D. had cooperated with their investigation.

This was why we cooperated with the Knapp staff, why we gave them just about everything they asked for. Up to a point, the Knapp probe was essential to the reform. Both inside and outside pressures were needed. The very existence of the Knapp effort reduced in Headquarters and in the precincts the strength of the case *against* Murphy; because they could see my reform moves as necessary: "He's got Knapp . . ."

I did not care what motive the officers attributed to me; all I cared about was that they changed their behavior. I did not worry that many would come to resent the reform and even have strong feelings of animosity for me personally. If I had wanted to win a popularity contest, I would not have taken the job; I might have stayed in Detroit, made the Detroit P.D. into the best municipal police department in America, and died rooting for the Detroit Pistons, Lions, and Tigers.

Thus I was in secret league with the Knapp Commission; I was using them as they were using me.

At one breakfast, Armstrong raised the question of Seedman. "You're not going to make him Chief of Detectives, are you, Commissioner?"

Well, the answer was, of course, yes; but the bluntness of the question was most disconcerting, so I did not answer it.

We fenced about Seedman.

They had "heard" all about Seedman.

I asked for some particulars.

"Well," said Armstrong, "a little of this, a little of that."

"That's not enough," I said.

They raised the name of a prominent jeweler in the Midtown diamond exchange. He was also a prominent fence. Armstrong said he was a good "friend" of Seedman's. Armstrong delivered this to me as if informing me that my high command was loaded with transvestites. Armstrong and Knapp waited for my response. I thought the insinuation was a terrible injustice to Seedman.

The truth was that there were rumors about Seedman—that he was this or that, that those diamond pinkie rings hadn't been purchased with Master Charge, that he knew this or that underworld character. But Seedman never seemed to care about these rumors; he still wore the diamond pinkie ring, and as far as I knew he still occasionally had a conversation with this, that, or the other underworld figure. The reason that he made so little effort to hide these little failures of judgment was that there was nothing else there; it was a case of less than met the eye. The rumors were nothing more than that—rumors. During Seedman's long career in the department he had not once been charged with, much less convicted of, the slightest offense. But if you were a novice and you waded into the N.Y.P.D. grapevine, you'd hear before the first hour was out this or that rumor about Seedman—all unsubstantiated, and in my opinion untrue.

Finally I told Armstrong that, yes, I was thinking of making Seedman Chief of Detectives. I even told him the true reason: Seedman was the only man in the bureau with the stature and savvy to finesse the massive changes I wanted to make in the bureau.

Armstrong and Knapp stared at me with mouths wide open.

Often I left the Yale Club wondering how much more they really knew about Seedman that they were keeping from me. Certainly for the corruption investigators the Detective Bureau had to be proving a rich hunting ground. Poorly supervised, ripe with opportunities, the bureau, the plainclothes units, and the Narcotics Division were real problems areas in the N.Y.P.D.—as they were in many big-city police departments. The Knapp Commission, under Armstrong's guidance, would have to be totally incompetent to miss all the bodies buried there. But was Seedman one of them?

I knew where the newspapers had gotten their story about the probable selection of Seedman as Chief of Detectives. Not long ago we had had lunch. Al was entitled to it, not just as the bureau's most famous and flamboyant detective but as a longtime colleague from the days when we were instructors at the Police Academy.

The lunch provided considerable grist for the N.Y.P.D. rumor mill. Nothing that happens at the level of the P.C.'s office can be permitted to remain in its proper perspective. Instead it must be polished and blown up into a hugely attractive rumor masquerading as inside dope. Then the rumor hits the papers. The rest of the week is spent denying it.

The rumor mill got a lot of mileage out of that one lunch with Seedman. Like the seating arrangement on the reviewing stand at Red Square in Moscow on May Day, the P.C.'s luncheon bookings were closely watched for what they might reveal about the P.C.'s intentions. And so when I lunched with Detective Commander Seedman, we just about brought Headquarters operations to a stop.

The rumor mill, conversely, offered certain advantages. The astute P.C. could tap out all sorts of messages, over great distances, reaching the farthest Queens precinct, simply by virtue of whom he had lunch with, whom he spent more than ten minutes with in his office (through the peephole the rumor carriers could catch a look at whoever was entertaining the P.C.), who was or was not asked to attend this or that hush-hush meeting.

As with the Seedman luncheon, the reality was both less and more than met the eye. We did discuss the vacant Chief of Detectives spot toward the end of the luncheon when Seedman could no longer contain himself; but he was promised nothing. I suppose he was teased unmercifully. I explained that I wanted someone at a high level to reorganize the department's training programs; and when Al realized it was only this that I was immediately offering, he almost, I think, died. But I doggedly and truthfully explained that training, like planning, was one of those functions that was more than a frill, and in troubled times was actually of great importance.

Are our officers trained professionally for hostage crises? (No.) What about small-scale street demonstrations? What is the full range of our options? How about detective training? Is it sufficiently job-related? (Some, not all.) Have we adequately trained the detective supervisors and commanders? (No.) Have we convinced the bosses to use training and reject the notion that the Police Academy has the total responsibility in this area? (Absolutely not.) Can we assume field commanders know how to use training to raise ethical standards? (No.) What about our rookies? Are we throwing them to the wind? (Yes.) Are we putting them at the mercy of the craven old-timers? (Yes.)

My task was therefore to convince Seedman that being in charge of training for the department—*all* training—was not entirely the same thing as being made a vice president in a corporation and being given responsibility for paper clips. At the same time, I mentioned as casually as I could that the position of Chief of Detectives would remain vacant until Seedman's temporary assignment with training had been completed to my satisfaction, and until I'd had enough time to consider the choices.

"What sort of person do you have in mind, Commissioner," asked Seedman, eyes glistening.

I explained that I was troubled by the organization of the Detective Bureau. We were still operating in the old manner, with hardly the slightest justification for the status quo either in our success in clearing cases, or in the effectiveness of our deployment of manpower. I suggested that the heart of the problem could be in the system by which detectives were assigned cases.

Seedman stirred. The cigar began to wag nervously out of the corner of his mouth. "Yeah, they catch squeals," he said.

This was detective parlance for the process of case assignment. It worked this way. The detectives sit in the detective squad room waiting for the phone to ring. A woman rings up; her cat was stolen. This was a squeal. Whoever was "up" caught the case. Say it's Detective Seedman's turn. The phone rings, and whoever it is or whatever it is, Seedman gets the case. The detectives take turns answering the phone like batters in a lineup awaiting their turn at the plate. Whether or not the case is important, it is assigned to a detective not by any rational process but by the luck of the draw.

The system was silly. Even baseball managers arrange their players into some sort of lineup to maximize offense, and they assign their players different positions in the infield and outfield to maximize defense. So our detective work wasn't even as "scientific" as baseball. At least a manager knew who the pitcher was and who was going to bat against which pitchers in what order. Nothing so rational or considered was built into, as Seedman put it, the squeal system of the N.Y.P.D.

The antidote for this silliness was a system in which one lined up the appropriate players for the appropriate pitches: a system of detective specialization. In this system, developed many years ago in other departments and widely deployed in the larger police agencies by

1970, certain types of cases would be handed over to detectives with specialized knowledge of the type of criminal activity involved.

"I like the specialization idea, Al," I said, adding that we could divide up the detectives not into precinct squads but into specialized units—detectives for homicide and sex crimes, for robbery, for assault, for burglary-larceny.

"Yeah," said Al, chomping furiously now on the cigar. "They have something like that in the Bronx."

Seedman was referring to a pilot program begun under the previous administration. "Right, Al, but I was thinking of going a little further than the Bronx. You know, the whole route."

Seedman's eyes widened. The cigar did not quite drop from his mouth. "That'd be," he said, "staggering."

"Well, maybe *you* could look into that while you're in charge of training. We need someone with your experience to check out the possibilities. We don't want to go into this thing half-cocked."

Al's cigar was momentarily motionless. He was feeling the air to see if he had heard right. And he had. The route to being Chief of Detectives had now been mapped out.

"Sure, boss," he said, "I'll look into it right away."

I smiled, he smiled. The outline of a deal had been tendered.

But the specifics of the deal would not yet be spelled out. Seedman could not yet sense the totality of the reorganization because, purposely, I had remained vague about details. At the moment we were only in the "experimental" stage, looking to develop the possibilities of reorganizing the detectives along the lines of specialization.

The specialization concept was not a new one; it assumed that detective work, like medical work, was susceptible to improvement by the development of specialized fields of technical knowledge. If detective work was the "science" of removing from the community undesirable organisms, then different sorts of organisms could be treated by different types of specialists—detective specialists. It was simply a matter of deciding on the kinds of specialization to be represented in the bureau and dividing up the detectives according to ability and interest. This, as I saw it, would be Seedman's area of authority.

For myself, I was less interested in specialization per se than in the elimination of the precinct detective squads. For reasons which should become clearer later, I wanted desperately to get those detectives out of the precincts. This was what I was really aiming for.

What I had told Seedman, in effect, was that detective specialization was very important to me, that the person who could put the program all together would be the natural choice for the job of Chief of Detectives.

Some time later I suggested to Seedman that he visit a few detective bureaus around the country. I wanted the future Chief (though he did not yet feel he had it locked) to see detective specialization at work elsewhere and to open his eyes to the truth about the N.Y.P.D.—which was that, for all its sophistication, it was behind many other police departments in key respects.

In the back of my mind was the ultimate goal: the abolition of the seventy-six separate detective squads now housed in the precinct buildings and the substitution of specialized squads to cover the territory of one district—each district being considerably larger than the territory of one precinct, but not quite the size of an entire New York borough, with several districts, for example, in one Manhattan.

Detectives would be assigned to these specialized units (for example, burglary or robbery) and would work out of one central district office, with area-wide responsibility for the particular crime assigned.

At the same time, some of the bureau's squeals would be handled by the Patrol Bureau. In certain cases precinct officers would be responsible not only for preparing the initial on-scene reports but also for follow-up.

At first look, the reorganization seemed designed to give the bureau a break. Why soak up the detectives' time with uninteresting squeals? But in reality we were less concerned with the detectives than with the precinct officers. We wanted to give them a fair share of the department's more consequential work, as well as to blur the heretofore clear line of distinction between the detective and the beat cop or patrolcar cop.

In this reorganization, logic was clearly on our side. But what about the Detectives Association, the police union representing the gold shields? The union's response to the new concept might be cyclonic.

But would the union openly oppose a man like Seedman who had such popular support in the ranks? This was why we needed Seedman as Chief.

Resistance from police unions was traditionally an obstacle to reform. In my master's thesis on police unions, I wrote, "Police employe organizations have traditionally labored for higher pay, shorter hours and more liberal pensions. Promotion on the basis of seniority has been one of their consistent goals. . . . Organizations [like this] with significant strength gained through political alliances may have resisted efforts of administrators to rid their departments of corruption. Rather than promote high morale, they would, thereby, have hindered it. . . . The employe organizations have often cooperated with corrupt political forces."*

Every police chief with reform on his mind understands this. The relationship between police unions and anti-corruption chiefs was never symbiotic. And the unions knew how to drum up opposition—to plant stories damaging to the reform in the papers, to alert politicians that some due chits were coming up for collection, to scare off the Mayor, frighten the devil out of the Police Commissioner. These unions had political clout.

Seedman was conducting the business of "studying" the specialization idea with considerable skill, and I was impressed. Somehow he was managing to keep a step or two ahead of the Detectives Association. But there were others in the city tuned in on detective affairs, and they were powerful. The Police Commissioner might fiddle with the lives and careers of twenty thousand uniformed patrol officers, but if he looked the wrong way at the powerful Detective Bureau he could find himself in political trouble.

Big-city detectives as a whole were enormously resourceful. They had lines of communication out to all the important power centers: to the politicians, who controlled the budget; to the district attorneys, who controlled cases and headlines (and sometimes, if you let them, the Police Commissioner); and to the press corps, which in the city of New York was truly a power broker in police affairs.

And detectives would work assiduously to cultivate these relation-

*Patrick Vincent Murphy, *Police Employe Organizations*, Thesis for Master of Public Administration, College of the City of New York, 1960.

ships. They would spend more time bar hopping with reporters than working on cases. They would devote unbelievable man-hours to the D.A.'s pet case, one on which the D.A. might run for re-election, but they would deep-six hundreds of other cases that directly affected the lives of miserably uninfluential people. And should a judge's daughter get mugged on the way home from school, they would turn the city upside down and shake their informants to death until they got someone.

They were both resourceful and powerful. They would let these little favors pile up and then one day call the politicians, call the judges, call the reporters—and create their own political lobby.

The police commissioner who did not sniff the wind for detective counterinsurgency was living in an *Alice in Wonderland* world. I knew. During my career at Headquarters, when I was in charge of the Inspection Squad, I had the pleasure to observe, in awe, the consummate skill and relative ease with which detectives routinely outmaneuvered one police commissioner after the other.

I was not anxious to be numbered in that grand tradition. Yet the past could easily become prologue. Even now—as Seedman was out in the field reorganizing the bureau along specialized lines, presenting the specialization idea in soft-sell one-on-ones with detectives and their commanders—negative feedback was coming from City Hall. Lindsay's aides were raising "innocent" questions, "routine" queries. "Gee, Commissioner, about this specialization thing, I was wondering . . ."

The questions were obviously inspired. A City Hall aide, with the world on his mind, could not have had the time to so familiarize himself with the intricate internal workings of a big-city detective bureau to raise highly informed questions of fact and procedure about the reorganization. Obviously the aides were getting very competent briefings, from the only possible source, and they had probably fallen for the line.

It was not unusual, I knew, for otherwise mature and adult people to be captured by the mystique of the Detective Bureau. The world of the detective is, or seems to be, an adult fantasy world, a Disneyland of law enforcement. The gates open and one is inside an enchanted world, of "leads" and "informants" and "interrogations" and "poip-a-trait-uhs" and "blind alleys" and "breaks." Time and again I had watched outsiders come into contact with the detectives; and if they were assessed as being worth the time, they received the full "treatment" from the bureau.

For high City Hall aides, then, contact with the bureau must have been an irresistible, exotic excitement—practically a religious experience. And as with many recent converts, they could become avid proselytizers to whom it was difficult to say no. The very fact that City Hall had picked up on the program to institute controls over detectives illustrated the extent to which the bureau had become politically active, like a lobby.

So now the phones were ringing. Jay Kriegel was a Lindsay aide who had graduated from Amherst, one of the finest Eastern colleges, as well as Harvard Law School, and had drawn the assignment from the Mayor as principal liaison with the P.D. Kriegel was both bright and obtrusive. He had also been through, I suspected, the Detective Bureau's charm school. Fully programmed, he was now calling frequently "for information." Just to "check out" various "rumors." Of course such requests were nothing more than barely concealed rerouted queries from my friends in the bureau.

Under the previous police administration, City Hall aides like Kriegel may have enjoyed control over the operations of the department, at least at some consequential level; and perhaps they may even have made important management decisions normally the prerogative of the P.C. As much as civilian control over the police is mandatory in a democracy, direct internal intervention in the authorized business of a police department is not desirable, especially when a reform is being advertised. Either extreme—total independence from the political community, or total imprisonment—would inevitably be a political time bomb.

On one call Kriegel said bluntly, "Commissioner, what's going on with the Detective Bureau? You got some kind of revolution going on?"

Kriegel was very smart and had put his finger on what was happening, but exactly. "Yes, Jay," I said, "and this is a hot one. Do you think *we* can get away with it? Are these guys going to be trouble for *us*?"

My comeback gave the aide pause. I had put it in such a way as to raise the grave question of which side the Hall was actually on.

"Well, Commissioner," said the aide finally, "in my view you're off your rocker to mess with the bureau, but I suppose my chief gripe is that you haven't been keeping the Hall informed of what you're up to."

"Jay, this is a very hot one. I don't know whether the Mayor would really want to get close to it. He might get in trouble if he tries. Neither of us wants that. So perhaps we should keep the Mayor isolated from it, and let me go out on the limb. That way, if someone does try to saw the limb off, I'll be the one who takes the fall, not John."

There was a pause. Kriegel, who had a mind like a pocket calculator, was adding up the pluses and minuses, doing the long division.

Finally he said, "I don't see how it can work, Commissioner. There are too many bugs in this specialization business. Boy, you take these guys out of the precinct houses and you could be inviting disaster."

"Now, Jay, it's only an experiment. That's why we have it on an experimental basis, to locate the bugs. Then we can ditch the whole darn thing if we see that the experiment's not working."

Long silence.

"Okay, Commissioner."

To be sure, City Hall knew full well that the reorganization was much more than some study-group experiment. It was a systematic effort to reform the content and the style of big-city detective work. In addition, the very fact that Kriegel (who was very close to Lindsay) was calling meant that the detectives themselves had recognized what was at stake. Even Seedman continued to refer to the reorganization as "staggering." By describing the reorganization as an experiment, I was simply covering my tracks, seeking to throw the opposition off balance by implying impermanence, to give them jelly to hit rather than a solid, immovable target. Like those "temporary" buildings in Washington constructed during World War Two which lasted for decades, the "experiment" was designed to be a monument. I was as serious about the reorganization as anything in the reform; and if City Hall decided to cut me down on it—and they had the power—I knew I would resign.

But the issue had not been shaped into either-or. I had given the Hall a graceful exit. The Mayor was released from responsibility. It was Murphy's program. The Hall could put out the word, as far as I was concerned, that the Commissioner was flying on his own with the detective reorganization and that City Hall was being kept out of it.

Lindsay, it seemed to me, *should* stay out of the fray. There was nothing in it for him. He had gotten burned previously in reaching so deeply into the department. And why should he risk the resignation of a reform commissioner? Even more significantly, Lindsay had learned the hard way that police administration was a highly complex matter. If he really wanted a better police department—and I believe he was very sincere in this wish—he could only hope for the best from his new commissioner.

Of course, I kept my own doubts from the Mayor. I preferred his praise, often expressed in cabinet meetings in full view of other commissioners and aides, to fully disclosing the thin ice I was skating on.

I knew that without Lindsay behind me there was little hope of lasting long enough to make the changes. Because the more I fiddled with the various bureaus and divisions of the N.Y.P.D. the lonelier, emotionally and politically, I was becoming. (I also saw what could happen when you fell out of his favor. On several occasions I witnessed him after a cabinet meeting with his hand, literally, around some commissioner's throat. John was perhaps naive in certain respects, especially about cops, but he was no cream puff.)

Lindsay knew that the detectives had powerful allies around town. Cops in general, he believed, were unmanageable and unpredictable. But detectives? Who knew what they were capable of?

The "job action" was a momentary setback. It occurred, for my purposes, at a most inopportune time. Because of fundamental dissatisfaction with the basis on which their salary raises were set by city wage negotiators—it was known as the "parity" issue, by which the city's uniformed services were all tied up in one comprehensive and politically explosive formula more complicated than the fission equation for the atomic bomb—the N.Y.P.D.'s patrol officers one cold January day staged a semi-walkout. They would respond to emergencies, but they would not engage in the routine business of the department—walking or riding patrol, responding to non-emergency calls, taking crime reports. The job action, which came very close to being a genuine police strike, lasted through six days and nights of deep anxiety (it seemed more like six months), and during the ordeal, Detroit and Mayor Gribbs had never seemed more attractive.

As all sides went to the mat on the crisis, the Police Commissioner had to reach for all available manpower to maintain a police presence in the city. To this end, I had to enlist the three-thousand-man Detective Bureau. It had not joined in the labor protest. Would the detectives be willing to man patrol cars? They responded like Marines, and for six days, along with hundreds of brass who also went out on patrol, held the city's hand until the situation ran its course and things returned to normal.

But in the request for the extraordinary help of the detectives, I worried about owing them a big political debt. Would the price I would have to pay involve a delay of implementation of detective reorganization?

The city had to be policed at any price, but my hope was that the reorganization would not be the cost. After the dust from the job action settled, I called in Seedman, now fully installed as Chief of Detectives.

Seedman had his dream job, and he carried it well. He had made his pact with the devil, had gotten what he wanted; all I could hope was that he would not try to back out of the deal.

Seedman, as usual, was smoking a smelly cigar. He was wearing, as usual, an expensively tailored suit, the diamond ring, the cuff links, but he was smoking the cheap cigar. (The fact that Seedman always smoked a cheap cigar was curious. How would Mike Armstrong explain it? If he was making so much money under the table, why not a Royal Jamaican, or better yet a smuggled Havana?)

"You wanted to see me, boss?" said the new Chief, vaguely resplendent under a cloud of cigar smoke.

There was nothing about Seedman that did not exude confidence. The former detective commander of Manhattan South—it was one of the glamour jobs in American policing—had been proving that he was the best possible choice for the specialization reform. My goal was to have Al reposition the Detective Bureau under the umbrella of the Police Commissioner before the final Knapp report came out. As of July 1 of that year, all eleven Manhattan South precinct detective squads had been reorganized into four area-wide teams, one each for homicide-assault, robbery, sex crimes, and burglary.

Chief Seedman was now pushing the program throughout the city. His resiliency and persistence were the currency of the transaction. He was patient but tough with the troops. This was the program. This was what the Commissioner wanted. This was how it had to be. The tremendous effort hardly seemed to be taking a toll, but Al was a stoic.

Like all of us in the high command, the Chief had come up from the streets, through the hideous Depression and the ups and downs of a cop's life; but the scars were hidden, the wrinkles all smoothed out. His emotional requirements were fortunately limited. Unlike some aides, who seemed to need constant reassurance that the P.C. loved them, Chief Seedman asked nothing of me save that I deliver what I promised, which was to take upon myself any and all political static from the Hall on the reorganization. Which I was trying, desperately, to do.

At high-command conferences, Seedman took some pretty rough shots. By now the top echelon was filled up with commanders with Murphy-like reservations about the Detective Bureau. But Seedman never flinched or shared with any of us the bitter details of the struggle within the bureau to fight the reorganization. We might say something like "So-and-so must be giving you a hard time." Seedman, disdaining the opportunity to unburden himself, would respond, "Hey, this is a great commander out there. He really takes care of his squad; he never goes home."

In the back of my mind I'm thinking, Right, Chief, he never goes home because he's making too much money; or he's always at some bar gathering "information"; or out on the links with the judges or the D.A.'s.

Without the Knapp probe, I might not have been able to get a handle on the detectives. The specialization program, which was being advertised as a productivity measure, was also a cover for dealing with detective corruption. This was the part of the program that I had not emphasized to Seedman. When I first began discussing specialization, I got Seedman's commitment to a vague program; the specifics were not spelled out. I did not want to give Seedman the full sense of the project before becoming Chief, because I did not wish him to have the opportunity to state that he was taking the job with misgivings.

The specialization program was a deep cover for assaulting the territorial system of detective corruption. The root of the problem was actually precinct territoriality. The precinct system—and the lack of accountability—gave the corrupt detective too little work and too much time to engage in corruption. The opportunity for the shakedown artists to work over the merchants, the bar owners, and the restaurateurs in their turf was enormous. There was simply no check over it. In providing them with a small piece of turf, the department was maintaining ideal conditions for a manageable system of extortion.

The key to detective corruption was the imperative of the precinct territory. The profit motive, macho, the generalized climate of corruption, cynicism—these were all wrapped up in the corrupt behavior. To deal with the problem, we proposed to spread out the grafters over a larger territory—territory that would now have to be *shared* with several other teams of detective's, in that there were four sets of specialists per area. The goal was a breakup of the detective monopolies within the precinct.

Seedman was attracted to specialization for a variety of motives; none of them really had anything to do with anti-corruption. In this he was absolutely consistent. His justification for implementing specialization was grounded in the logic of fitting individual talents to individual problems. This made sense to that side of Seedman's intelligence that appreciated intellectual tidiness. The anti-corruption angle either did not occur to him, did not interest him, or was felt to be of minor consequence. Of the three interpretations, the second was one which one could document. A series of messages on the need for more action against corruption in the Detective Bureau seemed not to have stirred any interest among Seedman's corps, but no one could have expected otherwise. The Office of the Chief of Detectives could not possibly have generated much interest in the subject, because it was its position that in the Detective Bureau there was no corruption of significance.

Thus, the specialization program was ideally designed to address itself to the problem without speaking directly about it. As long as Seedman was 100 percent behind the specialization, the P.C. was 100 percent behind him. With detective specialization, a merchant or bar owner or restaurateur would now have to "know" not twenty detectives from the precinct squad but at least a hundred from the area-wide special units. In breaking down the exclusive precinct system, specialization made it more difficult for the detective to deliver protection (or whatever else was being bartered in exchange for the graft) to his "client," because he could no longer speak for the precinct detective squad; it no longer existed. And he could hardly speak for all four area-wide detective units. In broadening the territory at issue, specialization pulled the rug out from under the monopoly basis of corruption.

"Any problems, Al?" I asked the Chief, after we reviewed the areas of progress, like conquering commanders looking at a map of captured enemy territory.

"No, boss," he answered, exuding that old-school charm and confidence.

Seedman left the office, and I immediately buzzed special aide Peggy Triplett on the intercom: "Please find out when Chief Seedman is scheduled for vacation."

The reorganization of the bureau was an endlessly complex and serious matter, perhaps the most important single move of the reform. If successful, it would serve as a model to other police reformers around the country, demonstrating not only the importance of the effort but even more basically the fact that it might be done. Few knew outside of police circles the extent to which detective bureaus were feared by the average police administrator or the average mayor, or how little they had to do with crime control, or how much discretion they enjoyed over the management of their own affairs.

In the jargon of the bureau, the unpromising cases under the catch-a-squeal system were assigned to "Detective McCann," a mythical figure and stand-in for an actual detective. Detective McCann represented the wastebasket, i.e., trash *can*. If you ever had the experience of calling a detective squad to inquire about the status of a case which you felt was not moving along with sufficient speed, you might have been told that it had been assigned to Detective McCann, who would get back to you as soon as possible. If you were persistent enough, one of the detectives might even have impersonated Detective McCann on the phone.

Seedman stood up well to the mounting pressure. A New York reporter called requesting an interview with a detective who *favored* specialization. It caused a big laugh at Headquarters. Various wags began quoting odds as to whether the Chief would be able to find one. By now the full anti-corruption impact of specialization was clear, and some detectives were not happy about it.*

Finally, one detective commander returned Seedman's call. Yes, he found a detective who would be willing to be quoted by name as favoring detective specialization. Of course there were others— sincere, dedicated detectives who (a) liked the specialization idea and (b) loathed the corruption. But did they want to be identified publicly with Murphy's reform?

Also troubling the detectives was another element that had not yet been made public. Unlike the Patrol Bureau, there was a tier system of salaries in the Detective Bureau. A first-grade detective earned the equivalent of a lieutenant's pay; second-grade, sergeant's pay; and third-grade, 10 percent more than a patrol officer. At this time, about 5 percent of the N.Y.P.D.'s detectives were first grade and 85 percent were third grade.

During the previous month a regrettably small number of first-grade detectives had retired. (Because the position was so lucrative and/or interesting, many detectives, especially first grade, hung on well beyond their twenty years, even though they were eligible for retirement with pension.) In the ordinary course of things, the P.C. would have rather quickly promoted some second-grade detectives to first-grade slots. But I did nothing.

I wondered how long it would be before Chief Seedman requested an interview. I didn't have to wait too long.

"Hey, boss," he said, nonchalantly. "You didn't fill those first-grade slots. Maybe it slipped your mind?"

Not exactly. I had no intention of filling those vacancies. Seedman perhaps sensed this. My informants in the field were reporting back with amusement that the detectives were all astir. "What's the prognosis?" was the worried query in the detective locker rooms.

And now Seedman was wondering about the prognosis. When would these plums be handed out? The vacant first-grade positions were part of the leverage of the power conformation around the Chief's office. To have them taken away might prove very embarrass-

---

* To be sure, not everyone who opposed specialization was a closet grafter. There were those who simply did not believe that specialization of detectives was a good practical idea.

ing and might weaken the Chief's hold over the troops at a time when he needed all the leverage I could give him.

"Al, I don't know what to say," I began. "We've got money problems."

This was correct. By this time, a job freeze was in effect. As a result of the city's poor fiscal picture, all city agencies had had to cut back. When I began, there were approximately 37,000 full-time employees in the department, including 5000 civilians, of whom a sizable number were police trainees.* During my first two years, the size of the department was to shrink considerably, from 32,000 sworn officers to 29,500; and from 5000 civilian employes to 2500. The reduction would add up to a 13 percent loss in personnel strength.

I had readily accepted these losses on the basis of my long-held belief that what we needed were not more police but more productive ones. I supported the Mayor and Henry Ruth, the Director of the Office of Criminal Justice (which had been funneling most of the federal grants into the prosecutors' offices and the courts). I believed that, with 90 percent of the city's criminal justice budget, the Police Department would have to live not with more but with less. So the appeal to comparatively impoverished circumstances in front of Seedman had the ring of truth to it. We did need to economize, and first-grade detectives were a luxury item at best.

"Maybe," I suggested, "for the time being we could fill those slots with some third-grade detectives. You know, bring some new blood in."

Al's eyes brightened at the hint of the compromise. The costly first-grade positions would remain unfilled, but the Chief of Detectives would, in conjunction with the P.C., retain the equivalent number of strings for less expensive third-graders. The Chief would save face. The P.C. would save money.

---

* Indeed, the civilian loss was almost exclusively in trainees. They had been recruited directly from high school, required to take some college courses, and would be appointed police officers upon reaching twenty-one. The concept was good in theory but in practice was fatally flawed. These new police recruits had a lower percentage of racial minorities than the rest of the department, which was bad enough. In 1972 this was intolerable. A high percentage of minorities was necessary among entering officers to correct this serious imbalance. But contrary to the general assumption inside the city as well as nationally, the N.Y.P.D.'s record was anemic compared to Chicago, Philadelphia, Washington, and some other large-city P.D.'s.

And here again my ultimate goal was designed to be not immediately visible. It was to abolish the three-tier system entirely. Not filling the vacant first-grade slots was just the first step. As second-grade positions became vacant, they too would remain unfilled. Over the very long run, as the first- and second-graders put in for retirement, their slots too would remain unfilled. Before too long, the only vacancies being filled would be the third-graders. By a process of attrition and personnel control, the bureau, without demoting a single detective, a step which was well within the P.C.'s power, would be transformed into a single-grade outfit—still more advantaged than the rest of the department but not quite as overprivileged as before.

But the conversion had to be made quietly, without fanfare. If you announced it on *Eyewitness News*, the Detectives Association would have to take a public stand, and the long knives would be drawn.

Seedman's eyes, intense and cold, indicated that he may have understood the shape of things to come. Rising from his chair, fighting through a cloud of cigar smoke as tall as a storm cirrus, Seedman looked as if he had seen the rough weather ahead. "Okay, boss," he said, "I'll go ahead and fill them with third-graders for the time being."

"That's great, Al."

Nothing is ever so easy as it logically should be.

Not long after, the phones started heating up on the detective issue. Kriegel wanted to know what was going on—again. Even the Mayor put in a call. (I half expected the President's domestic adviser to check in next.)

But my line of defense was an aggressive one. To sit still for the impending attack might jeopardize the entire reorganization. Instead of retreating, I put out a new order. This froze vacated second-grade positions. (This raised the level of quiet hysteria.) For good measure we added an additional twist. In the near future we'd be putting uniformed cops out on the streets *with gold shields*.

The goal was to blur the distinction between detective and patrolman. If patrolmen, in uniform, were capable of detective work, and detectives, out of uniform, were incapable of solving many cases, then why the distinction? What was the difference? If there was none, then what could be more symbolic than a detective in uniform?

One afternoon I was at City Hall and Kriegel said hello. He also said, "I'm getting some heat on the detective reorganization."

I replied with a briefing on my latest plans.

Kriegel feigned astonishment and surprise, but of course he knew all about it. The detectives were leaking everything to him.

Kriegel had an odd look in his eye. Quite uncharacteristically, he didn't say anything for several seconds. This was about the most worrisome thing Kriegel had ever done in my presence: remain silent.

Then he walked out of the office, ostensibly on another errand. I left the Hall and returned to Headquarters.

Later that day the Mayor called. "Commissioner," he began, in the tone that meant this was business. When he wanted me to substitute for him on some television or radio show that he could not get to, he would call me at the last minute and begin with "Pat"; this meant personal.

"Commissioner, I see that you have a big thing going with the Detective Bureau. Why can't you tell us about these things, Commissioner? You know, so at least we could know what to make of the heat when it comes in on us? Hell, Pat!"

"Mr. Mayor"—now I'm businesslike too—"this is a risky one we're undertaking over here. I really don't know how it's going to work out. So I decided not to involve the Hall on this. I don't want you to get burned. This is really rough. Why don't you let me go out on the limb on this one?"

Pause. Lindsay was thinking it through. Although the line of defense was essentially the same as outlined months earlier to Kriegel, it still retained a forceful freshness and logic. It also seemed grounded in a basic decency, because I was sincere in wishing to protect the Mayor from being drawn into a bloody fight.

Finally: "Okay, Commissioner, maybe you're right. Good luck with it. I'm behind you, as usual."

I hung up and breathed more easily. The detective reorganization had put me on tricky ground. The Mayor was saying, Okay, I won't undercut you. It was, in my view, one of the best mayoral decisions John Lindsay had ever made. I was very thankful.

Indeed, there was no turning back now. The first month in office we had moved quietly to remove from the Bureau the famed Bureau of Special Services (known as BOSSI). This was the secret Headquarters unit concerned with subversion and other matters. For what BOSSI was involved with, the loose supervision of the Detective Bureau seemed the worst possible place for it. We took it away from the bureau and placed it under a reorganized Intelligence Division. This move had attracted attention, but the next move would be even more widely noticed. It concerned the narcotics effort. And, if only for Seedman's own benefit, the propitious moment for the move would be while the Chief was out of New York—maybe on vacation.

In the past, there had been an understanding in the department that it was crucial to insulate the Police Commissioner from the distasteful but inevitable corruption in the lower ranks. The understanding was unstated but was enthusiastically accepted by all concerned. Great, masterful maneuverings sailed forth from the high command to this end, over the decades establishing a grand tradition of insulation in the classic fashion.

An elegant insulation was accomplished by the wide disperse-ment of the most corruption-prone units throughout the department. These units, especially gambling (plainclothes) and narcotics, were treated much like leper colonies and were isolated in cultures far from Headquarters. There, in relative obscurity and untouched save by the occasional Headquarters "John Walsh" raid for dramatic effect, these units could proceed under the assumption that the Police Commis-sioner was operating on a cloud of innocence, an angel with his harp in the company of other angels.

This insulation of the Police Commissioner led, however, to mis-management. The Police Commissioner could make strong anti-corruption appeals in the press and before the ladies' auxiliaries; he could conduct the political business of the Hall and front for the department with various other constituencies; but in the face of the sometimes grisly realities of police power, the P.C. was a pet rock.*

Together with First Deputy Smith, I decided to make a major break with tradition. As it stood now, the borough and division patrol commanders were responsible for the plainclothes squads. But they spent so much time worrying about these non-uniformed officers that

---

* The phrase "pet rock," to my knowledge, was first used in connection with American police chiefs in a sharply-phrased speech on police leadership delivered by Robert di Grazia when he was Boston Police Commissioner.

there was little energy or time left for directing or controlling the more than 97 percent of their personnel doing patrol duty and responsible for street crime and basic services. Therefore, it made sense to bring together all of the plainclothes units under a single command, directly responsible to one of the P.C.'s top aides.

The proposal rocked Headquarters. The feeling was that the consolidation would pack so much dynamite in one place, such a short distance from the Commissioner's office, that the P.C. might be blown out of office. Old-timers at Headquarters, even the honest ones, had to shake their heads. This was suicide.

But the consolidation did not stop with gambling plainclothes.

When Chief Seedman returned from vacation, he no longer had to worry about the 800-man Narcotics Division, half of them white-shield officers under the Detective Bureau. Narcotics was now, as was gambling enforcement, under an entirely new creation, the Organized Crime Control Bureau.

To the public, the reorganization was advertised for what the bureau's new title suggested: organized crime control. New York's organized crime families operated with near impunity in the areas of gambling, loansharking, narcotics, political corruption, union infiltration, and superficially legitimate businesses ranging from carting to pornography. But underneath the obvious logic of consolidating in one bureau the various department efforts to control the growth of organized crime, there was an internal goal. The new Organized Crime Control Bureau (O.C.C.B.) was going to be involved not only with organized crime outside the department but also with organized crime inside the department—whether the monthly pad, the entrepreneurial shakedown, or the unsolicited but accepted bribe. Thus, under one bureau and one new deputy commissioner, both sides of the fence would be under surveillance.

To Chief Seedman, of course, the removal of narcotics enforcement from under his command while he was on vacation was, perhaps, a rebuff. But Seedman was privately troubled by narcotics, recognizing as we all did that the amount of money available in bribes from organized crime interests to police officers was unprecedented.

He may even have believed that there was not a great deal one could do about narcotics corruption, and may therefore have been greatly relieved by the loss.

Seedman, when he came back from vacation, predictably made a big show of irritation over the abrupt and clandestine change; but his performance, while duly noted, was not at all troublesome. It may not even have been sincere. Seedman was above all smart. What did he want with narcotics smoldering in his bureau now that the Knapp Commission was out hunting for bad cops and good copy?

Our choice to head the new Organized Crime Control Bureau was William McCarthy. The selection stirred up considerable comment around Headquarters and in the precincts. McCarthy, who had retired from the department and who had to be lured back to New York from the Florida links, had a well-deserved reputation as a terror on the corruption issue. Known as "Knock-em-over Bill," he made his reputation as a sergeant who was not one of the boys. "Is McCarthy riding?" officers would ask the precinct switchboard operator before going into a coop to sleep or relax. His reputation was widely known, and it stood in marked contrast to that of the sergeants who belonged to sergeants' clubs in the precincts and would let the troops coop and pick up a few crumbs as long as they didn't interfere with the bosses' money. Even sergeants who didn't belong to the clubs tended not to rock the boat. But McCarthy, the idealist, was a boat rocker making waves. Considering what the O.C.C.B. represented, a commanding officer who didn't rock this new boat might very well sink with it. McCarthy, the new O.C.C.B. head, was given the title of a deputy commissioner, and he organized his work to mesh closely with that of First Deputy Commissioner Smith. Now the department's narcotics, vice, and gambling plainclothes units, once as far away from the Commissioner's office as Bangladesh, were only a few doors away. The buck now stopped at the high command.

In his first moves, McCarthy went directly to management mistakes. Narcotics officers, in any effort to move in an undercover fashion in upper-level dope circles, needed money, sometimes a great deal of hard cash. The long-standing and growing abuse resulting from insufficient departmental "buy money" or "flush money" was that officers would hold back some of the narcotics seized in an arrest rather than turn it in as evidence. The officers could then trade some of the dope to junkies in return for information; or, considering the high street value of the merchandise, they could sell it and either pocket the proceeds or buy their way (legitimately or otherwise) into a narcotics operation. By insisting on having adequate buy money, an insistence which Mayor Lindsay and Jay Kriegel not only understood but to their credit supported fully, McCarthy hoped to remove from narcotics officers the initial temptation to hold back seized dope, for whatever motive.

A second area of concern was the incredible lack of supervision. In the Special Investigating Unit of the Narcotics Bureau, where there was great corruption, too many officers were going their own way. Management had no idea what they were doing and seemingly did not want to know. But the new police administration was confronting the problem for what it was, win or lose. McCarthy wanted many more sergeants in order to increase the supervision of plainclothes and narcotics work; chaos and individual entrepreneurship were to be replaced by management. From a ratio of fourteen narcotics officers to one sergeant—an ineffective and absurd ratio—we made more sergeants out of patrol officers and brought the ratio down to eight to one.

The benefits of appointing new supervisors were twofold. In McCarthy's conception of organized crime, it was far better to spend a great deal of time concentrating on an underworld David Rockefeller than to fill monthly arrest quotas by booking betting clerks. Thus the choice of targets, once entirely the prerogative of the plainclothes officer, now became a management-level decision, with many factors involved. One factor was whether the target under discussion was worth the department's time and the public's money.

But there was another factor in the calculation, and this was entirely novel. In my view, eliminating or reducing police corruption was always more important than convicting organized crime figures, even the overlords—the dons. The minimization of corruption opportunities came first. Taking a high corruption risk as a trade-off for improving the odds of hooking a big fish was a confusion of priorities. In many major organized crime investigations the odds of building a case that would stand up in court and all the way through the appeal process and result in the imprisonment of a major organized crime figure were much lower than the chances of creating conditions leading to further corruption of the Police Department.

Therefore, all serious forays into the big time of organized crime had to be weighed with great care. The higher and more consequential the target, the further up the chain of command went the decision making. I told McCarthy that he would have to approve the very big cases. One investigation actually involved the placement of a bug in a trailer where substantial organized crime business was conducted, and resulted in cases against not only big-time mobsters but also some of our corrupt cops working with the mob.

But case-approvals were now going to be made with enormous, painstaking premeditation. The integrity of the department could not be compromised for the sake of shaky cases that had little chance of making it through the courts. The decisions of consequence could no longer be made by the plainclothes undercover officers. They would now be made on the apron of the Commissioner's office. It was a new ballgame.

The final twist in the saga of the reform and reorganization of the Detective Bureau occurred late on a Friday afternoon. As was my custom, I had ducked out of Headquarters early on this occasion for dinner with some old friends, carrying to the Mercury the usual stuffed attaché case of weekend work. When I arrived home in Great Kills, Staten Island, I received a nervous phone call from the First Deputy: "Call Mike Armstrong." So I called.

The essence of the conversation with Armstrong was that the Knapp Commission had uncovered evidence that Chief of Detectives Seedman had accepted a free meal from a famous Manhattan hotel for himself, his wife, and a second couple. The hidden threat in this message was: What were we going to do about it?

First Deputy Smith didn't know, and at first neither did I. We were both very troubled. Smith set up an emergency task force back at Headquarters to think the problem through and come up with a recommendation. I told him too to find out what Seedman had to say about this thing. Then I sat down by the phone and waited for either Seedman or Smith to call.

Seedman never called. In the crisis of that long weekend, the Chief of Detectives kept his silence. Smith called about an hour later. A task force had thought through the problem and recommended that Seedman be temporarily relieved as Chief of Detectives and reassigned to the Office of Chief Inspector, pending an investigation by Chief Sydney Cooper, head of Inspectional Services. The recommendation was a compromise between the hard-liners who favored suspension and the soft-liners who favored an investigation but no change in status.

I mused at home on the irony of the commission's eleventh-hour move. Here they were, taking aim, over the issue of a single free meal, at the chief who had been quietly engineering one of the most massive reforms in the recent history of the N.Y.P.D. Of course, both the timing and the content of the message were extremely suspicious, because after all those breakfast sessions with Chairman Knapp and Chief Counsel Armstrong I was programmed toward paranoia. Obviously, a free meal of this kind was not insignificant; but what else did they have? If this was just a piece of the Seedman investigation, what other allegations of misconduct or even corruption against the Chief did the commission have up its sleeve?

The phone call from Armstrong came late on Friday. On Monday —just two days away—the public hearing of the commission was scheduled to begin. Would my Chief of Detectives be called as the first witness, and would the riot act be read to him?

If the commission had any substantial evidence against Seedman, the hard line made sense. Harsh action would show that we were willing to discipline not merely the poor hapless patrol officer or third-grade detective but a commander as high and as powerful as the Chief of Detectives.

On the other hand, if Armstrong and Knapp were bluffing—if they had nothing more and the dumb free meal was the only card they held —then relieving Seedman could appear to be excessive and might suggest that in the desire to appear in control of my own administration, I had overreacted, even panicked. But the critical question just would not go away: What were the circumstances surrounding the free meal? An eighty-four-dollar meal was very different from a free cup of coffee, or even a three- or five-dollar meal.

I thought over the situation for several hours—maybe the longest ones of my commissionership—and came to the intuitive conclusion that Armstrong and Knapp were bluffing. Indeed, it was entirely possible—in fairness to the two men—that they felt that I had some secret dirt on Seedman which I was hiding. (But, of course, I had none.) Armstrong's strategy may well have been to reveal the free meal in an effort to scare me into believing he had learned about some dirt I might be hiding. I would then be faced with the dilemma of hanging tough or cutting my losses (Seedman).

But I believed that Seedman was truly not guilty of anything more monstrous than bad judgment—assuming it *was* an isolated incident that could be justified. Also in the forefront of my mind was the recognition that Seedman had carried on the detective reorganization skillfully and courageously. Therefore, considering the possibility that Armstrong might be playing games and the fact that Seedman was a valued member of the new management team, the middle-ground recommendation was the least I could do for Al, and perhaps the most I should do in response to Knapp. Approved, therefore: temporary reassignment pending completion of an investigation by Sydney Cooper—and while we awaited further information or allegations from the commission.

Thus we called Mike Armstrong's bluff, and by late the following week—the first week of the public hearings—Armstrong folded.

For Chief Seedman was not called to testify, and our investigation showed that the only free dinner discovered was given by the hotel in appreciation for assistance unrelated to the Chief's official duties. Of course, if Cooper's investigation had not justified the meal, it would have been a very serious matter, especially for someone who was Chief of Detectives.

And so by week's end Seedman was fully reinstated, and I felt that the humiliation of having been relieved of command for a few days was more than adequate punishment for his being caught in the position of looking bad without actually being bad.

Seedman later explained that the meal was in compensation for advising the hotel's security staff on some anti-burglary and anti-prostitution measures. The meal was actually in lieu of a fee, even though acceptance of a fee would have been entirely within Seedman's right, since the consultation had been performed while Al was off duty.

Even today, with all the corruption that we knew had occurred in the Detective Bureau, it is hard to believe that this was the strongest hand Armstrong was able to play on the eve of the hearings. In retrospect, it almost seemed like a case of headline hunting.

Chapter Eight

The Management of Cops

There is, I admit, something theatrical about macho police management, but the huff-and-bluff style is theater of the absurd. If America's police chiefs do not possess a clear understanding of what they are doing, at least they possess a patently pure motive. They are protecting America from the bad guys, and they are doing it with the deep sincerity of Boy Scouts on Saturday morning maneuvers. If nothing else, their hearts are in the right places. They are the good guys.

The chief characteristic of American police management is "toughness." Like the front-office of a sports team, the police chiefs often mistakenly view themselves as coaches; the answer to a poor first half is to knock some heads together and then follow it with a locker-room peroration. I remember a famous, popular chief with a similar Vince Lombardi approach to corruption in the ranks. An officer identified as corrupt would be summoned to the Chief's office. The tough Chief would read him the riot act, get up from the desk, and then sock him in the jaw. This was the Chief's system of integrity control: the knockout punch.

Charming as it was, a system for controlling graft it was not, except possibly, remotely, in a small department where roughhouse one-on-ones might have some impact. The chief under discussion here was a commander in a big-city police department. And yet even the leaders of our biggest, most consequential police departments continue to run things as though all of America were still a small town, and Matt Dillon an appropriate role model for a metropolitan police chief.

To be effective and relevant, police forces must necessarily be complex and sophisticated. The institution must reflect the problems to be regulated. The management of such an institution will be difficult but interesting. Very interesting.

One of the first things I reflected on after becoming Police Commissioner in New York was how few lawyers there were in the department. (My sensitivity to this problem was undoubtedly heightened by my experience in Detroit, Washington, and Syracuse, whose police departments similarly lacked sufficient legal manpower in staff and line positions.) The scarcity of legal talent was of course ridiculous. After all, a police department traffics in the law the way a hospital's currency is medicine. What would one say of a hospital without a pharmacological capability?

At the Headquarters level there was a deputy commissioner for legal matters; but out in the field, in the precincts where the real police work was being done, there was nothing.

At Headquarters, I noticed immediately, the Deputy Commissioner for Legal Matters functioned in a very traditional manner. From my first day, I had urged all at the top management level to come forth with some new ideas and proposals. Of all the responses, the least consequential came from the D.C.L.M.

What we needed at the Commissioner's level was a heavy hitter to deal with the district attorneys and other legal potentates. The department was constantly, routinely, getting into areas that required legal expertise of a very high order. We were making arrests that the district attorneys were failing to prosecute. We were trying new policies that the Corporation Counsel was raising serious legal questions about. In the everyday affairs of the department, legal questions arose for which we had no answers. Accordingly, I raised with the high command the question of whether we weren't taking a real beating because we had so few lawyers—and so few good ones—to grapple with so many of the complicated legal issues that seriously affected our everyday performance. But the response was "What's wrong with the way we've always done it?"

At City Hall I raised the problem with Jay Kriegel. I told him we needed more legal input at the Commissioner's level. Kriegel was sympathetic and helpful. He had recently interviewed a number of lawyers with an interest in city government. Indeed, he was meeting with just such an applicant now.

.Ordinarily, this P.C. would not have accepted referrals from Kriegel. But the candidate in the aide's office that afternoon was one of the products of the Mayor's Talent Search, a system based on competitive merit rather than political connection.

It was by grace of God that I happened to be at City Hall that day, for it led to the hiring of Philip Lacovara, who had been first in his class at Columbia Law School.*

Civilian professionals of Lacovara's caliber were rare to police departments. When police chiefs speak of the need to hire more civilians, they usually have in mind not qualified professional lawyers, systems analysts, or administrators, but switchboard operators, clerks, typists, meter maids, and crossing guards. Consequentially placed civilians were more to be feared than cultivated.

The acquisition of Lacovara was instructive. From the moment we found a makeshift office for him, right down the hall from my own, our ability to deal with the fundamental business of the department improved perceptibly. In the frequent and sometimes intense congress with the district attorneys, who had been in the habit of lording their legal expertise over the department, the Special Counsel represented the department with great force. The N.Y.P.D., like anyone else, needed a good lawyer, and we had found a very good one.

In an epoch when police corruption was obviously going to be the front-running issue, the presence of a very competent legal adviser to the Commissioner was probably crucial to whatever success we may have had. It was necessary for us to demonstrate to all concerned that we could police our own crime problem. The centerpiece of the internal effort was the department's trial room, where police officers accused of improper or illegal conduct could be brought up on charges and, depending on the ultimate disposition of the charge, dismissed, fined, suspended, or reinstated.

The integrity of this effort was crucial to the credibility of the reform. Although I believed that the presence of the Knapp Commission was a powerful stimulus to the reform, I publicly took the posi-

---

* Lacovara later went on to greater fame and fortune; among other things, he became a prosecutor with the Office of Special Prosecutor, investigating Watergate.

tion that any police department ought to have the capability of policing itself. But when I came to the N.Y.P.D. from Detroit, after an absence of five years from my home department, if I had not known any better I might well have thought that the N.Y.P.D.'s internal system of justice had been purposely sabotaged.

In the New York Police Department the commander in charge of the trial room and the attendant power and process was the Trial Commissioner. It was not only an important job and a terribly sensitive job; it was also a thankless job. But if I had not been familiar with the astonishing and sometimes hilarious ineptitude at the highest levels of policing in America, and had not understood the haphazard way in which the most consequential decisions were often made, I would have thought that the system had been deliberately designed not to work.

With appropriate urgency, Benjamin Ward, the former Trial Commissioner who was now Deputy Commissioner for Community Affairs (and one of the fairest, most reliable aides at Headquarters), and the studious Phil Lacovara, the new Special Counsel, launched a study of the effectiveness of the internal trial system.

In any police department, what you wanted was neither of two extremes: neither a kangaroo court on the one hand nor a system of fixing cases on the other. Before Ward and Lacovara jumped into the situation, my secret fear was of the latter.

What I had observed was that the recommendations from the trial room often seemed to be strained—as if trying to avoid a finding of guilt in a case where ordinary prudence and intelligence would have led to the conclusion that the respondent was indeed guilty as charged. Another worry was that the recommended penalties often seemed curiously lenient, even in cases of incredible misconduct where outright dismissal would hardly have struck anyone as irrational. The one thing I did not wish was the appearance (or the reality) of the department bending over backward to keep on the payroll corrupt or otherwise wholly undesirable police officers. On the other hand, we did not want to have a system for railroading accused cops, but every instinct was telling me that this was not the problem.

Special Counsel Lacovara sent over to me a five-page memorandum on the trial room situation that fortunately never got outside to the press. In a series of disturbing but penetrating observations, the

Special Counsel raised the sort of issues about the department's trial counsel function that every major police department in the United States ought to raise about its own but, in my experience, so often failed to do. In part, police departments may not wish to raise such troubling questions; but mainly, in my view, what we have is an unplotted failure of imagination and professional management.

In Lacovara's view, one of the most serious deficiencies in the disciplinary system seemed to be in the department's trial counsels. Wrote the Special Counsel: "These men are, for the most part, policemen first and lawyers second. This means that they view their present assignment as prosecutors as a temporarily distasteful interlude in the development of their police careers. With rare exceptions, they have no outside trial experience and no opportunity to observe, much less to develop, the arsenal of professional skills that distinguish effective trial lawyers from clerks. Faced with leaders of the criminal defense bar, it is no wonder that the Department's lawyers find themselves consistently outgunned. Indeed, this is especially evident in the most serious corruption and brutality cases, where the Department's interest in adequate presentation of the facts is gravest."

The average trial counsel was of relatively low rank. The vast majority of the corruption investigators would clearly outrank the prosecutors. In a police department rank is everything. In essence, the message of management to the trial counsel was: What the investigators bring in to you to prosecute, that's what you go with; don't ask any probing questions; you have no stature. Special Counsel Lacovara continued: "This attitude manifests itself more critically at the stage when the charges are drafted. Especially in major investigations, it is a ranking line officer [the investigator] who decides what the charges will say, and it is this package that is, for better or worse, presented to the hapless trial counsel to attempt to prosecute. No federal or state prosecutor could responsibly let investigators draft *and* file an indictment, yet this is precisely what we do now."

Evidently, some funny things were happening in the trial room. An investigating officer preferring charges would allege a classic case of corruption even though the evidence would only support a lesser charge. In another case, the allegations of a criminal complaint or indictment that had resulted in acquittal were mindlessly copied for use at a departmental trial on the theory that the accused cop "really" did what he was originally but unsuccessfully charged with, and therefore the department should try to prevail where the district attorney had failed.*

The Special Counsel's proposal was for the improvement of the procedures and of the effectiveness of our disciplinary system from top to bottom. In this recommendation I was entirely supportive. Any reform commissioner would have been. The situation in the trial room, as well as in the precincts, was absurd. We had to do something about it if we were to have any hope of raising standards of integrity and performance to some reasonable level.

A few months later we solved some of our problems with the acquisition of Philip Michael as the new Trial Commissioner. Michael came to us from San Francisco, where he had been a top prosecutor in the U.S. Attorney's office, and where he had attracted some attention as the chief prosecutor for the government in the corruption case against Mayor Joseph Alioto. (Alioto was ultimately acquitted by the jury.) Under the system developed by Michael, the Trial Commissioner's office became responsible for approving the content of all departmental charges before they were served. Investigators were required to forward a draft of the charges along with a memorandum describing exactly what alleged improper behavior was observed and what the witnesses could be expected to say. Prior to serving charges, the Trial Commissioner or a member of his staff was now empowered to interview investigators and witnesses.

"In this way," as Lacovara wrote of the new system, "a relatively experienced, professional and dispassionate litigator can frame the charges to the practicalities of proof." Under the new system, he pointed out, "trial counsel might decide to allege and prove only the seemingly minor violations. Little is lost and much could be gained, since the exceedingly suspicious circumstances could be taken into account in determining the punishment on the ostensibly 'minor'

---

* A departmental trial is not the same thing as a criminal trial in a courtroom. It is an administrative proceeding within the Police Department for the purpose of removing cops from the department, or denying guilty officers rights, privileges, benefits. We were anxious not only about winning our cases in the Departmental trial, but also about the inevitable appeal in the courts, because all Departmental decisions were subject to judicial review. How could we be tough, therefore, in the trial room without running a risk of being reversed in the courts?

charges. This is precisely what a judge does with a probation report in making the punishment fit the criminal rather than the crime."

Lacovara's contribution led to stunning improvements. The police department which has itself as its lawyer has a fool for a client. Civilian expertise like Lacovara's is essential.

In the same way, our precincts needed full-time civilian attorneys on call. In my own mind, I saw the day when there would be an attorney inside the actual precinct building. The advantages were numerous. The district attorneys were constantly complaining about the legal quality of our arrests. With a lawyer working with the arresting officers, better cases could be prepared right from the start. Police officers faced the constant risk of civilian suit for false arrest or even police brutality. With an attorney's supervision every step of the way, the hazards could be reduced. But under traditional Matt Dillon police management, such suggestions were thought of as fancy trimming. The idea that legal guidance might be useful to the cops in the exercise of their arrest discretion, and in the performance of their duties, was really one that had scarcely been considered. In this way we can illustrate the sense in which the term "police management" has been practically a contradiction in terms.

The management of a police bureaucracy is made up of the bitter, the ridiculous, and the fascinating. From the standpoint of logic, the most surprising thing about police departments is that so much good work gets done.

Municipal politics and bad management are the two main reasons why the struggle of the honest, effective police officer to do good work is a heroic one. In every department of substantial size in the United States there are enough incredible inconsistencies built into the operating system to provide plently of material for comedy script-writers. From this perspective, the most honest television portrayal of police work is not perhaps *Kojak* or even *Police Story* but *Barney Miller*.

The New York Police Department, which many believe retains, for all its bad publicity, the right to be considered one of the most important law enforcement agencies in the world, displays contradictory qualities which reach the high and the low. For example:

• In the city of New York, as in most American urban centers, serious crime occurred with the greatest frequency from six in the evening to two in the morning. This was our American high crime period. This was when people coming home from work were mugged, stores held up, drunks rolled, johns fleeced, family quarrels broke out. At roughly ten o'clock in the evening the crime curve reached its peak. Between ten and midnight all hell broke loose. At roughly the same time the four-to-midnight shift, tired, exhausted, irritable, was looking forward to heading home or to a bar. Thanks to the way in which we had fitted our work schedule to the incidence of crime, the period of maximum lawlessness just about perfectly coincided with a change in the eight-hour shifts.

• Crime occurred with greatest density in New York, and probably in many other cities as well, between six P.M. and two A.M. The rest of the twenty-four-hour cycle was less critical. However, until we tried to do something about it, the manpower of the N.Y.P.D. was carved roughly into three equal platoons. In this stroke of management genius, the four-to-midnight platoon, which got socked with tidal waves of crime, was assigned more or less the same troop strength as the midnight-to-eight A.M. platoon, which presided over a comparatively quiet and exhausted city. It was with a management policy like this that the war on crime could be lost.

• The personnel function of a modern police department sounds boring, but its work is vital indeed. It is through the personnel department that top police administrators can (sometimes) manipulate the bureaucracy and make things happen. In most police departments personnel is a forgotten lost art, and the commander assigned to it is perhaps even humiliated by the assignment. But under the reform administration, Personnel was reborn, and the new commander, Sydney Cooper, was one of the most astute and most respected (and feared) career officers in the N.Y.P.D. With Cooper in charge, the possibilities for creative rather than routine management were developed.*

But the job was enormous. There were so many things to correct.

---

* And the big management stick was brandished for effect. When patrol officers went out on strike during the job action, Cooper took careful notes, and months later, invoking the Taylor Law against strikes by public employees, docked more than twenty thousand striking officers pay for every day they were out.

For instance, under the personnel system of the N.Y.P.D., the police officer who during his career did little or nothing had the least to lose. This was how the system worked. A cop could be dismissed from the force for doing the wrong thing—for example, an improper or suspicious arrest. But the one thing he could not be disciplined for was for doing nothing. Plainclothes officers, under an arrest quota system, might be penalized, yes; but not a uniformed police officer of the patrol branch, which force constituted more than 50 percent of the manpower of the department. Indeed, there were cases on record (kept secret, of course) of police officers who emerged after twenty years on the job without having made a single arrest! This was yet another example of how not to conduct a crime control campaign.

• Possibly one of the most emotionally debilitating and intellectually puzzling theories about American policing is called "stranger policing." Under this concept, a police department is not so much a public service as an occupation army. The department seeks to reduce an officer's sense of personal identification with his beat by regularly rotating him or her into different sectors. The theoretical idea was that the officer ought not to get too familiar, i.e., corrupt, with the people on his turf. The idea, which had long been policy with the detectives, was pushed to a final absurdity with the beat cops. In the end, the cop had little or no personal identification with, or emotional stake in, the quality of life in the territories he or she would be serving.

The concept was refined by establishing weekly rotation of tours of duty. No attention was paid to the fact that police problems and the people that the police interact with vary enormously at different times of day as they come and go at schools, bars, stores, and factories—youths, street people, day people, night people, et cetera.

At one point, I authorized precinct commanders to set up a non-rotating schedule of straight tours rather than weekly rotation, which can destroy the stomach. Were there, we asked, any police officers in the department who would volunteer to work straight shifts in an effort to maximize our ability to fight crime? The answer to our question was gratifying, and we got more volunteers than we had anticipated. Although New York cops were conditioned to believe that rotating tours were of the essence in policing, some of the volunteers grasped the logic of normal non-rotating working schedules. After the reshuffling, we staffed the first platoon (midnight to eight A.M.) with only 15 percent of the force, and that was all that was needed. The second platoon (eight A.M. to four P.M.) got 35 percent, and a full 50 percent went to the third (four P.M. to midnight)—with enough flexibility to stretch some of the 50 percent over to two A.M. by starting them at six instead of four in the afternoon. A built-in dividend: fewer people after midnight cooping because they had so little to do while the city slept.

• The most difficult element to overcome in the fight against corruption in the department was the code of silence. For a variety of reasons, including the fact that in their view police corruption was no worse than widespread corruption in the courtrooms or in the prosecutors' offices, police officers were rarely inclined to testify against the corrupt acts of their brethren. But what strengthened this code of silence was the policy top management had always followed of not offering officers caught in corrupt acts lenient or sympathetic treatment in return for assistance in cleaning out the larger nest. For as long as anyone can remember, police and prosecutors have "turned" criminals—i.e., treated them leniently in exchange for information and/or testimony against their partners in crime. But in law enforcement, crooked cops have not (or only rarely) been "turned" against their cop partners in crime.

This was hardly a condition unique to the N.Y.P.D. Even at the state and federal levels, "turning" those who violate their oath of office was far from being a well-developed act.

A cop might voluntarily, like Frank Serpico, come forward with incriminating information; it was therefore thought prudent to make such a move as difficult and worrisome as possible by taking the line that all violators would be fully prosecuted with no exceptions and no deals. This way everyone was warned not to rock the boat.

• Next to Fort Knox, the Property Clerk's office of the New York Police Department probably contained more wealth per square foot of office space than any other building in the country. In addition to a great deal of cash, there was also a tremendous amount of narcotics seized and stored as evidence which in the street was convertible into a fortune. Therefore, under the management system of the N.Y.P.D., the employee in charge of this storage room was a civil servant— literally a clerk who was not exactly handsomely reimbursed for his honesty. When this situation came to my attention early in the reform,

I practically had a heart attack; soon after, an inspector whom I had known since my days in the Police Academy* was put in charge, with the mandate to make a thorough survey of the system of storing evidence to determine its susceptibility to corrupt practices. Under this new administrator, the problem, we hoped, could be dealt with. But imagine a ten-thousand-dollar-a-year clerk in charge of a billion-dollar property room, with no administrative control over him!

• Your municipal police department, if it's like the N.Y.P.D. (and many are), operates under civil service constraints. Once upon a time this was an admirable idea. But the idea has soured. Entrance into the force and promotion up the ranks to the level of captain is entirely by virtue of performance on a competitive written examination. Forget whether the candidates are good officers, possess leadership qualities, are of high integrity, or even if they can write an intelligible report. The only thing that counts is how well they test, on an examination whose fairness to non-white applicants is decidedly suspect. Is this any way to run a police department?

The successful management of a police department is probably a subtle combination of intelligence, guts, and knowing when and where to bend with the wind. It may also require a great sense of humor.

Before too long, in the continuing effort to bring civilian professionals into the department, we had brought on board a number of high-powered systems-analysis types. They were able to analyze the entire width and breadth of the N.Y.P.D. and then, as problems arose, to break down the N.Y.P.D. system into smaller, constituent parts. Two important acquisitions in this regard were Michael Landi, for whom we created a whole new position as an assistant commissioner, and Paul Canick, Deputy Commissioner for Administration. Over at City Hall Edward Hamilton, the high-powered Director of the Budget (and later Deputy Mayor), provided similar counsel.

---

* He had a reputation for being a pillar of honesty. Once, as an instructor, he had caught a recruit cheating on an examination. The inspector, then a lieutenant, made a federal case out of the incident and had the cheater drummed out of the department. At this time such a response to cheating was considered far-out and excessive. In his view, such a measure was the least that should have been done. I had agreed then, and I still agree now. Letting cheaters remain in the department was not exactly an ideal way to build a base of integrity and honesty.

I'll never forget Deputy Commissioner Canick's heroic little struggle against gas runs. It was not exactly an issue that was going to make the cover of a news magazine, but to me it so clearly illustrated the way in which traditional practice was often at odds with better policing that I was very much amused when Canick first raised the question of gas runs in a memorandum in July of 1971.

In the City of New York there were a small number of official gas dispensing stations at which official vehicles were required to gas up. Forget that in a sector of an R.M.P. (radio motorized patrol) there were dozens of gas stations where a stop might not only produce a fill-up but also perhaps some intelligence information or gossip useful to preventive patrol. Police cars had to go to the gas dispensing points. Canick complained in the memorandum that these stations were often so few and far between that "it is not uncommon for sector cars to be pulled out of position, out of their precincts, divisions and, occasionally, out of their borough commands." To Canick, who possessed an orderly, composed mind, the gas runs seemed pointedly inefficient. In his analysis, if 2 percent of all sector cars at any given time were on a gas run, then it would follow that for six hundred cars* the R.M.P. function would be shy about twelve cars at any given moment. To compute the dollar cost of the waste, Canick then used as the multiplier yardstick the statistic that it required *eleven* patrol officers to provide continuous round-the-clock police coverage in a sector.† Therefore, in his analysis, city taxpayers were spending about $2 million annually on unproductive labor—just to get the R.M.P. cars to the gas points and back to their sectors. And this was not figuring in the wasted gas getting to and from the gas dispensing points!

More germane perhaps were Canick's figures showing that if we could keep from making costly gas runs the department would realize a substantial increase in on-duty patrol cars over the course of a year. In other words, instead of running after gas the R.M.P. units could be chasing crooks.

Inevitably, Canick's solution raised some practical difficulties. The

---

* Very roughly what the N.Y.P.D. would have out on the street, city-wide at any given moment.

† Very roughly, two in each car per shift; three shifts to a twenty-four-hour period. Then, one officer off for the day, one on paid vacation, two in court, one on some other assigned, possibly emergency, duty. Total eleven.

recommendation was to provide a system of gasoline credit cards that could be used at any commercial gas station. As I recall, we were still fiddling with that one when I left in 1973. But the essential idea could not have been sounder. "It would put," as Canick phrased it, "the police into welcome commercial contact with retail gasoline vendors in their assigned areas."

Another area rich for exploitation by the systems analyst was the Motorcycle Division. In the middle of 1971 the N.Y.P.D. maintained a fleet of approximately 160 motorcycles, operating out of four motorcycle precincts. Five hundred and thirty-five uniformed personnel were assigned to the division; the annual budget was $6.6 million.

The basic purpose of the motorcycles was moving-traffic enforcement, although escort and emergency courier duty (e.g., transporting rare blood) were possible with them. Other than this, they were not very useful. For one thing, they were hardly all-weather vehicles. The six-cylinder R.M.P., which only cost about five hundred dollars more per unit than the motorcycle, was far more useful; the eight-cylinder R.M.P. made the motorcycle look sickly. The R.M.P. was an all-weather vehicle. It could be used safely for many purposes. Its sole drawback in comparison to the motorcycle was its inability to maneuver through heavily congested traffic with ease.

The motorcycles were costly not only because—with the exception of traffic work—they were useless; they were also dangerous. Motorcycle-related injuries, though never satisfactorily quantified, were probably costing city taxpayers a small budget deficit in retirement pay. One survey suggested that the three-fourths-disability retirement rate* among those assigned to the Motorcycle Division was, not unexpectedly, quite high. In one memo, Budget Director Hamilton recommended "a gradual phase-out of motorcycles." He could see no possible justification for them after reviewing the data on injuries and disability retirements which surfaced. I knew, however, that because it was needed for presidential motorcades and those of heads of state

* Under the provisions of the police pension system, an officer permanently disabled in the course of performing his duties could retire immediately after appropriate certification on a pension equal to three-quarters of salary—on the theory that he could probably earn little if anything to maintain his standard of living.

as well as for untangling expressway traffic jams, we would not want to eliminate this unit completely. But we did want to increase productivity with the darn motorcycles, and minimizing their number meant reducing costly injuries and costly early disability retirements.

Clearly even more suspect from every conceivable angle was the pet Mounted Division. In one memo Hamilton pointed out, "There was a period of time when the horse was useful to law enforcement. That period passed into history shortly after Ford started producing the horseless carriage."

The department's Mounted Division consisted of 220 horses, maintained by some fifty civilians, with 206 uniformed officers assigned to the division. The annual cost to taxpayers was $5.7 million. Besides the cost and the marginal contribution to crime control, another fact not to its credit was that the ratio of maintenance attendants to horses was about one to four. By comparison, the ratio in the R.M.P. fleet was one to twenty-one (160 civilian attendants for a fleet of some 3300 cars). This meant that the horses were a better supervised division than narcotics detectives, where the ratio had finally been gotten down to one supervisor for eight officers. And this at a time when the horses were perhaps the only foot soldiers in the N.Y.P.D. that we were absolutely certain were corruption-free!

In almost everything you read about the N.Y.P.D. and other police departments in those days, the primary focus was on the corruption, heroism, or inefficiency of the street cop or lone detective. Out of the limelight were Headquarters and the high command, except when they wanted you to see that they had done something which made them look good. But in truth American policing was in a troubled state not only in New York and not only in the other big cities but also in virtually every nook, cranny, county, village, town, and duchy of the United States because of failures of management. It was one thing to hold the individual police officer responsible for his own corruption or incompetence. But that officer could hardly be held accountable for a climate of corruption, much less for patterns of corruption and absurdly inept performance throughout the department. This had to be laid at the doorstep of top management.

The quota system—used in many forces—was a pretty good example. In narcotics, as in gambling enforcement, the quota meant that the least consequential street criminals were snapped up in an end-of-the-month rush and offered to Headquarters as sacrifices on the altar of paper efficiency.

The Headquarters quota not only reinforced crime control inefficiency but it may have cemented an alliance between plainclothes officers on the take and underworld entrepreneurs. Under the numerical quota—for instance, four gambling arrests per plainclothes officer per month—Headquarters was demonstrating interest not in crime control but in body counts. Like Pentagon policy in Vietnam, the top brass, seemingly indifferent to the reality in the trenches, was fighting its own real failures of leadership and command with fictions.

In the trenches the reaction was always one of cynicism—and the occasional flash of resourcefulness. Take, for example, the "Phantom." This end-of-the-month phenomenon illustrated neatly how abstract grand designs at Headquarters often assumed hilarious shape once they sank down to the street level.

At the end of the month the arrest reports were due. Always there was a certain amount of scurrying around at the last minute. One of the ways of meeting the deadline was to call in the Phantom.

The Phantom was a different low-level betting clerk each month. The honor was rotated from book to book. When a clerk's turn came up, he'd receive a call from a plainclothes officer telling him to stay put, that it was his turn.

The plainclothes officer would arrive to arrest the clerk for violation of the gambling laws and then take him to the precinct house for booking. There the desk officer would take down the charge and the name of the arrested person, who would be promptly bailed out.

The arresting officer, conscious that colleagues might well be scrambling around for some arrests to meet their quota, then would get on the phone. "Need a collar?" he would inquire, and offer his own arrest.

The colleague could indeed use a gambling arrest. The betting clerk would then be driven to that precinct and booked again—under a different name. In the first precinct he was, say, Johnny A. In the second precinct he would be Sammy A. By the time the night was over, the gambler might have been booked in a half dozen different precincts under as many different names. It was the night of the Phantom, and it was thus that Headquarters' minimum gambling quotas were met.

And at the end of the next month a different phantom would be conscripted for duty. Month after month, for this reason and for many others, the gambling arrest statistics bore little relationship to the effectiveness of the gambling law enforcement of the department.

Arrest statistics and crime statistics could be terribly misleading. Sometimes it was hard to know what to make of them. One program that tackled the problem of statistics involved the planning sergeant, a new breed of police officer. We ordered every precinct commander in the city to select one sergeant as the precinct's planning officer.

This officer was brought into the Police Academy for a crash course in what amounted to statistical probability. The course taught the newly selected planning sergeant to correlate the frequency with the topology of crime. To simplify matters, the sergeants were shown how to use a precinct map and brightly colored pins. The underlying thought was simple: What was past was prologue. Certain criminals were not only recidivists, but certain crimes tended to repeat in time, place, and character. With an informed crime topology, the planning sergeant could help the commanding officer of the precinct deploy the troops closer to the scenes of crime.

This use of crime statistics made sense. What did it mean to say Philadelphia was down, and New York was up? Very little indeed. What did make sense was to say that at 16th and Market in Philadelphia, between certain hours, certain sorts of crimes were likely to occur, thus justifying a certain configuration of manpower deployment. Indeed, in New York we watched over and over again as planning sergeants, with the sophisticated use of these data, were able to guess times and locations of crimes.

The planning sergeant can be an important person in a police department. As I once wrote to precinct commanders: "Can we pinpoint one or more sectors experiencing unusual increases in crime? I am trying to learn more about the problem by dividing it into smaller pieces—*analyzing* the crime. The Planning Sergeant should be encouraged to analyze the problem in several ways: time, space, population change, patrolmen in sector (new; unchanged; eager; indifferent, et cetera). . . .

"As has been made clear to us by Professors LeFave, Goldstein, and the National Crime Commission, police officers have very broad discretion, police policy is not very well defined, and the patrolman's activities are poorly controlled . . ."

The planning sergeant was a key figure in the long-overdue reform of the precinct; the precinct could make the difference in American policing. For in the necessary and inevitable move toward consolidation of policing, the danger was a loss of immediacy of contact with local communities. The planning sergeant might relate a larger "science" of modern policing with local conditions and community needs. For the commanding officer beset with a lot of difficult, even losing propositions, the planning sergeant could be the saver. He could help management decide what kinds of arrests to make.

The compleat planning sergeant was also a key figure in my ideal conception of the police precinct. In this utopian conception, the precinct would be free of corruption, and virtually virtuoso in crime control; and it would have adept management.

But the wish is father to the thought; and in New York we put together an "experiment" in systematizing decency. In my view, as you know by now, police officers are not born corrupt; they are converted by a larger climate. We therefore composed, in perhaps too theoretical a manner, a long-range method for converting our precincts from what they were to what we wanted them to be. Besides being free of serious corruption, we wanted them to be free of ineffectiveness.

The trick was to fiddle with Personnel's policy of assigning rookies. At that time the policy was to assign rookies out of the Police Academy as needed to fill vacancies in the various precincts. This in essence was to scatter them to the four winds.

The new program was called the "model precinct." (This was where utopia would try to remain as far away from reality as possible.) In the model precinct the ranks would be filled as completely as possible by a direct pipeline from the Police Academy. We wanted the rookies clean, idealistic, anxious to please, not yet cynical. In this culture of idealism we would try to add nutrients, control the temperature and other environmental conditions, and seek to strengthen the antibodies, which over time we could inject into other precincts in the manner of a miracle drug.

Naturally, it was necessary to keep inside the culture some experienced officers, but they had to be hand-picked by the precinct commander. It seemed irresponsible to leave the rookies utterly alone with the minefields, time bombs, and waves of kooks and vested interests that infested any precinct.

By staffing the culture with rookies, we were isolating in the model precinct uninfected organisms. (There was no way to graft in the Academy. Corruption was not an elective course; Detective McCann was not an instructor.) This was a qualitatively different peer group than in most other precincts. In this nurturing environment the rookies would not be exposed to the cigar-chomping cynic of a sergeant, the "cut-me-short-but-don't-cut-me-out" lieutenant, the weary, hopelessly drained captain.

It was an idea, obviously, whose time had not yet come, but it was an attempt to break with tradition.*

To backtrack a bit, the first actual police patrol force was created in thirteenth-century Hangchow. Patrol was the primary function of the police. It was evidently no more successful then than it is now, and today we have advanced from the rickshaw to the radio car. In twentieth-century America some $5 billion is spent every year for the maintenance and operation of uniformed and superbly equipped patrol forces.

The main point of aimless police patrol seems to be to reassure the citizen that the police department, like the city zoo, exists. As one

---

* The first sergeant in the model precinct was a relatively young officer named David Durk. Durk had figured prominently in the Serpico incident; he had worked closely with Officer Serpico in attempting to bring allegations of corruption to the attention of police authorities—and then to the New York *Times*. Durk, additionally, was a very bright person—a graduate of Amherst and a real student of police work. He made a significant contribution to the effort to attract college-educated persons to police work, and was both sincere and deeply committed to the control of corruption in the N.Y.P.D. He was also very ambitious indeed, and tended to lose interest in projects that seemingly were not clearly related to career advancement. This trait is hardly unusual among police officers but it is not always completely desirable. In the case at hand, Durk soon lost interest in the model-precinct assignment.

management study of police work concluded, "For the greatest number of persons, deterrence through ever-present patrol, coupled with the prospect of speedy police action once a report is received, appears important to crime control." In this view, the answer to a rise in crime is simple: more uniformed patrol. It was a view that was hardly ever challenged—at least not in public—so great was the fear of public outrage over pricking the great Goodyear blimp of policing.

It was not until quite recently that the myth of routine police patrol was attacked in a scientific, conclusive way—and publicly. A major experiment, conducted under the auspices of the Police Foundation in Washington, was initiated in 1972 in Kansas City, Missouri. Fifteen police beats in the city were selected to test the proposition that routine patrol affected crime.

The study was fascinating in both its simplicity and its complexity. The fifteen beats were randomly grouped into three categories of five beats each. Each of these categories got a different dose of patrolling.* In one category police officers were under strict orders to abandon routine patrol and to respond only to citizen calls for service. In the second category the instructions were to conduct business as always, responding to calls for help and doing routine patrol. And for the third category routine preventive patrol was intensified by a factor of two to three times the usual level, with additional patrol cars reassigned from the first, "no-patrol" category.

This stunning experiment ran for a period of twelve months. It was conducted by qualified social scientists under strictly controlled conditions. The structure of the experimental design and the precision of the execution compared favorably with the most rigidly prepared and conducted social science experiments. It had to be at least as valid as any previous experiment in policing because a great deal was at stake: the demolition of an American myth.

After the data were analyzed with care, and the results studied by all sorts of experts, two major conclusions emerged: Crime in Kansas City over the twelve-month period did not vary significantly over

---

* The negotiation with the Kansas City P.D. was necessarily difficult. Neither the foundation nor the P.D. wished the study to create serious problems. Therefore, it was agreed between both parties that in the event of a crime wave in category one, the experiment could be scotched. But no such catastrophe developed.

the three categories; and, perhaps even more incredibly, citizen perception of safety and police service was unaffected across the three categories despite the secret redeployment of patrol cars and manpower.

The study concluded: "Some of these findings pose a direct challenge to traditionally held beliefs. Some point only to an acute need for further research. But many point to what those in the police field have long suspected—an extensive disparity between what we want the police to do, what we believe they do, and what they can and should do."

One possible misinterpretation of the study was that the answer to crime was to reduce police departments by some 25 percent and use the funds elsewhere.* But the implication that makes much more sense is that if police officers, instead of blindly patrolling on the basic of a misguided belief in the omnipotence of a uniform, would spend the time obtaining citizen cooperation, cultivating informants, analyzing crime patterns, tracking offenders and suspects, conversing with youths, even developing tactics to trap criminals, they could be more effective.

The power of the study was enhanced by the typicality of Kansas City. Its problems are national problems. The city ranks close to Detroit in terms of aggravated assault rates, and close to Los Angeles, Denver, and Cincinnati in murder and manslaughter rates. It seems safe to assume that if routine undirected patrolling does not work for Kansas City, there's no reason to believe it will work anywhere else in the United States. In my view, in fact, undirected patrolling doesn't even make sense in a small town, perhaps even *less* sense than in the city. But in either place, aimless, monotonous, pointless patrol does not help the good people of America cope with the bad. My own basic instinct says not only that good police work can be executed without it but quite possibly it can't be done with it.

We came at the corruption from the top and from the bottom.
From the top we increased accountability. Prior to the reform, the

---

* Patrol usually consumes about half a police department's budget. About half of the patrol officer's time is spent riding or walking to "prevent" crime.

N.Y.P.D. had more unsupervised police officers running around the city doing who knew what than a Keystone Kop film. The lack of supervision was especially apparent in the Detective Bureau and in the plainclothes and narcotics units. Not surprisingly, this was where the corruption was most noxious. If we could just reduce detective and narcotics corruption to the bare minimum, hell, I might even be able to legitimize the free cup of coffee.

In narcotics we reduced the ratio of investigators to supervisor from fourteen to one to eight to one. Previously the department had asked a sergeant to supervise fourteen officers; this was absurd. Anyone who knows the first thing about police work knows that it is no more possible to supervise fourteen police officers at once than to teach eighty children a course in advanced math. Besides, we were now holding supervisors *accountable* for the conduct of their officers. It would have been very phony of us to institute that sort of requirement if in fact it was entirely impossible to fulfill.

To increase first-line supervision, we had to create many additional sergeants; and for this we had to go to City Hall. The response from Lindsay was magnificent; we got everything we asked for.

From the bottom, we tried some new approaches. Perhaps the most terrifying was Bill McCarthy's field associates program. This was really one for the books.

The field associates concept was your basic double-agent system. New graduates of the Police Academy on their first day out would be assigned to the Office of the Deputy Commissioner for Organized Crime Control. In theory, at some point Deputy Commissioner McCarthy would invite the rookie officer into his office for a little chat. During that chat McCarthy would ask if the young officer would be willing to enroll secretly as a field associate.

A field associate worked not for one but for two masters. He worked, naturally, under his direct supervisor, usually a sergeant. But on the cuff he also worked for one of McCarthy's men as a sort of secret Serpico, an undercover anti-corruption investigator. During duty hours the field associate was the average cop, but once off duty he would phone in reports from the field on what was happening and who was doing it.

McCarthy's twist was in not deputizing *every* rookie assigned to his office for the day. Some rookies would sit in his outer office and never get asked inside. But the next day, when they reported for the first regular tour of duty, they would often be asked by their supervisor or maybe by their new colleagues, How'd it go in McCarthy's office? What'd'ya tell him? What'd he say?

And when the recruit who was not asked inside answered truthfully that nothing happened, that he had spent the entire day outside his office and no one spoke a single solitary word to him, his denial of complicity in the field associate program would seem incredible.

Before long McCarthy had everyone out in the field believing that *all* the rookies were double agents. Naturally this fouled up organized corruption systems, because those involved never knew for sure who was working with McCarthy and who was not.

It was a devilish, even ruthless, scheme, but this was what we had to do. We were not only racing the Knapp Commission; we were running against losing the confidence of the public in our basic integrity as an institution. I knew we could get the jump on the Knapp Commission, but I also knew that we could not fool all of the people all of the time—and it was high time indeed to stop fooling around.

Frankly, I could do less with the bottom rungs than with the top. Up through the rank of captain all members of the N.Y.P.D. were shielded by civil service tenure. Above that level there were at the mercy of the Police Commissioner. And this P.C. was being merciless. I wasn't running for office or for a spot on the P.B.A. slate or even to win a popularity contest. I was trying to change the job.

But I was also getting as little cooperation at the top levels as at the bottom. This confirmed my suspicion when a person came into the N.Y.P.D. he was ready to become a model police officer, that few came in corrupt. But as the years go by and the frustrations, disappointments, and reversals add up, the corruption sets in like arthritis; and it becomes harder to change, to move with the times.

The executive ranks—those above captain—were a disappointment. Were they taking the reform seriously? Could I make them take it more seriously? Toward the end of the summer of 1971 I sent out this memorandum:

CONFIDENTIAL

Memorandum: To all Captains and Above
I am determined to make basic changes concerning corruption. If you fail to believe that, or fail to act aggressively against corruption, you do so at your own peril. I have not expounded the "rotten apple in a barrel" theory. The problem has been a barrel which fails to protect and encourage the good apples while permitting the bad ones to operate without sufficient control. My predecessors continued a system of attempting to control corruption almost exclusively with a relatively small Headquarters unit. That system could not work. I have discarded it.

The current system places responsibility in field commanders. They have been and will continue to be held accountable, and to an ever-increasing degree. Field commanders must learn to hold their subordinate superior officers, including sergeants, accountable.

This system can work. I am determined to make it work. Commanders who fail to act vigorously against corruption will be removed to make room for the advancement of those who will.

You should anticipate being called upon to describe what you have done to reduce corruption within the authority you possess. All that I know about accomplishing major change in large police departments in the United States convinces me that the key is change in the higher ranks. . . .

It is unhealthy for leadership to become stagnant. Opportunities for advancement must be made available to the many capable younger men who have reached the rank of Captain. Experience indicates that the higher the rank an officer achieves, the longer he or she remains in service.

An analysis of the opportunities for advancement, or even command, for our Captains is discouraging. The tendency for those above Captain to remain in service far beyond the average constitutes a heavy lid on the aspirations of promising young potential executives. . . .

I cannot permit friendship or respect for long years of satisfactory service to deter my obligation to place in top positions those most qualified and determined to accomplish the long overdue changes I have planned, regardless of seniority. . . .

It has been said that the Police Commissioner must bite the bullet,* regardless of how much it hurts. I intend to do just that, even taking the most personally painful step when necessary of removing any executive who fails to identify and correct his problems.

* "Bite the bullet" was one of the Knapp Commission's contributions to the recycling of clichés.

By the end of my administration, I doubt that many in the executive corps questioned the sincerity of this confidential memo. By then a turnover of more than 90 percent had occurred in those ranks, principally from retirements. The "bullet biters" were promoted. A few not willing to retire were demoted. But no one at that level was caught in corruption—a quite different situation from the last big scandal twenty years before, when several of the brass were caught. The Wagner era reform had brought integrity to the top but failed to build the organization and the management capability to impose it at the bottom.

Leadership was essential to the reform, and leadership was essential to the improvement of policing not just in New York. In truth, an organization cannot be any better than its leadership. This crisis in leadership was the single most important factor behind the failure of American law enforcement to perform better than it has.

The most disheartening incident of my administration concerned the Property Clerk's office. It illustrated dramatically the state of management in modern police departments. The incident occurred more than a year after the distasteful and incredible Seedman affair, and it could have forced me to resign if the story had leaked before we announced it.

It was the sort of incident that fiction writers in their wilder imaginings could not produce without some critic chiding them for being preposterous. The *Times*, in an editorial comment on the incident, wrote properly, "This strange sequel to 'The French Connection' strongly suggests that stranger things go on in the department than are conceded by the P.B.A., or dreamed up by a Knapp Commission."

The story began one cold December evening at LaGuardia Airport as I disembarked from a plane. Dave, my driver, met me at the gate, obviously concerned. "Call the First Dep," said Dave. "It's urgent."

Somehow I was able to locate a pay phone that was available, and I dialed Bill Smith's private office number, which by now I had committed to memory. I preferred the coin-box line to my car radio-telephone for security reasons.

Bill seemed as tense as Dave had been out of breath. He said, "We're missing about ten million dollars' worth of heroin from the Property Clerk's office, boss."

I said, "What?"

The story was this. In the New York Police Department, evidence seized in a case was stored by the department until final disposition of the legal proceedings—appeals and all. Whether the merchandise was a stolen car, a string of pearls, a lock of hair or a multi-million-dollar cache of heroin, it had to be marked as evidence and stored.

For the purpose of centralizing the storage process, the department eons ago had put together a Property Clerk's office. By 1970, what with all the old cases banging around the courts with loose ends everywhere, the place looked like a cross between a flea market and a three-ring circus.

As a new commissioner I was very worried. As I have said, my first move was to appoint as new commander of the storeroom a full inspector—indicating the importance I attached to the assignment—with an impeccable reputation for honesty. Then I requested a full report from the inspector on conditions inside the huge storeroom. I expected the report to be a chronicle of horrors, but in fact the new commander was relatively sanguine about the security situation. "Nothing to worry about," his report said in effect. "Everything's fine here." So I didn't worry.

But I should have. The origins of the Property Clerk theft, as it turned out, went back to 1962. It was then that a joint federal-N.Y.P.D. investigation uncovered a major heroin-importing ring operating out of Marseilles. There, raw opium from the Far East and Turkey was refined into water-soluble heroin for exportation into the United States through various smuggling devices. The ring was not only run by professionals; evidence was later uncovered of a possible link between the smugglers and present or former officials of the French government. It was a highly sophisticated ring, exporting a yearly amount of narcotics whose value could match the gross national product of many developing countries. Nevertheless, in 1962 the ring was collared by American law enforcement, and about ninety-seven pounds of heroin was confiscated, marked and sealed as evidence, and assigned to a bin in the Property Clerk's office.

Sometime between 1962 and 1972, when an audit was conducted, the narcotics disappeared, as if into thin air. The disappearance might never have been detected without the audit. The audit was not initiated by the All-Is-Well inspector in charge of the storeroom but by Inspector William Bonacum, who was now commanding officer of the Narcotics Bureau. Inspector Bonacum possessed what Chief Inspector Mike Codd once characterized as "all the lovable qualities of a lightning rod." Bonacum also possessed, in a more charitable view, tremendous integrity. It would have been inconceivable to him—as I dare say it would not have been to many of his predecessors—to react to the discovery of the missing fortune in narcotics with the instinct for coverup. Bonacum was serious about law enforcement and was deeply disturbed about the flagrant, unforgivable corruption in the S.I.U.—the Special Investigating Unit of the Narcotics Bureau. After a spate of federal, state, and city investigations and prosecutions, it became evident that S.I.U. probably deserved the distinction of being the most corrupt single unit in the history of American law enforcement. Bonacum, because he was a Murphy man as well as his own man, and with mandate from me and McCarthy, was not just a lightning rod but practically a moving electrical storm.

Bonacum had evidently become worried about the post-arrest disposition of narcotics. He knew only too well the incredible street values of illegal drugs (the newspaper estimate of the missing *French Connection* eighty-one pounds was $10 million). He knew that supervision of the entire N.Y.P.D. narcotics "crackdown" had been almost criminally negligent. Bonacum was not about to be made a fool of. Instinctively, he zeroed in on the Property Clerk's office as a big hole in the dike that might have to be plugged.

How did the fact come to light that the heroin was missing? There was no investigative series in the paper. The Special State Prosecutor, created a short time before by the Governor's executive order at the suggestion of the Knapp Commission's final report, did not have to be given a key to the Property Clerk's office. The "scandal" was exposed as a result of our own initiative.

But would you think a great deal less of me to hear that I almost wish Bonacum hadn't been such a hero, that a previous commissioner, over all the years that the heroin was supposed to have been stored there, had exercised some similar initiative and spared me the consequences of a theft for which my reform administration was not responsible?

The next day at Headquarters I was worried to death not about a coverup but about a leak. Outsiders sometimes gave police departments unwarranted credit for being able to sweep their dirty work under the rug, but in truth it is quite difficult to keep a secret among cops. My worry machine was now in second gear precisely because of the possibility that first word of the missing cache would come not from the reform administration but as a sensational scoop or leak. If others appeared to have pried this story out of the N.Y.P.D., there would be hell to pay. And it was not as though after two full years of a bloody, enervating reform I had not made enemies in the department.

At Headquarters nothing else was now important. The specter of total humiliation on something like this was a total preoccupation. To me the only way out was awfully obvious: complete disclosure of the truth as soon as possible. It seemed not so obvious to my colleagues, however. According to Smith, McCarthy, and Bonacum, the Property Clerk's office was such a disaster area that it was entirely possible that more than eighty-one pounds had been pilfered. Until the audit was further extended, any announcement might subsequently appear misleading if not deceptive. They were for holding back until we were absolutely certain of the final magnitude of the theft.

I said nothing but waited. Deputy Commissioner for Public Information Richard Kellerman, an old pro, argued vehemently that we were all in a car perched precariously on the edge of a cliff and that the slightest change in the weight distribution or even a strong wind could doom us all. In his view it was better to give the press half a loaf now than to have to deal with the unofficial disclosure of even a few crumbs.

In rebuttal, the Smith-McCarthy-Bonacum team was understandably worried about being made to look foolish because, as Bonacum explained, the procedures in the Property Clerk's office were so incredibly lax.

But we would look foolish in any event. At least if we went public with the truth now we would look honest, and perhaps generate some sympathy on the basis of our forthrightness.

I did not want to humiliate Smith or McCarthy, two very good officers, so we sat on the scandal for several days. Finally I could no longer stand the tension of waking up each morning wondering whether it would be all over the papers. I phoned Mayor Lindsay and told him about the extraordinary theft and what we planned to do about it.

When I was Public Safety Director in Washington, D.C., the Mayor there—Walter Washington—taught me well. It was always better, he had said, to get out in front on a story, put it out yourself before your enemies did, and let the chips fall where they may.

Besides, Bonacum had had more time for his audit, and the count still stood at eighty-one pounds. This was what I was going public with.

The press conference was a torture for me. But at least the Police Commissioner, not an investigative reporter, was breaking the story. Still I was ashamed. In essence, the theft meant that for some time the N.Y.P.D. had been one of the city's major suppliers of dope. At one point in the press conference I was asked whether the theft of the eighty-one pounds was the greatest amount of heroin ever lost in one pop by a law enforcement agency in the United States. "It is to my knowledge," I replied.

The reporters filed out of the auditorium in a big hurry. There was obviously not going to be a bigger story that day.

But there was to be one a few days after. For as I left the auditorium, Bill McCarthy rushed up to me and said, "Bonacum's found more missing." I was almost crushed.

At the follow-up press conference we gave out the happy news that also missing was an additional eighty-eight pounds of heroin and thirty-one pounds of cocaine. We looked bad, but at least we looked forthright.

The mystery of the theft was never solved. The state's special anti-corruption prosecutor, Maurice Nadjari, swiftly entered the case, but as this book goes to press neither he nor his successor, John Keenan, has offered a convincing explanation or an indictment. The M.O. of course was grasped instantly by Bonacum. By forging a detective's name to withdraw the drugs "for a court hearing," a person or persons over a period of time managed to substitute a harmless, worthless white powder for the high-priced heroin, eventually removing a fortune and leaving behind sacks of sugar.

In an editorial, the *Times* pointed out, "Commissioner Murphy . . .

is not responsible for what happened, and his candor in revealing the story does him credit. But he is clearly responsible . . . for discovering how deeply his force, even the smallest part of it, is involved in the drug traffic, which is the very fountainhead of the city's crime."

What we ultimately discovered was that the narcotics units under the previous police administration had made major contributions to the city's drug traffic. It was this area of corruption more than anything else which most shocked me upon my return from Detroit. Bonacum had been given a free hand to clean the bureau up; and he was surely getting a great deal of help from city, state, and federal prosecutors, who found easy hunting among our narcs. For a time, the situation was so bad that I worried that the federal narcotics agency might want no further part of joint federal-N.Y.P.D. co-operation, but McCarthy and Bonacum prevented that from occurring, and soon had gained so much confidence that joint operations were more common than ever.

Perhaps I should not have been so shocked by the growth of corruption in narcotics enforcement. After all, it had long been my contention that the single most dangerous feature of organized crime syndicates was their ability to corrupt or co-opt local law enforcement. From this illicit relation so much that was wrong with American policing flowed, including the growth of narcotics corruption. The growth of drug use and abuse in America was not a product of this corruption; more\ realistically, the corruption was a symptom of a deep-seated, permanently encrusted social problem. The corrupt narcs hardly created the huge demand for heroin, nor did they provide more than a small piece of the total supply; but they did profit from it. No recent development in American policing has been so dispiriting, or ugly.

In New York, as in Detroit, Washington, and many other police departments, internal and external racial tensions had been pushed down under the surface. They were a big worry. We set up some encounter-type sessions between white cops and black cops, with the idea of getting things out into the open, but we were still worried. Reports continued coming in from the precincts about racial antagonisms, exaggerating the usual organizational tensions in precincts over desirable assignments, selection of patrol car partners, rewards, and disciplinary practices. A typical problem involved a black officer driving home after completing a tour at midnight, "forgetting" the speed limit, and being stopped by a team of white officers. When he identified himself and was denied the "usual courtesy" (no ticket, just a warning) accorded a fellow officer, he shouted, "Racist!" And so another internal racial confrontation was put on the escalator moving toward a "federal case."

At first glance it seemed that our white officers were doing an exceptional job of law enforcement on their off-duty black brethren, but like most stories, this one had two sides.

We struggled, naturally, to keep these ugly incidents out of the papers. Benjamin Ward, the Deputy Commissioner for Community Relations, went out to the precincts to sort out the fact from the fiction. In a short period of time, with the help of field commanders, who in the N.Y.P.D., whatever their other faults, were almost without exception highly sophisticated in race relations, he turned the problem around.

Another feature of life in the N.Y.P.D. that we discussed with Ben Ward, the highest-ranking black commander in the department, was the question of a white officer's assignment to a high-crime precinct; that is, a precinct with a high percentage of minority residents. With so few black officers, even those precincts with almost totally black populations would be staffed by a large majority of white officers, and the problem was similar in Puerto Rican precincts. As a result, many young white officers began their careers in black precincts. While some enjoyed the high level of activity, others preferred reassignment to quieter places as soon as possible.

The question for management was how to develop a policy that was fair to both the individual and to the department. How to encourage and reward those willing to serve in the most demanding and dangerous precincts in order to match the best people with the most sensitive assignments? The consequences of an error in judgment in Harlem were likely to be far more destructive than in, say, Flushing. How to deal with the problem of the officer, sergeant, or lieutenant whose performance indicated he might, as a direct result of his racism, make a bad decision in Harlem and was therefore, even though he could perform well in a white middle-class precinct, a risk?

Back in the 1950s, the question of equal rights led to an administrative decision to scatter black officers into every precinct in the city. This was just to prove a point! The point under conveyance was that, simply, there was no difference between black and white. Of course, this is, from the standpoint of police work, nonsense. All other things being equal, a black officer is much more valuable in Harlem than a white officer. So once the point was made in the 1950s that black officers could work in any precinct in the city, they should no longer have been added to the white neighborhoods, where their value was a fraction of what it could have been in black areas. But once again astutely unthinking management perpetuated what should have been a once-only demonstration. It was important to make the point, but more important to redeploy future manpower once that point had been satisfactorily made. It was frustrating to have hundreds of black officers where whites could have been—and vice versa.

The ultimate solution was the creation of a career development program which rewarded service in high-crime precincts with promotions and desirable assignments, such as detective work. The new program therefore gave the individual officer a choice in determining whether he preferred minimum service in a high-crime precinct, to the possible long-range detriment of promotion and assignment, or longer service, which would, we told him, benefit his career.

In minority relations, I tried to help Ben Ward as much as I could, appearing frequently on Harlem radio talk shows and similar programs in an effort to present myself as concerned and sensitive. But on more consequential levels, such as recruitment, my hands were tied. My prison keeper was the civil service system, which, unlike Detroit, operated outside the sphere of influence of the Police Commissioner and his high command. It was a law unto itself. The culturally biased civil service examination for entrance, even when the passing grade was lowered to (in theory) accommodate minority applicants, served to let in more white high school drop outs.

A better answer was probably to be found a step in the opposite direction: to reduce the size of the force by retirements of officers with more than twenty years of service, among whom was a very low percentage of minorities. As I wrote, in a moment of wishful thinking, to Peter Ring of the Personnel Bureau (Ring was one of the civilian outside experts we had hired and whose presence considerably improved the degree of professionalism in N.Y.P.D.'s top management): "In my dream world, police officer attrition would continue until we were down to 28,000 positions maximum rather than hire more high school dropout policemen. That alone would slightly increase the percentage of blacks and Hispanics in the department. Dozens more civilian professionals could be hired, including a high percentage of blacks and Hispanics. In order to obtain more blacks and Hispanics for future appointment as police officers, new programs for community service officers, aides, trainees and/or Model Cities police, et cetera . . . would be started."

Today, in the late 1970s, our experience in the deployment of black officers serves to illuminate some of the issues now involved in the question of the role of women in a police department.

In theory, there is nothing inherently less defensible about the idea of an all-*female* police department than there is about an all-male department. In the absence of evidence to the contrary—and I do not believe such evidence will ever be forthcoming—we shall take it as axiomatic that women have as much right to be police officers as men.

In practice, the resistance to women in policing is fierce, though it is ever so gradually diminishing. The resistance stems from a variety of concerns—ranging from sheer male chauvinism to the perhaps more understandable worries of the wives of officers thrust into a work-companionship situation with a female officer. Nevertheless, whatever the reason, resistance to the sexual as well as racial integration of police departments is a losing battle. Indeed, many departments have hired women officers solely as a result of legal action; they were unable to prove in court that, in essence, it takes a man to do police work.

For some time, Chief Ed Davis of Los Angeles believed that he had the courts outmaneuvered. He said he wouldn't hire *anyone* whose height was under five feet eight inches. Then, however, he had the burden of showing the relationship between minimum height and maximally effective police work. Not surprisingly, and with some rapidity, the courts adjudged the height requirement for what it was—discriminatory.

In truth, police departments will never be able to demonstrate that police work is inherently or necessarily a man's job. On the contrary, there is some evidence that female officers perform police duties not only as well as men but in certain circumstances even better. Of course, police departments have for some time utilized women in youth work, in aiding young victims of sex crimes, and in dealing with instances of brutality against females. But beyond these obvious cliché roles, women have demonstrated unusual competence in areas where they might have been expected to be incompetent. For instance, one study showed that in the experience of the Cincinnati Police Department, female officers were especially adept at defusing potentially violent situations among emotionally charged combatants. In one particular low-life saloon, the study showed, female officers time and again proved themselves skilled negotiators and clever mediators in situations where serious violence could have resulted. The study suggested that the very physical presence of the women officers had a disarming, calming effect. In other words, instead of the lack of macho being a handicap, evidently it was a plus.

With these new kinds of data coming in, police administrators are faced with the delightful situation of having on their hands not a problem but a golden opportunity. Women, the data now suggest, make satisfactory cops. With this in mind, the police administrator must then try to get around a problem all too reminiscent of the question of black cops in the 1950s. The problem is that female officers today are not seen as a valuable resource but as a civil rights pilot project. They have been reduced to an equal rights question.

My own pet wish is to pass over as quickly as possible the demonstration that women officers can do everything as well as men (et cetera, et cetera) and move to a more intelligent level of discourse and personnel deployment where women are used for the special capabilities they possess. Women would be extremely desirable acquisitions for a police agency even if equal rights litigation had never forced the issue. Indeed, coming at the question of the role of women from the legal and constitutional point of view has tended to obscure the point that women are in fact somewhat different from men, and that, as far as we can tell, in certain situations may actually be more competent than men. Since none of our police departments sport a fifty-fifty ratio of men and women, is it discriminatory and sexist to suggest that we ought to be using those few women we have in the best possible way?

The police officer who started the chain of events that led first to the Knapp Commission and then to the appointment of a reform police administration was Patrolman Frank Serpico. I was in Washington when the Serpico revelations broke in the New York *Times*—courtesy of the solid investigative reportage of staff reporter Dave Burnham. I was an instant convert to the Serpico legend. (Indeed, was I not even a bit rueful that *I* hadn't thought, when I was in plainclothes centuries ago, of teaming up with someone as resourceful as Sergeant David Durk, the Amherst graduate who had a friend at the New York *Times*?) Thus it came as quite a surprise when, as Police Commissioner, I found that my admiration for Serpico was not universally shared in the high command, as indicated by this memorandum which I circulated to the brass early in 1971.

CONFIDENTIAL

When Patrolman Frank Serpico was shot recently a question arose as to whether he should receive a gold shield soon.

There is some feeling that his involvement in misconduct investigations has been considered a negative factor.

I'm inclined to favor a gold shield if you see no objections.

But there were objections—a hell of a lot of them. No issue touched off quite the intensity of emotional debate at Headquarters as the question of whether Frank Serpico ought to be rewarded for his efforts in exposing corruption by awarding him the coveted gold shield. Certainly, no other personnel issue facing the high command came close to matching the Serpico promotion issue for sheer viscera and sustained suspense.

The root causes of the controversy, which we kept rather well hidden from the public eye, were many. One was the inevitable resentment caused by Serpico's public confessions about the department. The gut instinct of all bureaucracies and professions is to wash one's own laundry—if it gets washed at all—in great privacy. But another factor may have been my own management style.

That style places a premium on the delegation of authority and responsibility. The goal is to achieve a consensus on an issue or policy, even when I have made up my own mind on the issue. Projecting an illusion of indecision thus was an element of that style; on occasion, I would even refrain from personally partaking in the deliberations for fear my presence might intimidate frank discussion, or worse yet might tip the real hand that I held. I preferred even the illusion of indecision to an immediate decision for which there was no high-command consensuality. This practice became more frequent, naturally, as the high command more and more took on the Murphy look—when we had several high-powered people knocking heads together.

Thus I allowed the Serpico question to be kicked around, and it almost turned into a soccer match. Most surprising of all, I think, was the reservation of Sydney Cooper, now the feared Chief of Inspectional Services.

Cooper, as the former Bronx borough commander, had worked with Serpico in an effort to clean up the plainclothes corruption in the Bronx. He knew Serpico better than any of us at Headquarters; indeed, Smith and I had never met him. I had expected that Cooper would be gung-ho for the promotion, but his position was quite lukewarm.

At a series of high-level discussions the nature of Cooper's lack of enthusiasm began to show. In brief, without going into every detail, Cooper felt that Serpico was unreliable and uncooperative. Not that he was dishonest, not that his allegations of corruption were not generally true and important, not that Serpico in some sense wasn't an important person; but that, in the final analysis, Frank Serpico was, well, unreliable. The phrase Cooper used over and over again at this meeting was that Serpico was a "reluctant dragon."

The nub of Cooper's deep and sincere reservations about Serpico was that, time and again, Serpico's allegations of corruption, upon examination, would evaporate into thin air. Of course, we knew he had seen and had been anguished by corrupt behavior; he was not a Don Quixote. But he was so light on specifics (in some cases he would not even show up to give testimony) that he began driving Cooper . . . well . . . crazy. Also, Serpico would not allow himself to be "wired" with a body radio transmitter.

Anyone who doubted the sincerity of Cooper's commitment to professional integrity was either insane or grievously misinformed. Thus when Cooper began expressing real doubts about the promotion of Serpico, we were all a bit thrown for a loop.

Finally, as the dust began to settle, I sent a memorandum to First Deputy Smith and Chief Cooper.

CONFIDENTIAL

What about Serpico?
Should he be made a Detective?
Should he be assigned to Internal Affairs?
   —overtly?
   —covertly? (i.e., assigned to a field unit—detective squad, for
      example—but identifying hazards and corrupt members of the
      force)
Should he be assigned within the 10th Division area so he can work
with Inspector Delise?*
The "New York Magazine" article and other articles put me on the
spot to demonstrate I'm bigger than "the system" and willing to reward
Serpico.†

A few days later we held an unusual promotion ceremony at Headquarters. Six police officers were advanced to detective for their anti-corruption work. A senior adviser noted that this was the largest group of officers ever rewarded for catching *criminals who were cops*. One of the six was Frank Serpico.

When I left the ceremony, I felt good about myself. I felt I had, in a symbolic stroke, changed the rules of the game. In the past nothing was ever done to encourage honest officers to expose corruption or identify criminals in uniform. Now, under the reform, officers were

---

* Inspector Paul Delise was introduced to the general public because of the film *Serpico*. Delise was the police official who accompanied Serpico and Durk to the New York *Times* to add weight to Serpico's presentation. But Delise was well known in the N.Y.P.D. well before that—by some, resentfully, as "Saint Paul." In truth, Delise was a genuine twentieth-century hero. Under the Murphy administration he would receive temporal rewards—a promotion.

† This was for Cooper's benefit. Translation: Even if I agree with you about Serpico, I'm under an awful lot of pressure to bend with the wind. The truth was that, back then, I didn't agree with Cooper's reservations. I was a Serpico fan.

being rewarded—and with the highest accolade of all—for taking the initiative in coming forward.

But today I am not so sure. Today, a half dozen years after that promotion, four years out of the N.Y.P.D., from the perspective of Washington and the Police Foundation, I have very grave doubts.

On the surface it was the right thing to do, but almost *too* right. Now, after the film and the book, I just do not know.

What troubles me most is the impression in the film that Serpico was set up for the kill by police officers anxious to silence him forever. I am greatly disturbed by this because I just do not think it is true.

In the twelve months prior to Serpico's being shot while on a narcotics raid, literally dozens of police officers had been shot, and many of them were narcotics undercover officers. Indeed, for some time in the early 1970s it was practically open season on police officers—a dirty, horrible ordeal for all of us, including the Police Commissioner, whose attendance at the death watch outside the hospital room and at the funeral was mandatory, part of the job. Indeed, like so many others, I waited for a while outside Serpico's hospital room after he had been shot, and I returned the next morning for a short visit.

Thus, Serpico's tragic misfortune was not something that stood out, unfortunately. Indeed, at the time of the shooting, no one even raised the question of whether Serpico had been set up. Certainly, none of the police officers—several dozen, as I recall—who waited outside to give blood as Serpico's life wavered in the balance believed that he had been set up. If there had been any such substantial possibility, the times were such that not only the P.D. but the district attorneys, the B.N.D.D. (federal narcs), and other state and federal agencies would pursue more vigorously than normally any allegations or leads. But there were none. Not a single New York reporter came across even the slightest evidence.

To be sure, there may have been some hate mail sent to Serpico. I do not know this for a fact, but I'm willing to take it as true. But you must remember that there are nuts in the N.Y.P.D. just as there are in the U.S. State Department or the Motor Vehicle Department; and surely Serpico's revelations rubbed against the grain of many cops. But the fact was that at the time of the shooting, to put matters entirely callously, Serpico seemed like just another cop shot that year in the line of duty—and in a very, very scary and dangerous line of duty: narcotics undercover work.

It was only after the book and the film that the impression became widespread that Serpico had been set up in that hallway in Brooklyn by police officers. The impression, understandably, made a good cinematic resolution for the film, which claimed only to be *based* on fact. But the impression is so widespread now that almost every place I go I am asked questions about why Serpico had been set up.

I do not believe Serpico was set up, and, even more, I do not believe that Detective Serpico believes it either.

Chapter Nine

The Future
of Policing

Despite all the activity, it was almost a routine morning at the Police Foundation in Washington. After the weekly staff meeting, a troubled police chief from a Midwest city telephoned long-distance. "Pat, I've got a big problem here with the D.A.," he said. "We're getting beat over the head every other day in the papers. Maybe I need a legal adviser or something. What do you think? Got any ideas." The chief said that he would be visiting Washington late the following week. Roberta Lesh, the Foundation's administrative assistant, booked the Chief into the schedule for a long chat.

That afternoon, the mayor of a Connecticut city telephoned with a problem that he was hardly the first municipal chief executive ever to suffer. "My chief just won't talk to reporters, Pat," he said. "He clams up. Maybe I need a new chief? He's over the hill anyway. Never was any damn good, for that matter. What should I look for? *Who* should I interview?"

The routine morning was followed by a full afternoon. Included that Monday was a joint meeting of staffs and minds—the Police Foundation's and the National Institute of Law Enforcement and Criminal Justice's. The subject was detectives. On Tuesday was an intensive staff discussion about police juvenile units—and our project on same, funded by the federal Law Enforcement Assistance Administration. For Wednesday a one-day trip to New Orleans to orchestrate a discussion group of twenty-five mayors on the subject of urban policing, chiefs, and crime. Thursday a big meeting back in Washington on how to measure police productivity. Arrests? Citizen contacts? Crime statistics? Radio-car runs? Friday a meeting in the Foundation's conference room with four police chiefs recently constituted as the "research committee" of the Police Executive Research Forum—a Foundation creation that could go far. That afternoon a private session with the head of the National Organization of Black Law Enforcement Executives. Concern about L.E.A.A. policies—and funding decisions.

This is a rather typical week in the life of the Police Foundation, a non-profit research center established in 1970 with a $30 million grant from the Ford Foundation and through the leadership of its president, McGeorge Bundy. I became the Police Foundation's second president in May of 1973. It turned out to be a fortuitous move.

There is nothing like the Police Foundation in the United States. The underlying thought for everything it does rests not on the proposition that American policing, with minor modifications, is in good shape but on precisely the opposite. The overall effect of the Police Foundation may be symbolic and inspirational as much as anything else. For its very existence is probably reassuring to those in this country who are either intuitively or through experience persuaded of the need to improve policing. Its very existence means that there are persons in this country who care deeply about this improvement. It means there is every reason to hope that someday quantum improvements will come. It means that there can be institutions like the Police Foundation that may someday help transform policing into, if not a profession, then at least into a legitimate calling.

However, the future of policing, unhappily, will not be decided at the Police Foundation. To me, the quality of policing is so essential to the solution of our critical crime problem that it is both heartening to come to the realization of a shared concern and disheartening to realize how relatively little that concern seems to be shared. The total problem, at the moment at least, seems far greater than the totality of the movement toward correction. If the orthodoxy of American policing is the immovable object, then the unorthodoxy of reform seems not quite the irresistible force.

Under these circumstances, the Police Foundation has taken on a significance that perhaps far exceeds its means. When the private Foundation was created in 1970, everyone sensed that against the colossus of the federal Law Enforcement Assistance Administration, with its annual $800 million budget, the modestly funded Foundation might look like a weak sister to big brother. Therefore, rather than set its sights all over the landscape, it made more sense to pick the shots selectively. The research targets selected were (1) the basic daily activities of police officers on the street, and (2) the effectiveness, or ineffectiveness, of these traditional functions in controlling crime.

The accuracy and success of our targeting, it was understood by all involved, would rest quite simply enough on the quality of our research, not the quantity. Instead of grantsmanship, the Foundation would become associated in everyone's mind with a kind of thinksmanship, and concentrate accordingly on re-examining some of the basic assumptions on which American policing is built. Unfettered by the political and bureaucratic constraints of a government agency, the small Foundation could contribute some things to police improvement that L.E.A.A. could not.

A good example of the Foundation's unique role occurred in the spring of 1977, with the release of a study on firearm abuse. The study, which drew on police records in ten of the nation's fifteen largest cities, was an eye-opener in its revelation that the famous Saturday Night Special (the cheapest of handguns) played no dominant role in the commission of violent crime. On the contrary, according to our study, higher priced brand-name handguns are used as crime weapons every bit as frequently as the cheaper firearms. In consequence, any police or law enforcement strategy that is focused on the Saturday Night Special to the exclusion of other types of handguns will inevitably miss the mark. Yet, prior to this study, it was practically an axiom of American law enforcement that most gun crimes were committed by the Saturday Night Special.

The study also contained implications for federal, state, and local law enforcement agencies on the subject of gun control, an advance in American civilization which I have advocated ever since my days as an instructor at the Police Academy in New York. For example, evidence accumulated for the study suggested strongly that the primary source of supply for firearms was not organized crime or firearm bootleggers but the private gun-possessing citizen. "The apparent high volume of firearm theft suggests," the study concluded, "that enough firearms are now stolen each year from law-abiding citizens to fill most criminal needs." This astounding conclusion adds, of course, to the argument for serious gun-control legislation, which would perhaps even include requirements to force licensees to take specific security measures to guard against thefts.

The firearm study was only the first step toward establishing a body of useful knowledge about the problem of firearm abuse and policy alternatives for dealing with it; but at least it was a start, for it destroyed another of the many unfounded assumptions of American law enforcement.

Perhaps an even more significant contribution by the Foundation in this respect was the now famous Kansas City patrol experiment.

While still Commissioner in New York, I had been invited out to Kansas City for one of the original planning sessions held by the Foundation's staff. It was a freewheeling, penetrating, and at times even intoxicating free-for-all; and when it came my turn to speak, I naturally held forth on one of my favorite themes: patrol.

Ever since foot patrol in Red Hook in the 1940s, I said, I yearned for some hard research to test the blindly held belief that patrolling the streets, on foot or by car, per se prevented crime.

At the Urban Institute in 1968, I explained at the meeting, I had developed a design for reorganizing patrol at the basic level. The design relied little on mechanical tin-soldier patrolling and heavily on friendly interaction between citizens and police.

I believed, I said, that it was the citizen who contributed most substantially to arrests. It was the citizen, after all, who most frequently phoned in the location of a crime or identified the suspect for immediate arrest or later apprehension. Any patrol design that regards as marginal or superfluous the valuable criminal intelligence that citizens possess is necessarily self-defeating. For this information obviously becomes useless, even worthless, if police officers fail to go after it.

I mentioned too that when I went to Detroit, the Urban Institute design was implemented on a trial basis in one small area—the Beat Commander project. For the first time one person would have total command of a beat—a sergeant would direct the work of the officers in obtaining citizen cooperation, thereby reducing traditional undirected patrol. I also mentioned that in New York—this is 1971 now—we would be trying an expanded version of the Beat Commander, to be known as "neighborhood policing."

So, at this early planning session I raised, as did others, the question that was perhaps the hallmark of my continuing critique of American police and crime control: "Patrol is the most expensive police function. People just do not realize that the great bulk of police manpower is assigned to patrol, and yet its value is only assumed— and the assumption has never been tested. If the assumption is wrong, therefore, we are facing a situation of enormous waste on a national scale. My question: Is that patrol assumption valid?"

My audience in the conference room seemed to agree that I had raised an important issue (though of course I was hardly the first ever to raise it). The Foundation was already into discussions with the Kansas City Police Department and Clarence Kelley, then its chief— and an outstanding one. He had been serving as K.C. Chief for more than ten years but, unlike so many other entrenched chiefs, was not threatened by research. After a long period of internal discussion, considering various routes and strategies, it was decided to test preventive patrol.

Thus was the famous Kansas City patrol experiment launched— the Foundation's first truly far-reaching research project. By the time I came to the Foundation in 1973, the experiment was well under way. And when the results were released, they struck the police world like a tsunami hitting a coastal town. Even today the results of that study, described in Chapter Eight, are still making waves.

Understandably, the police world is not research-oriented. It is necessarily a world of action—or perhaps, more truthfully, a world of *re*action. But it should make room for more thinking and research; it should give no quarter to mindless, complacent anti-intellectualism. But in the police world, opposition to any serious research at all is intense.

The chiefs generally are too comfortable with the assumptions handed down through the ages—patrol prevents crime, detectives solve most cases on which they work diligently, more police out on the streets in uniform establishing a visible presence can reduce crime, and so on. Thus "eggheads"—the police word for those who raise penetrating questions about police work—are terribly threatening to the police establishment, which like an ostrich solves the problem by hiding from it. While most observers would probably agree that the work of the Police Foundation has added considerably to the state of knowledge about policing—our reports have been praised for their quality and professionalism—our findings have not been accepted by most chiefs, much less implemented by most police departments. This has been at once the most serious disappointment and most pressing personal challenge since the N.Y.P.D. commissionership.

Accordingly, the Foundation has had to do more than simply publish reports. It has also had to promote them, defend them, fight for them—all as part of the effort of filling the role of communications hub for police careerists and public officials who are not at all happy with the police establishment's unquestioning acceptance of the status quo. "What's wrong with the way we've always done it?"—to quote some high officials in the N.Y.P.D. in 1970.

The answer, of course, is the condition of American society in the 1970s and the failure of American policing to have had a more consequential impact on crime. Failure speaks for itself (there is usually no one around to speak for it), yet in a way it has been the difficult job of the Foundation to articulate the nature of that failure, even at the risk of losing popularity points in certain quarters.

The police alone cannot solve the crime problem. Neither can the combined police and criminal justice "system"—even if it were improved to merit the "system" label. But the police could do far better if they understood their potential, as well as their limits, and spoke clearly and honestly to the public about both. They have failed to understand. They have failed to educate the public. They have contributed more to the problem than to its solution by defending the status quo when basic change is needed.

The Foundation, then, has not been playing games; it has been fighting, quietly, a war. About a year ago some two dozen police chiefs from the three hundred largest departments around the country, under the auspices of the Foundation, met and put together a new organization designed to move the police world forward. Working as both advisers and participants in Foundation work, they have become a positive force for police improvement and reform. Incredibly, it is the first organization of police leaders in the United States. The traditional state and national associations of chiefs have included—and in fact been dominated by—chiefs who are in truth the equivalent of sergeants and lieutenants, men who head the small to tiny departments.

As a result, what the Foundation has tried to represent has now become virtually a new school of thought in American policing. Its findings, in its studies, reports, and conferences, are no longer just academic matters; they now attract the attention not only of the serious police leaders, criminal justice researchers, and concerned academics, but also the attention of city managers, mayors, city council members, and even budget directors. Occasionally, a Foundation report even finds its way to the pages of the American press, contributing to the neglected education of the public who pay for police service and protection.

This turnabout is important, and not just to the Foundation. For instance, one of the policy alternatives now open for inspection by enlightened chiefs visiting Washington is an experiment in the San Diego P.D. concerning one-officer versus two-officer patrol cars. This West Coast experiment is an important one, because many officers believe sincerely that a one-officer car is unacceptably dangerous. In New York, for instance, the P.B.A. has refused to countenance one-officer cars. But is the one-officer car actually less safe? One questions the assumption. Since violent crime tends to be heavily concentrated in some parts of cities and relatively rare elsewhere, it can probably be demonstrated satisfactorily by statistical methods that officers in one-officer cars in low-crime areas are in fact safer than officers in two-officer cars in high-crime areas. Under such circumstances, then, one-officer cars could be used in many areas, helping to conserve a great deal of money in many police budgets.

For American policing, technology—hardware—is the great modern god that failed. Its impact has not only been overrated, it has been misunderstood, especially in the police world.

A good example is the computer, a very expensive item. POLICE DEPARTMENT USING COMPUTERS TO PREDICT CRIME, the newspaper story will headline, with a picture of the beaming chief and the computer company representative shaking hands in the chief's office with an American flag in the background. But the sad unwritten story behind this picture is that, while companies are hard-selling these expensive toys all over the country, the chiefs really have no idea what to use them for. In some departments the computer is nothing more than a high-priced adding machine—a pocket calculator picking your pocket. It may help collate arrest figures, deployment statistics, and so forth, but it is not "predicting crime."

In other departments a computer system may be designed to expedite the process by which a squad car responds to the scene of a crime. In New York they called this program SPRINT, and it was advertised as the biggest innovation in policing since the nightstick. The only trouble with it is that the victims of crime don't generally call the police as fast as the computer can digest the call. That is, the hapless victim, in shock and panic, will first call his wife, or his mother, or even his doctor; *then* he'll call the police. Experience has shown that it takes the victim, on the average, a full seventeen minutes to notify the police. By this time the several-hundred-thousand-dollar computer system has become a several-hundred-thousand-dollar irrelevancy.

One Foundation study on response time demonstrated that in effect the whole business—and indeed it has become just that—of improving police response time has been vastly oversold. So have other types of hardware, like the helicopter, which in a fiscal crunch, because of its incredible consumption of fuel, becomes the first item to be axed by the hard-pressed police administrator. In many departments these costly machines have become virtual museum pieces. Only a few of the very largest city departments can justify having them.

On the whole, technological "improvements" in policing tend not to be just expensive and at their best marginally useful; sometimes they can, because of unthinking overreliance on them, have quite a destructive effect on the *art* of policing, especially in the fine texture of citizen-police relations. Take two seemingly harmless technologies long established in policing—the radio and the automobile. As these "improvements" became available to the police over the past forty years, the friendly style of policing that existed naturally when officers walked among the people in the commercial zones and shopping streets and other densely peopled sections was gradually replaced by a more mathematical, technological style: the patrolling of America from behind closed doors, on wheels, in communication with the outside world through a windshield and over a radio frequency.

At the time, no one really knew any better; the use of the car and the radio on the face of it seemed like an unobjectionable idea. What little was written on the subject reassured the police that they were preventing crime by their increased presence (the car covering much greater distance in any period of time). Quality, it seemed, was to be measured in quantity.

The actual effect of the technology was to increase the distance between the community and the police, and thereby dilute the quality of the police service, even though the intention was otherwise. Being closer and friendlier, the foot officer knew much more about crime, delinquency, criminal associations, and ex-offenders on his relatively confined patrol beat; he could be held more accountable for controlling crime. It was virtually impossible to hold accountable those who had never known foot patrol; and since the smallest unit of the police department had been so organized as to be beyond accountability, in essence the entire police department could not be called to account. Everything had been so organized that at no one level, low or high, could blame be affixed or total authority conferred. It was in this way that police departments were, perhaps inadvertently, organized around a totality of irresponsibility. The motorized officer necessarily possessed less criminal intelligence, was remote from crime, was frequently dispatched beyond his assigned sector, and covered great gobs of territory—all the consequences of a new technology from which so much benefit was predicted.

The important new "technologies" today, in my opinion, are better management systems: reorganizing the structure and refining the procedures by which the country is policed. The answer lies not in gimmickry but in smart, friendly policing.

As the white middle class left the cities for the suburbs and was replaced by poor blacks and other minorities, the predominantly white police officers literally rolled up their car windows and behaved more and more like visitors to a strange planet. Without the people on their side, and lacking the criminal information, intelligence, and citizen cooperation essential to control crime, a tragic new chemistry was brewing: (a) populations that largely for socioeconomic reasons committed more crime, and (b) police relying on ineffective, irrational crime control policies. This brew helped create the crime explosion of the 1960s and '70s.

The police, unfortunately lacking introspection and the ability to exercise honest self-criticism, could only reply with a simplistic explanation: The decisions of the Warren Supreme Court were at fault.

With some changes now in the air, the future looks less bleak than it did even five years ago. The movement away from "stranger policing" has begun and should continue. Variations on neighborhood team policing are now being tried throughout the country, as white police departments have had to learn to relate to black communities without rancor or testiness.

The shift would not necessarily involve less motorized patrol and a spectacular increase in foot patrol. We have probably passed well beyond the era when total foot patrol would not be an anachronism. But the shift should mean a lot less time wasted on so-called preventive patrol, whose chief effect seems to be only to waste manpower. It means American policing is moving finally in the right direction.

Ideally, there could come the day in America when each neighborhood will have its own identifiable police officer playing the lead role in managing the control of crime. That officer's only function would be to relate to the community, gather criminal intelligence information, and serve the neighborhood in the fashion of a very local chief of police. For that neighborhood officer there would be no aimless patrol, no answering calls (especially those that would take him out of his turf). Nothing that headquarters could give that officer to do could possibly take priority over the provision of intimate police service to the community to which he is assigned.

From the loneliness of the solitary beat officer, to the collectivity of the larger police department, the changes we are now seeing are almost all for the better. The recruitment of more minorities and women could make neighborhood policing less difficult. A much higher percentage of civilian employees, including professionals— lawyers, planners, analysts, computer specialists, personnel administrators, and so forth—should enable a police department to cope with the increasing complexity of crime. As the mythology of detectives continues to be discredited, better use could be made of their time, and their efforts could be more closely coordinated with those of neighborhood officers. The quality of management should greatly improve. State and federal governments could get involved, and standards could be created, and incrementally raised. As part of the movement, more police chiefs will be selected from outside departments. The insularity and narrow provincialism that currently exist because of police inbreeding should begin to break down.

As policing is improved—with better-educated, more articulate personnel, especially in management, where the problem is greatest—the improved status should strengthen policing's hand in the effort to eliminate partisan interference and corruption. In the improvement of quality of policing, as opposed to quantity of police, the work of police departments should be more finely in tune with that of other branches of the criminal justice system. Heads of different branches now do not understand the aggregate effect of their work because they do not know what is occurring in other parts of the system, and therefore cannot tell whether they are working at cross purposes or in a team fashion.

The police in some localities produce more arrests than the system can reasonably handle; by the same token, the courts often produce rulings which mystify, in the sense of confusing and demoralizing. Better data systems—and here is where a touch of technology could indeed help—should be able to orchestrate the system to minimize frustration and maximize crime control. And as the data produced by these systems become more usable, the police should become much more productive and direct their activities in a way that will make more sense not only to themselves but to those who must work with them.

Up until now, the police have tended to take satisfaction in the mere completion of arrests, and then feel they can walk away, having done the job. But all too often the offender who returns to the street and the community to become a recidivist is cited by the police as evidence of the failure of the courts or the correction system. Living in a glass house, the police should be wary about taking positions which might create a rock storm. Why haven't the police devoted enough time to the offender who after being arrested returns—whether through bail, parole, or probation—literally to the scene of of the crime; i.e., the community? Because they have not been working closely with probation and parole officers, the police have undercut their own effectiveness. In the future the system will work better if every part of it works together systematically. Are we all on the same side, or aren't we?

Curiously, the two most serious problems are located at the bottom and the top of policing—at the level of the neighborhood and at the level of the chief's office. It may be only my own personal prejudice that of the two the problem at the top is the more severe. This conclusion arises from the axiomatic proposition that the work of police officers—no matter how idealistic, energetic, and motivated—can never transcend the caliber of their leadership. Leadership will either be constant inspiration or instant depression. Cops at the lower rungs cannot escape management.

The problem at the top is not solely with the chief, though by now it should be clear that the relative lack of mobility and the abundance of insularity have produced a less than distinguished national corps of chiefs. But even where the chief is a prince, that often is not enough. One of the louder laments of thinking police chiefs concerns the unsatisfactory level of management ability among the deputy chiefs in their departments. This second echelon of deputies contains those upon whom the chief depends for carrying out policy. Even good chiefs who have risen to the top of the department in which they started echo the same complaint.

The problem is a symptom of the nationwide civil service system. Regrettably, it is common under civil service for every position, ranging up to the chief's, if not including the chief's, to carry tenure. Tenure means that it is often impossible to fire people for poor performance. Even misconduct, short of a serious crime, can be inadequate in some jurisdictions to support a dismissal. The result is often a good top manager functioning under the severe handicap of a management team that in essence can tell him where to go. "Just try to make me work!" one has heard high-ranking second-echelon brass to say. "I've got tenure."

Even less seemly is the specter of the top chief who pulls his civil service rank and defies elected officials, reporters, and the public in their attempt to hold him accountable or to persuade him to meet changing problems or conditions: "I'm here for life, and I'll do it my way."

An ideal civil service system would be one in which the worst excesses of all extremes would be minimized, in which there would be neither total political control nor total insulation from performance, realities, or public demands for accountability.

In many jurisdictions the situation is even worse. Neither civil service nor any other kind of merit system has been tried; this is of course unfortunate. It often means straight political appointments, and a total lack of standards or integrity. Without tenure or pension benefits, incumbents often make the most of a short term by lining their pockets or extending special privileges that can be redeemed later.

And even where civil service has been introduced, it can be nothing more than a phony veneer intended to conceal favoritism, politics, payoffs, or kickbacks in hiring and promotion. In some places one can get the job by purchasing it, or receive the promotion by paying off the promoter.

But perhaps the most frustrating problem for police administrators is the civil service guarantee of tenure in both entry-level appointments and promotions. As a result, performance is weak at lower levels, productivity improvement is extremely difficult to achieve, and necessary changes are resisted. Effective policing in the 1970s is hindered more by overly protective civil service than it is aided by the independence of civil service tenure.

In defense of the American police officer, our society clearly gives him more to do than can be humanly accomplished. In the future, police performance will probably increase only as we decide on the priorities of those things we want accomplished by our policing. This will require sorting out among crimes and among criminal behavior. How seriously are we offended by gambling, public intoxication, marijuana use, and prostitution? By comparison, would we say that gamblers and prostitutes are actually more offensive and dangerous than the perpetrators of consumer frauds, or even drunk drivers? If we know that our police cannot possibly take on all the crime problems, which ones do we want them to go after first? It seems to me that if we go after all of them more or less indiscriminately, we may wind up empty-handed.

In essence, the future quality of policing probably depends on the instructions and choices of the citizens as much as anything else. It could be that in the decriminalization of some behavior, police work will become both more discriminating and less scattershot. But some choices have to be made before better police work can proceed.

Curiously, the future of police work may depend somewhat less on the competence and vision of the commissioner or chief. As the demonstration of police ineffectiveness and inefficiency continues, the power of the head of police will decline, and in the vacuum the city council, the mayor, the city manager, or the budget director will be swept in to take control of or have substantial leverage over deployment, budget, manpower levels, and planning. This development would largely be the result of the failure of the police world to admit its limitations honestly and do better what it can do well. At the same time, from below, militant police unions will grow in strength and size, to the point where any significant change in departmental policy may be subject to union veto. With some police unions affiliating with the Teamsters, this may not be an ideal development.

It is entirely arguable that police departments are no more egregiously managed than many other government institutions; cops certainly have no monopoly on incompetent organization. It is conceivable that the production of license plates and official papers by a motor vehicle office and pointless paper by the State Department may not be inherently less serious examples of bureaucratic juvenilism than anything produced by police departments. As with police corruption, police mismanagement floats in a larger sea; it is less an exception to the general rule than yet another manifestation of it.

But the analogy is at the same time somewhat misleading. There is presumably some difference between having to stand in line hour after hour for papers to be processed, and having to endure the psychological and even physical costs of a local police agency that may be seriously mismanaged or perhaps even corrupted. Like hospitals, police departments are life-and-death institutions, and in their mismanagement vast tensions can be created which cut the texture of society—and our peace of mind—into shreds. The abstraction and extraction of the police officer from the context of the community that his presence was designed to elevate is only one example of how our police have failed; but in a manner similar to the *over*specialization of modern medicine—in which the "new" specialization of family doctor had to be created—it is one that tells a wide and deep story indeed.

The failure of management of police institutions has had a harrowing effect not only on the lives of our citizens but also on our police officers. It may hardly be the fault of dumb police administrators that the police have one of the highest rates of suicide of any occupation in the country. After all, the inherent conditions of the job and the streets—the physical dangers, psychological pressures, et cetera—have a lot to do with it. But it is probably correct to say that dumb police management contributes generously to exceedingly high rates among police officers of alcoholism, nervous breakdowns, family breakups, heart disease, and other stresses that we see now as the almost inevitable concomitants of modern policing. While better management would hardly wipe out all the stresses, as if with a magic wand to erase reality, it would surely help alleviate some of the strains. In New York, you will recall, we found that cooping on the job was most extensively practiced during the midnight-to-eight shift. This, we knew, was also the most boring shift of all, and yet management had consigned to this dungeon many more officers than were needed. The boredom was reduced by simply offering interested officers the other two shifts, where more manpower was needed. The result of that offer was practically a mass migration of cops. The problem was therefore in its essence not a product of "cop genes" but of the environmental situation that police management had helped create.

Poor management is a terribly onerous burden for cops to have to live with. Perhaps equally as much as inefficient (and sometimes corrupt) courts and incompetent (and sometimes corrupt) prosecutorial offices, an inefficient (and possibly corrupt) police administration can make an ordinarily difficult job virtually impossible. There is no doubt in my mind that the general level of poor management in American policing adds substantially to the level of stress at the street level.

In its essential form, even without the debilitating and often demoralizing accoutrements of managerial stupidity, the job of the American police officer is a terribly emotional one. Nerves are on edge for every moment the officer is on display—or on undercover or plainclothes assignment. The police officer is probably in closer contact with the failures and rejects of American society than anyone, and the impact on his psyche is sometimes devastating. In the police role as a sort of grand mop-up operation, the police often see society for what it is at its worst—not as society likes to see itself. With this closeness to the face of horror, the police can develop a weird psychological combination of extremely shrewd street insight and Kafkaesque disorientation.

What the police chief—behind his big oak desk in his private office, insulated from the outside world by hordes of officious aides and layers of bureaucracy—must do, by all means, is to focus the entire institutional effort around one job: that of the police officer closest to the communities. Everything else should be secondary. It's a bosses' job only if we permit the bosses to make it one, if we permit both the institutions of the police and the officers themselves to become alienated, literally and figuratively, from their primary role in society, which is to keep the peace and maintain order in a sophisticated, humane, and Constitutional way. Policing should not be a bosses' job but rather a cop's job, because it is my view that perhaps the American police officer in this last quarter of the twentieth century has the most important job around.

Index

Long Island Police Department, 50, 73–74, 90, 153, 248

Los Angeles Police Department
Hoover and, 90
stranger policing in, 39
as successful police bureaucracy, 49

Lucas, Bill, 137

Lussen, Fred, 189

McCarthy, Bill, 125*n*., 168, 212, 237–238, 243, 245

Machiavelli, Niccoló, 109

McMillan, John, 108–09

Mafia, F.B.I., and, 86

Management problems, in police institutions, 268–70

Manhattan Rackets Squad, 137, 140

Markham, James, 181

Media, *see* News media

Meet the Press, 64

Mental health breakdown, crime and, 78

Mercury automobile, 11–12, 17

Metropolitan areas, crime growth in, 80

Miami Police Department, 40

Michael, Philip, 222

Michigan State University, 66

Misner, Gordon, 35

Model Cities police, 248

"Model precinct" program, 233–34

Mohammed Temple Seven incident, 173–175

Montgomery County (Md.) Police Department, 66

Morgan, Tom, 171–72

Motorcycle Division, 229–30

Mounted Division, 169, 230

Muggings, 51

Murders, 51

Murphy, Betty (Mrs. Patrick V.), 12, 15, 17, 45, 51, 60, 107

Murphy, Michael, 153

Murphy, Patrick V.
accomplishments of cited, 13
typical day of, 13–14
joins N.Y.P.D. (1945), 19
education of, 21–22
as rookie patrol officer, 31, 44–45
as plainclothes officer, 46
resigns from plainclothes assignment, 47
sees Commissioner on gambling corruption, 47–48
becomes sergeant (1948) and lieutenant (1953), 48; captain, 55
as Training Officer at Police Academy, 48; as commanding officer of Inspection Squad, 49; becomes Police Chief of Syracuse, 55
addresses women's auxiliary on Syracuse homicides, 63–64
Syracuse political community and, 67
returns to N.Y.P.D., 77
as retiree from N.Y.P.D., 100
as Justice Department official, 100–102
and L.E.A.A., 100–02
as Director of Public Safety, Washington, D.C., 104–06
and Howard University shooting incident, 105–09
as Detroit Police Commissioner, 119–124
memo to Detroit precinct commanders, 127–28
as New York Police Commissioner, 139–82
gets "hands off" promise from Lindsay, 146–47
in new Commissioner's office, 148–49
problems with John Walsh, 154–55, 161
First Deputy Police Commissioner and, 154–55
accountability concept of, 160–61, 167
on narcotics problem, 162

Rural crime
  hidden, 74
  state legislatures and, 75
Rural police forces, 74–75
Ruth, Henry, 139, 207

Safe, Loft, and Truck Squad, 190
St. Ephrem's school, 21
St. John's College, 21–22
St. Louis County Police Department, 66
San Diego Police Department, 261
San Francisco Police Department, 50
Saturday Night Special, 257
Seattle Police Department, 65*n.*
Seedman, Albert A., 159, 183, 190, 192–93, 198, 200, 214
  bad judgment of, 215–16
  as Chief of Detectives, 202, 207
  Narcotics Division and, 211
"Sensitive location," defined, 176–77
Serpico, Frank, 21, 47, 154, 157, 237, 240, 250–52
  shooting of, 253–54
Signal-box system, 32
Silence, code of, 226
Smith, William H. T., 62, 100, 167–68, 210, 240, 251
Southern Congressmen, Washington (D.C.) Police Department and, 103
Special Agents in Charge, F.B.I., 88
Special Counsel, 218–22
Special Investigating Units, 127, 242
Special Services, *see* Bureau of Special Services
SPRINT program, 262
"Squeals," catching of, 194–95, 205
State police, corruption and incompetence in, 79
Stranger policing, 39, 225, 264
Strikebreaking, 72
Supreme Court decisions, on criminal procedure, 71

SWAT (Special Weapons Attack Team), 68–69
Syracuse, N.Y.
  murder in, 63
  political community of, 67
Syracuse Police Department
  blacks and, 69
  corruption in, 57, 62

Tamm, Quinn, 90
Teapot Dome scandal, 85
Technological improvements, 262–63
Temple Seven incident, 173–75
Ten-13 call, 174–77
Tenure, in civil service, 266
Thinking, need for, 12
Tocqueville, Alexis de, 74
Tour of duty, rotation of, 225–26
Traffic tickets, fixing of, 67
Tramunti, Carmine, 59
Treasury Department, 77
Trial Commissioner, 220, 222
Triplett, Peggy, 158, 205

Uniform Crime Reporting Index, 92, 128
Urban Institute, 119, 129–30, 258
Urban riots, *see* Race riots
U.S. Law Enforcement Assistance Administration, *see* Law Enforcement Assistance Administration

Vance, Cyrus R., 187
Vollmer, August, 71, 91

Wagner, Robert, 48, 153
Wall Street Unit, 190
Walsh, John, 153–54, 161, 167, 210
Walsh, William, 56, 67–68, 100
Ward, Benjamin, 177, 220, 246–47

About the Authors

PATRICK V. MURPHY, born in New York City, is the President of the Police Foundation in Washington, D.C. Previously, he had been the Police Commissioner of New York—and before that head of police in Detroit (1970), Washington, D.C. (1967–68), and Syracuse (1963–64). He has also served in the United States Department of Justice and was the first administrator of the Federal Law Enforcement Assistance Administration.

THOMAS PLATE, a New York City resident, is a magazine columnist and author. His books include *Crime Pays!*, a study of professional crime, and *Understanding Doomsday,* a study of the nuclear arms race.